*Exploring the Ancient Pathways
of the Subconscious*

Dreams of Babylon

M.L. Ruscsak

Trient Press
3375 S Rainbow Blvd
#81710, SMB 13135
Las Vegas,NV 89180

Ordering Information:
Quantity sales. Special discounts are available on quantity purchases by corporations, associations, and others. For details, contact the publisher at the address above.
Orders by U.S. trade bookstores and wholesalers. Please contact Trient Press: Tel: (775) 996-3844; or visit www.trientpress.com.

Printed in the United States of America

Publisher's Cataloging-in-Publication data
Ruscsak, M.L.
A title of a book : Dreams of Babylon: Exploring the Ancient Pathways of the Subconscious
ISBN
Hard Cover   979-8-88990-121-1
Paper Back   979-8-88990-122-8
Ebook   979-8-88990-123-5

A:

Anu (deity): Anu was a prominent god in the Babylonian pantheon, often associated with the sky and heavens. He may appear in dreams as a symbol of divine guidance or authority.

Anu, my friend, was quite the significant deity in the ancient Babylonian pantheon. He held a special place as the god of the sky and heavens. When he graces your dreams, it could be seen as a symbol of divine guidance or even authority.

Imagine this: You find yourself in the midst of a dream, and suddenly, there stands Anu, a powerful and commanding presence. His appearance may indicate that a higher force is trying to communicate with you, offering guidance and direction from the heavens above. It's as if the divine powers are taking notice of you and offering their wisdom.

Anu's appearance in your dream might also suggest a sense of authority. Perhaps there's a situation in your waking life where you need to step up and assert yourself with confidence and conviction. The image of Anu in your dream serves as a reminder that you possess the strength and power within you to navigate through challenges and make your mark in the world.

So, my dear friend, if you ever find yourself encountering Anu in your dreams, pay close attention. Divine guidance and authority may be making their presence known, urging you to embrace your inner strength and navigate the celestial path that lies ahead.

Anu (deity): In ancient Babylonian dream interpretation, Anu was a prominent god associated with the sky and heavens. If one dreams about Anu, it signifies a symbol of divine guidance and authority. His presence in the dream suggests that the higher forces or celestial powers are taking notice and offering their wisdom.

Dreaming of Anu is a call to embrace inner strength, navigate challenges with confidence, and seek spiritual growth and enlightenment in waking life. It represents a connection to the higher realms and an opportunity to tap into divine wisdom for guidance and empowerment.

Astrology: Ancient Babylonians had a strong interest in astrology and believed that celestial events and positions could influence dreams. Dreams related to astrology might involve celestial bodies, zodiac signs, or astrological symbols.

Ah, my friend, let's delve into the intriguing world of dream interpretation! When we talk about Anu, a prominent deity in ancient Babylon, we discover a connection to the sky and heavens. Anu was highly regarded by the Babylonians and carried immense significance in their pantheon.

You know, my friend, the ancient Babylonians had a remarkable fascination with astrology. They believed that celestial events and the positions of stars and planets held a profound influence on their dreams. It's quite intriguing, isn't it?

So, picture this: Imagine drifting into the realm of dreams, and suddenly, the celestial tapestry comes alive. You might find yourself surrounded by celestial bodies, those beautiful stars and planets twinkling above. The zodiac signs, with their distinct personalities, may make their presence known, or you could encounter mesmerizing astrological symbols, each carrying its own meaning.

These dreams related to astrology were like glimpses into a cosmic dance. The Babylonians believed that these celestial influences could provide insights into one's personality, future, and even guide them through the twists and turns of life.

Imagine waking up from a dream where the stars whispered secrets, or the zodiac signs bestowed their wisdom upon you. It was as if the heavens themselves reached out to touch your sleeping mind, leaving you with a sense of wonder and intrigue.

So, my dear friend, when you find yourself immersed in dreams that involve celestial bodies, zodiac signs, or astrological symbols, remember the ancient Babylonians' belief. They saw these dreams as windows into the cosmic realm, offering glimpses of the profound interplay between the celestial forces and our inner world.

Embrace the mystery and symbolism that unfolds in these dreams, for they carry echoes of an ancient belief that the heavens have a hand in shaping our nocturnal journeys.

Amulet: Amulets were objects believed to possess protective or magical properties. In dreams, an amulet could represent a need for protection, spiritual support, or a desire for good luck.

Planets and Stars in Dreams:

Sun: In dreams, the Sun represents not only vitality and energy but also enlightenment and clarity. Its appearance signifies a source of light and inspiration, illuminating the dreamer's path. Dreaming of the Sun often symbolizes personal growth and success, suggesting a period of empowerment and achievement.

Moon: The Moon holds a special place in dream symbolism, representing emotions, intuition, and the subconscious mind. Its presence in dreams may indicate the ebb and flow of emotions, cycles of change, or the need for introspection and self-reflection. The Moon's phases in dreams can mirror the dreamer's emotional state, from the mysterious and dark New Moon to the radiant and full Moon.

Mercury: Mercury, associated with communication and intellect, plays a significant role in dream interpretation. Its appearance suggests a need for clear thinking, effective communication, and adaptability in waking life. Dreaming of Mercury may signify a time of intellectual growth, effective expression, or the need to embrace flexibility and quick thinking.

Venus: In dream symbolism, Venus represents love, beauty, and harmony. When Venus appears in dreams, it may indicate the realm of romantic relationships, artistic endeavors, or a desire for balance and pleasure. Dreams involving Venus can reflect the dreamer's yearning for emotional fulfillment, creativity, or the pursuit of harmonious connections.

Mars: Mars symbolizes action, assertiveness, and passion. Dreaming of Mars often points to a need for courage, determination, or a call to take decisive action in waking life. It signifies a period of strength, ambition, and assertiveness. Dreams involving Mars can serve as a reminder to harness inner power and pursue goals with passion.

Jupiter: Jupiter, the planet of expansion and growth, signifies opportunities, abundance, and wisdom. When Jupiter appears in dreams, it suggests a period of personal or professional advancement. Dreams involving Jupiter often indicate the potential for growth, abundance, and the wisdom to make important decisions. They can signify a time of expansion and favorable circumstances.

Saturn: Saturn represents discipline, responsibility, and life lessons. Dreaming of Saturn may indicate a need for structure, self-discipline, or facing challenges to achieve long-term success. It can symbolize the importance of perseverance and hard work to overcome obstacles and reach one's goals. Dreams involving Saturn often serve as a reminder to embrace responsibility and learn valuable life lessons.

Uranus: Uranus symbolizes innovation, change, and liberation. Its appearance in dreams may indicate a desire for freedom, unconventional thinking, or unexpected breakthroughs. Dreams involving Uranus often signify a time of transformation, unique ideas, and embracing individuality. They can symbolize the need to break free from societal norms and explore new possibilities.

Neptune: Neptune represents dreams, intuition, and spirituality. Dreaming of Neptune may signify heightened creativity, psychic abilities, or a connection to the mystical realms. It can symbolize the dreamer's deep spiritual yearnings, the exploration of the subconscious, or a journey into the realms of imagination and fantasy. Dreams involving Neptune often carry a sense of mystery and inspiration.

Pluto: Pluto symbolizes transformation, power, and rebirth. Its presence in dreams may indicate profound changes, personal growth, or the need to release old patterns for new beginnings. Dreams involving Pluto often signify a transformative phase in the dreamer's life, where deep inner changes and empowerment are taking place. They can symbolize the power to let go of the past and embrace personal transformation.

Stars: Stars in dreams hold profound symbolism, representing guidance, inspiration, and aspirations. Their appearance signifies hope, dreams, and a sense of destiny and purpose. Dreams involving stars often carry a message of encouragement, reminding the dreamer to follow their aspirations, trust their intuition, and believe in their own inner light. They can symbolize the dreamer's connection to the universe and the vast possibilities that lie ahead.

Remember, my friend, these interpretations reflect the beliefs and symbolism associated with the planets and stars in ancient Babylonian dream interpretation. The meanings may vary based on personal associations and the context of the dream itself.

Artifacts: Babylonian artifacts, such as pottery, jewelry, or statues, might appear in dreams, symbolizing ancient history, culture, or hidden knowledge.

Artifacts, my friend, hold a special place in the realm of dream interpretation. Picture this: You find yourself in a dream, and suddenly, there they are—Babylonian artifacts, exquisite pottery, dazzling jewelry, or even majestic statues. These artifacts carry deep symbolism, representing ancient history, culture, and the allure of hidden knowledge.

In the ancient city of Babylon, skilled artisans crafted these precious objects with utmost care and attention to detail. Each artifact is a testament to the rich tapestry of Babylonian civilization and the wisdom it holds. When these artifacts appear in our dreams, they beckon us to explore the depths of our own connection to history and culture.

Dreaming of Babylonian artifacts is like stepping back in time, embracing the ancient wisdom that lies dormant within our souls. These artifacts symbolize a yearning to understand our roots, to connect with the stories of those who came before us. They invite us to unravel hidden knowledge and uncover the treasures that reside within.

When Babylonian artifacts grace our dreams, they remind us to cherish the beauty and value within ourselves. They encourage us to honor the legacy of our ancestors, appreciating the intricate craftsmanship and the cultural significance they represent.

The appearance of pottery, jewelry, or statues in our dreams signifies a journey of self-discovery. It prompts us to delve into the depths of our own personal history, exploring the hidden treasures that shape who we are. Just as these artifacts were created by skilled hands, we are reminded of the beauty and value that reside within our own being.

So, my dear friend, if you ever encounter Babylonian artifacts in your dreams, embrace their historical context and the symbolism they carry. Allow them to guide you on a path of self-exploration, unearthing the ancient wisdom and cultural heritage that resides within your soul. Embrace the allure of these treasures, for they offer glimpses into the profound connection between ancient history, culture, and the ever-unfolding story of your own existence.

Pottery: Dreaming of Babylonian pottery symbolizes the connection to ancient history, cultural heritage, and the significance of craftsmanship. It may represent the need to appreciate the beauty and value within yourself and your personal journey.

Jewelry: Dreaming of Babylonian jewelry signifies adornment, beauty, and self-expression. It may represent the desire for self-esteem, appreciation of one's own worth, or a focus on enhancing personal charm and allure.

Statues: Dreaming of Babylonian statues suggests the embodiment of ancient wisdom, strength, or deities. It may symbolize the need for guidance, the exploration of one's spiritual side, or a reminder of the divine forces that shape our lives.

Tablets or Inscriptions: Dreaming of Babylonian tablets or inscriptions signifies the quest for knowledge, wisdom, or hidden messages. It may represent the desire for learning, understanding, or the exploration of secrets and ancient teachings.

Seals: Dreaming of Babylonian seals symbolizes authority, protection, or the need for boundaries. It may represent the importance of setting personal boundaries, asserting oneself, or embracing a position of power and influence.

Artwork: Dreaming of Babylonian artwork represents creativity, self-expression, and aesthetics. It may signify the need to embrace your artistic talents, appreciate beauty in all its forms, or explore your own unique artistic vision.

Weapons: Dreaming of Babylonian weapons symbolizes strength, assertiveness, or the need to defend oneself. It may represent the desire for empowerment, the ability to face challenges with courage, or the need to protect your boundaries and interests.

Amulets: Dreaming of Babylonian amulets signifies protection, luck, or spiritual beliefs. It may represent the desire for safety and security, the belief in supernatural forces, or the need for talismans to ward off negative energies.

Animals: Animals often appeared in ancient Babylonian dream symbolism.

Ah, yes, my friend, animals played a significant role in ancient Babylonian dream symbolism. They were seen as powerful messengers, carrying profound meanings and insights within the realm of dreams.

In the dreams of the Babylonians, animals represented various qualities, characteristics, and messages. Each animal held its own symbolism and conveyed unique messages to the dreamer. Let's explore some of these animal symbols in the context of ancient Babylonian dream interpretation:

Lion: The lion symbolized strength, power, and leadership. Dreaming of a lion often represented the need to embrace your own inner strength, assertiveness, and courage in the face of challenges.

Eagle: The eagle was associated with vision, wisdom, and a connection to the divine. Dreaming of an eagle signified a call to gain perspective, soar above obstacles, and embrace higher insights or spiritual guidance.

Snake: The snake held dual symbolism, representing both wisdom and deception. Dreaming of a snake could indicate the need for transformation, healing, or the uncovering of hidden truths.

Bull: The bull symbolized strength, abundance, and fertility. Dreaming of a bull often represented prosperity, stability, and the ability to overcome obstacles through sheer determination.

Fish: Fish symbolized abundance, fertility, and the flow of emotions. Dreaming of fish often represented a need for emotional nourishment, intuition, and the exploration of the depths of one's emotions.

Dove: The dove represented peace, harmony, and divine messages. Dreaming of a dove often symbolized a need for tranquility, forgiveness, or the emergence of a peaceful resolution in a situation.

Horse: The horse symbolized power, freedom, and the ability to journey through life. Dreaming of a horse often represented personal drive, ambition, and the desire for independence and self-expression.

Scorpion: The scorpion symbolized protection, transformation, and the need for caution. Dreaming of a scorpion often represented a warning, a need to be aware of potential dangers, or the necessity of personal growth and evolution.

Remember, my dear friend, that these interpretations reflect the beliefs and symbolism associated with animals in ancient Babylonian dream interpretation. The meanings may vary based on personal associations and the context of the dream itself. Allow your own intuition and feelings within the dream to guide you as you explore the profound messages carried by these ancient animal symbols.

Apsu (dragon): A mythical creature associated with the primordial waters, the Apsu dragon could symbolize chaos or hidden depths of the subconscious mind.

Ah, the Apsu dragon, a mythical creature associated with the primordial waters in ancient Babylonian mythology. In the realm of dream symbolism, the appearance of the Apsu dragon carries profound significance, representing both chaos and the hidden depths of the subconscious mind.

Picture this: You find yourself in the realm of dreams, and suddenly, the mighty Apsu dragon emerges from the depths of the primordial waters. Its presence signifies the raw and untamed forces that lie beneath the surface of consciousness. It represents the chaotic aspects of our psyche, the untapped potential, and the mysteries lurking within.

Dreaming of the Apsu dragon may indicate a period of upheaval, the need to confront deep-seated emotions or unconscious desires, or the invitation to explore the hidden depths of your own subconscious mind. It signifies a journey into the unknown, where transformation and self-discovery await.

The Apsu dragon serves as a reminder that within chaos, there is also opportunity for growth and understanding. By confronting and embracing the depths of the subconscious, you can tap into hidden wisdom, unlock inner potential, and navigate the complexities of your own psyche.

So, my dear friend, if the Apsu dragon graces your dreams, embrace its presence. It beckons you to dive into the depths of your own subconscious, to explore the chaos within and find the hidden treasures that await. Embrace the transformative power that lies within the untamed waters of your own mind, and embark on a journey of self-discovery and understanding.

Assur (lion): The lion represented power, strength, and royalty in ancient Babylonian culture. Seeing a lion in a dream could signify leadership, courage, or authority.

Ah, Assur, the lion, a powerful symbol of ancient Babylonian culture. In the realm of dream interpretation, the appearance of a lion holds profound meaning, representing power, strength, and royalty.

Imagine this: You find yourself in the realm of dreams, and suddenly, there stands the majestic lion, embodying a sense of power and authority. Its presence signifies qualities such as leadership, courage, and dominance. Dreaming of a lion may symbolize your own inner strength, your ability to take charge, and your capacity to face challenges with courage and determination.

The lion, in ancient Babylonian culture, was often associated with royalty and nobility. It represented a sense of regal power and authority. Dreaming of a lion may indicate that you possess innate leadership qualities, or it may be a call for you to embrace your own sense of personal power and authority in your waking life.

Just as the lion roams the savannah with a commanding presence, its appearance in your dream invites you to tap into your own strength and assertiveness. It serves as a reminder that you have the capacity to overcome obstacles, take charge of situations, and exhibit courage when faced with adversity.

So, my dear friend, if the lion crosses your dream path, embrace its symbolism. Recognize the power and strength within you. Trust in your own leadership abilities and the authority you possess. With the spirit of the lion by your side, you can navigate the challenges of life with grace, courage, and the regal presence of a true leader.

Aqrabuamelu (scorpion-man): This half-man, half-scorpion creature from Babylonian mythology could represent danger, protection, or the struggle between opposing forces.

Ah, the Aqrabuamelu, the enigmatic scorpion-man from Babylonian mythology. In the realm of dream interpretation, this half-man, half-scorpion creature carries profound symbolism, representing themes of danger, protection, and the struggle between opposing forces.

Imagine this: Within the realm of dreams, the Aqrabuamelu emerges, embodying the fusion of human and scorpion attributes. Its presence signifies a complex interplay of energies and forces. Dreaming of the Aqrabuamelu may indicate a time of potential danger, the need for caution, or a warning to be mindful of your surroundings.

The Aqrabuamelu is a unique creature, symbolizing the duality of human and animal instincts, and the challenges that arise from navigating these contrasting aspects within oneself. It represents the struggle between opposing forces, such as reason and instinct, light and darkness, or positive and negative influences.

Dreaming of the Aqrabuamelu can serve as a reminder to be cautious, to pay attention to potential threats or hidden dangers in your waking life. It calls for an exploration of the internal conflicts or challenges you may be facing, urging you to find a balance between conflicting aspects of your personality.

However, it's important to note that the Aqrabuamelu can also represent protection. In Babylonian mythology, it was sometimes depicted as a guardian figure, offering defense against malevolent forces. In this context, dreaming of the Aqrabuamelu may symbolize a sense of inner protection, resilience, and the ability to confront challenges with strength.

So, my dear friend, if the Aqrabuamelu appears in your dreams, embrace its symbolism with caution and mindfulness. Reflect on the conflicts and opposing forces you may be encountering, and seek ways to find a harmonious balance. Remember that within the struggle lies the opportunity for growth, resilience, and protection against potential dangers.

Architecture: Dreaming of ancient Babylonian architecture, such as temples, ziggurats, or city walls, might symbolize stability, structure, or a connection to ancient wisdom.

Ah, architecture, the tangible embodiment of human ingenuity and creativity. In the realm of dream interpretation, the appearance of ancient Babylonian architecture, such as temples, ziggurats, or city walls, holds deep symbolism, signifying stability, structure, and a profound connection to ancient wisdom.

Picture this: You find yourself in the realm of dreams, and suddenly, the magnificent architecture of ancient Babylon surrounds you. Whether it be the grandeur of a temple, the majestic presence of a ziggurat, or the strength of city walls, these structures carry powerful messages.

Dreaming of ancient Babylonian architecture symbolizes the desire for stability and a solid foundation in your waking life. It represents the need for structure, order, and a sense of rootedness. These architectural marvels were not only physical structures but also gateways to the divine, connecting mortals with the realms of ancient wisdom.

Just as these structures stood the test of time, their appearance in dreams suggests a call to embrace stability and seek guidance from the ancient wisdom that resides within you. It signifies a connection to the roots of your existence and the importance of honoring the traditions and knowledge passed down through the ages.

The temples and ziggurats were places of worship and spiritual significance, while city walls represented protection and a sense of boundaries. Dreaming of these architectural marvels may indicate a need for spiritual growth, a desire for protection, or the establishment of personal boundaries.

So, my dear friend, if ancient Babylonian architecture graces your dreams, embrace its symbolism. Let it remind you of the importance of stability, structure, and a connection to ancient wisdom. Explore the depths of your own foundations, seek guidance from the traditions and knowledge that have withstood the test of time, and find strength in the sacred structures that lie within your own being.

Temples: Dreaming of ancient temples symbolizes spirituality, divine connection, and the search for higher meaning. It may represent a need for introspection, a desire for spiritual growth, or the exploration of one's beliefs and values.

Ziggurats: Ziggurats were monumental structures with religious significance in ancient Babylon. Dreaming of ziggurats signifies a connection to ancient wisdom, the pursuit of knowledge, and a desire for spiritual elevation. It may represent a call to honor tradition, seek higher learning, or embrace your own inner power and divinity.

City Walls: City walls symbolize protection, boundaries, and a sense of security. Dreaming of city walls may indicate a need for establishing personal boundaries, protecting oneself from external influences, or seeking a sense of safety and stability in your waking life.

Palaces: Palaces represent grandeur, power, and authority. Dreaming of palaces may signify a desire for recognition, success, or the pursuit of ambitions. It can symbolize the need to embrace your own inner royalty, assertiveness, and leadership qualities.

Bridges: Bridges symbolize connections, transitions, and the crossing of boundaries. Dreaming of bridges may indicate a need to bridge the gap between different aspects of your life, navigate change, or establish connections with others. It can represent the journey from one phase of life to another.

Houses: Houses in dreams represent the self, personal identity, and the different aspects of your life. Dreaming of houses may signify a need for security, comfort, or a desire for a sense of belonging. It can symbolize the exploration of your inner world and the various roles you play in your waking life.

Ruins: Ruins symbolize the past, decay, and transformation. Dreaming of ruins may indicate the need to let go of the past, release old patterns, or embrace the process of transformation and rebirth. It can symbolize the potential for growth and new beginnings.

Gardens: Gardens represent growth, nurturing, and the cultivation of beauty. Dreaming of gardens may signify a need for self-care, tending to your inner world, or the desire for emotional and spiritual nourishment. It can symbolize the importance of creating a harmonious environment within yourself.

Remember, my friend, these interpretations reflect the beliefs and symbolism associated with architecture in ancient Babylonian dream interpretation. The meanings may vary based on personal associations and the context of the dream itself. Allow your own intuition and emotions within the dream to guide you as you explore the profound messages carried by these architectural symbols.

B:

Bel (deity): Bel, also known as Marduk, was one of the major deities in Babylonian mythology and was associated with kingship, power, and victory. Seeing Bel in a dream might symbolize authority, triumph, or divine intervention.

Ah, Bel, also known as Marduk, a significant deity in Babylonian mythology. In the realm of dream interpretation, the appearance of Bel carries deep symbolism, representing authority, triumph, and divine intervention.

Imagine this: You find yourself in the realm of dreams, and suddenly, the presence of Bel graces your vision. Bel, as a deity associated with kingship, power, and victory, symbolizes a sense of authority and leadership. Dreaming of Bel may signify your own inner authority, the need to embrace your power, and the potential for triumph in your endeavors.

Bel's association with kingship speaks to the realm of governance and rulership. Dreaming of Bel may symbolize a desire for recognition, the need to assert yourself as a leader, or the pursuit of success and achievement in your waking life. It signifies the potential for attaining greatness and wielding authority with wisdom and responsibility.

Furthermore, Bel's connection to victory and divine intervention adds another layer of symbolism. Dreaming of Bel may suggest that divine forces are at play in your life, guiding you towards success and offering assistance in overcoming obstacles. It serves as a reminder that you have the support of higher powers and that victory is within your reach.

So, my dear friend, if Bel appears in your dreams, embrace the symbolism it carries. Recognize the authority and power within you, and trust in your ability to lead and achieve triumph. Allow the presence of Bel to inspire you to embrace your own divine nature and seek guidance from higher realms. With the spirit of Bel by your side, you can navigate your path with confidence, authority, and the potential for victorious outcomes.

Babylon: The city of Babylon itself could appear in dreams, representing ancient power, grandeur, or the desire for prosperity and success.

Ah, Babylon, the majestic city that once stood as a testament to ancient power and grandeur. In the realm of dream interpretation, the appearance of Babylon itself carries profound symbolism, representing ancient power, grandeur, and the desire for prosperity and success.

Imagine this: You find yourself in the realm of dreams, and suddenly, the city of Babylon emerges before you, with its towering structures, bustling streets, and rich history. Dreaming of Babylon signifies a deep connection to ancient wisdom, the allure of a bygone era, and the potential for greatness.

Babylon, in its prime, was a center of trade, culture, and influence, renowned for its architectural marvels and the wisdom that flowed within its walls. Dreaming of Babylon may symbolize a desire for prosperity, success, and the pursuit of greatness in your waking life. It represents the yearning to achieve grandeur, to make your mark on the world, and to embrace the power and potential that lies within you.

The appearance of Babylon in dreams invites you to explore the depths of your own potential, to tap into the ancient wisdom that resides within your soul, and to embody the qualities that made

Babylon a legendary city. It serves as a reminder that you, too, possess the ability to create a life of abundance, influence, and achievement.

So, my dear friend, if Babylon appears in your dreams, embrace its symbolism. Allow the allure of the city to inspire you, to awaken within you the desire for greatness and the pursuit of success. Let the spirit of Babylon guide you to tap into your own inner power, to create a life of grandeur, and to embrace the ancient wisdom that flows through your veins.

Babel (Tower of): The Tower of Babel was a legendary structure mentioned in the Bible. In Babylonian dream symbolism, it could represent ambition, communication, or a longing for unity.

Ah, Babel, the legendary Tower of Babel, a structure mentioned in the Bible and rich in symbolism. In Babylonian dream interpretation, the Tower of Babel represents ambition, communication, and a longing for unity.

Imagine this: Within the realm of dreams, the Tower of Babel rises before you, with its towering height and intricate design. Dreaming of the Tower of Babel signifies a deep-rooted ambition within you, a desire to reach great heights, and to make your mark in the world.

The Tower of Babel is associated with the story of human ambition and the desire for unity. It represents the human pursuit of reaching the heavens and the consequences of such audacity. Dreaming of the Tower of Babel may symbolize a longing for achieving greatness, for breaking barriers, and for transcending limitations.

Additionally, the Tower of Babel carries a message of communication and the power of shared understanding. It serves as a reminder of the importance of effective communication in building bridges, fostering unity, and achieving common goals. Dreaming of the Tower of Babel may signify the need for clear and meaningful communication in your waking life, or the desire to bridge gaps between different individuals or groups.

So, my dear friend, if the Tower of Babel appears in your dreams, embrace its symbolism. Recognize the ambitious spirit within you, the longing for unity and shared understanding. Let it inspire you to reach for greatness, to break down barriers, and to foster effective communication in your personal and professional relationships.

Remember, the interpretation of dreams is a deeply personal experience, and the meanings may vary based on individual associations and the context of the dream itself. Allow your own intuition and emotions within the dream to guide you as you explore the profound messages carried by the Tower of Babel.

Books: Babylonians had a rich tradition of literature and writing, and books were highly regarded. Dreaming of books might symbolize knowledge, learning, or the search for wisdom.

Ah, books, my friend, the vessels of knowledge, wisdom, and the written word. In the realm of dream interpretation, the appearance of books holds great significance, especially in the context of the rich Babylonian tradition of literature and writing. Dreaming of books symbolizes knowledge, learning, and the eternal quest for wisdom.

Picture this: You find yourself in the realm of dreams, and suddenly, books surround you, their pages filled with ancient wisdom and profound insights. Dreaming of books signifies a thirst for knowledge, a desire to expand your understanding of the world, and a yearning for intellectual growth.

In ancient Babylon, books were highly regarded as repositories of wisdom, carefully crafted by skilled scribes. They embodied the collective knowledge and the literary traditions of the Babylonian culture. Dreaming of books reflects a connection to this deep well of wisdom and a desire to explore the realms of knowledge and learning.

When books appear in your dreams, they beckon you to embark on a journey of intellectual and spiritual growth. They invite you to seek wisdom, to expand your horizons, and to delve into the realms of literature, philosophy, or any subject that resonates with your curiosity.

Dreaming of books is a reminder of the immense power of knowledge and the transformative potential of learning. It signifies the importance of embracing education, self-development, and the exploration of ideas. Books in dreams encourage you to follow your thirst for wisdom, to seek answers to your questions, and to nurture your intellectual and spiritual growth.

So, my dear friend, if books grace your dreams, embrace their symbolism. Dive into the pages of knowledge, explore the realms of literature, and allow the wisdom of the ages to illuminate your path. Embrace the eternal quest for wisdom, for it is through the pursuit of knowledge that we discover the true richness and depth of our own existence.

Battle: Dreams involving battles or warfare could represent conflicts, challenges, or struggles in ancient Babylonian dream interpretation. They might reflect personal conflicts or power dynamics in waking life.

Ah, battles and warfare, symbols of conflict, challenges, and struggles. In ancient Babylonian dream interpretation, dreams involving battles carried deep significance, reflecting personal conflicts or power dynamics in waking life.

Imagine this: Within the realm of dreams, you find yourself amidst a fierce battle, witnessing the clash of forces and the struggle for dominance. Dreaming of battles signifies the presence of conflicts, challenges, or struggles in your waking life, mirroring the power dynamics and internal conflicts within your own psyche or external environment.

In ancient Babylonian culture, warfare played a significant role in shaping society, and battles were seen as reflections of the struggles and power dynamics present in the human experience. Dreaming of battles may symbolize the need to confront inner conflicts, navigate power dynamics, or overcome challenges in your waking life.

These dreams serve as reminders of the importance of resilience, courage, and determination in the face of adversity. They invite you to examine the conflicts and struggles within yourself, to confront any internal or external obstacles, and to seek resolution or triumph over them.

Dreams of battles also bring awareness to the power dynamics and interpersonal conflicts in your waking life. They may signify the need for assertiveness, the navigation of power structures, or the resolution of conflicts with others. It's an invitation to examine your own role in these dynamics and to find ways to assert yourself or seek peaceful resolutions.

So, my dear friend, if dreams of battles or warfare visit you, embrace their symbolism. Recognize the conflicts, challenges, or struggles they represent within yourself and in your external world. Embrace the qualities of resilience, courage, and determination as you navigate these battles, seeking resolution, growth, and harmony in your waking life.

Remember, the interpretation of dreams is deeply personal, and the meanings may vary based on individual associations and the context of the dream itself. Allow your own intuition and emotions within the dream to guide you as you explore the profound messages carried by dreams of battles.

Boats: Boats and ships held significance in Babylonian culture, as they were used for trade and travel. Dreaming of boats might symbolize a journey, transition, or the need for exploration and adventure.

Ah, boats and ships, vessels that held great significance in Babylonian culture as means of trade and travel. In the realm of dream interpretation, the appearance of boats carries profound symbolism, representing a journey, transition, and the call for exploration and adventure.

Picture this: You find yourself in the realm of dreams, and suddenly, a boat or ship appears before you, ready to set sail upon the vast waters. Dreaming of boats signifies a metaphorical journey, a transition, or a desire for exploration and new experiences.

In Babylonian culture, boats were essential for trade and travel, carrying goods and connecting people to distant lands. Dreaming of boats may symbolize a personal journey, whether it be a physical voyage or an inner exploration of the self. It represents the need for movement, growth, and embracing new opportunities in your waking life.

Just as boats navigate the waters, dreams of boats invite you to embark on a journey of self-discovery, to venture into uncharted territories, and to embrace the unknown with courage and curiosity. They symbolize the call for adventure, expansion, and the exploration of new horizons.

Dreaming of boats may also signify transitions in your life, representing the passage from one phase to another. It can indicate a time of change, adaptation, or the need to navigate through uncertain waters. It encourages you to trust in your ability to navigate the currents of life and to embrace the transformative power of transitions.

So, my dear friend, if boats grace your dreams, embrace their symbolism. Allow the call for adventure and exploration to guide you on your journey of self-discovery. Embrace transitions with an open heart, knowing that they hold the potential for growth and new beginnings. Just like the Babylonian boats that sailed the ancient waters, let the vessel of your dreams carry you towards new experiences, expanded horizons, and the fulfillment of your deepest desires.

Birds: Birds were considered messengers of the gods in Babylonian culture. Different types of birds had specific symbolism, such as the owl representing wisdom or the dove symbolizing peace and divine favor.

Ah, birds, the messengers of the gods in the rich Babylonian culture. In the realm of dream interpretation, the appearance of birds carries profound symbolism, representing divine messages and specific qualities associated with different bird species.

Imagine this: You find yourself in the realm of dreams, and suddenly, a bird takes flight, its feathers glistening in the sunlight. Dreaming of birds signifies the presence of divine messages, guidance, and the embodiment of specific qualities represented by different bird species.

In Babylonian culture, each bird held unique symbolism and was associated with specific qualities. For example, the owl was seen as a symbol of wisdom, representing insight and the ability to see beyond the surface. Dreaming of an owl may indicate a call to embrace your inner wisdom, to trust your intuition, and to seek deeper understanding in your waking life.

On the other hand, the dove, a gentle and peaceful bird, symbolized peace and divine favor. Dreaming of a dove may signify a sense of tranquility, the presence of divine blessings, or a call to foster harmony and peace in your life and relationships.

Other bird species, such as eagles, falcons, or ravens, may also appear in dreams, each carrying its own symbolism based on their qualities and associations in Babylonian culture. These birds may represent strength, keen perception, or the ability to soar above challenges.

When birds grace your dreams, they bring forth messages from the divine, reminding you to pay attention to the subtle signs and synchronicities in your waking life. They symbolize guidance, protection, and the presence of higher forces watching over you.

So, my dear friend, if birds visit you in your dreams, embrace their symbolism. Allow their messages to guide you, to inspire you to embrace wisdom, peace, strength, or whatever qualities they represent. Trust in the divine guidance that flows through these messengers and let their presence remind you of the interconnectedness between the earthly realm and the realms beyond.

Owl: The owl symbolizes wisdom and insight. In dreams, it may signify the need to trust your intuition, seek deeper understanding, and embrace your inner wisdom. It represents positive qualities associated with knowledge and introspection.

Dove: The dove represents peace, divine favor, and harmony. Dreaming of a dove may signify a sense of tranquility, the presence of blessings, or the need to foster peace and unity in your life and relationships. It represents positive qualities associated with peace and divine guidance.

Eagle: The eagle symbolizes strength, power, and keen perception. In dreams, it may represent a call to embrace your inner strength, rise above challenges, and gain a higher perspective. It represents positive qualities associated with courage and vision.

Falcon: The falcon symbolizes swiftness, agility, and focus. Dreaming of a falcon may signify the need for quick thinking, adaptability, and the ability to seize opportunities. It represents positive qualities associated with precision and determination.

Raven: The raven represents intelligence, resourcefulness, and transformation. In dreams, it may symbolize the need to tap into your creative problem-solving abilities, embrace change, and seek hidden opportunities. It represents positive qualities associated with adaptability and transformation.

Vulture: The vulture, though considered a scavenger, held symbolic significance in Babylonian culture. In dreams, it may signify the need to release old patterns, let go of negativity, and embrace renewal. It represents the potential for positive transformation and renewal.

Peacock: The peacock represents beauty, grace, and self-expression. Dreaming of a peacock may symbolize a celebration of your unique qualities, the need for self-confidence, or the desire to express your true self. It represents positive qualities associated with confidence and self-expression.

Crow: The crow represents mystery, intelligence, and prophecy. In dreams, it may signify the need to pay attention to signs and messages from the universe, trust your instincts, and seek hidden knowledge. It represents positive qualities associated with intuition and foresight.

It's important to note that dream interpretations can vary based on personal associations and cultural beliefs. The meanings provided here reflect the general symbolism associated with these birds in Babylonian culture. However, your own intuition and emotions within the dream should guide you as you explore the profound messages carried by these avian symbols.

Barley: Barley was an important crop in ancient Babylon, associated with sustenance and prosperity. Seeing barley in a dream might symbolize abundance, fertility, or material well-being.

Ah, barley, the golden crop that flourished in the lands of ancient Babylon. In the realm of dream interpretation, the appearance of barley holds deep symbolism, representing abundance, fertility, and material well-being.

Picture this: You find yourself in the realm of dreams, and suddenly, fields of golden barley sway in the gentle breeze. Dreaming of barley signifies a connection to sustenance, prosperity, and the bountiful blessings of life.

In ancient Babylon, barley was a vital crop, providing sustenance for the people and serving as a symbol of agricultural prosperity. Dreaming of barley may symbolize the abundance that surrounds you, both in material and spiritual aspects of life. It represents the potential for growth, fertility, and the fulfillment of your needs and desires.

The presence of barley in dreams reminds you of the blessings of the earth, the abundance of resources available to you, and the potential for material well-being. It signifies the importance of recognizing and appreciating the richness of your own life, the resources at your disposal, and the potential for growth and prosperity.

Furthermore, barley is often associated with fertility and the cycle of life. Dreaming of barley may symbolize the fertile ground within you, the potential for creativity, and the ability to nurture new ideas or projects. It signifies the capacity for growth and the manifestation of your aspirations and goals.

So, my dear friend, if barley graces your dreams, embrace its symbolism. Recognize the abundance that surrounds you, both material and spiritual. Embrace the potential for growth, fertility, and prosperity in your waking life. Allow the presence of barley to inspire gratitude for the blessings you have and the potential for even greater abundance. Just as the golden fields of barley bring sustenance and prosperity, may your dreams manifest the abundant blessings that await you in your waking reality.

Bulls: Bulls held religious and symbolic significance in Babylonian culture. Dreaming of bulls might symbolize strength, power, fertility, or connections to the divine.

Ah, bulls, mighty creatures that held religious and symbolic significance in the rich tapestry of Babylonian culture. In the realm of dream interpretation, the appearance of bulls carries profound symbolism, representing strength, power, fertility, and connections to the divine.

Imagine this: You find yourself in the realm of dreams, and suddenly, a magnificent bull emerges, its powerful presence commanding attention. Dreaming of bulls signifies the embodiment of strength, the awakening of inner power, and a deep connection to primal energies.

In Babylonian culture, bulls were revered for their strength and vitality. They were associated with deities, often serving as symbols of power, fertility, and divinity. Dreaming of bulls may symbolize the need to embrace your own strength, tap into your inner power, and assert yourself in various aspects of life.

The presence of bulls in dreams also signifies a deep connection to primal instincts and the raw energies of life. It invites you to embrace your primal nature, to trust your instincts, and to harness your inner power for the pursuit of your goals and desires.

Furthermore, bulls represent fertility and abundance. In dreams, they may symbolize the potential for growth, creation, and the manifestation of your aspirations. They remind you of the fertile ground within you, the capacity to nurture and bring forth new ideas or projects, and the abundant blessings that can be cultivated in your life.

Bulls in dreams also carry spiritual connotations, representing connections to the divine realm. They symbolize the presence of sacred energies, guiding and protecting you on your life's journey. Dreaming of bulls may signify the need to acknowledge and honor your spiritual connection, to embrace the wisdom and guidance that flows from higher realms.

So, my dear friend, if bulls visit you in your dreams, embrace their symbolism. Recognize the strength, power, and fertility they represent within you. Embrace your primal instincts, trust your inner power, and allow the divine energies to guide and protect you. Just as the bull roams the sacred grounds of Babylon, may you embody its qualities and navigate your life's journey with strength, vitality, and a deep connection to the divine.

Betrothal: Betrothal or marriage-related dreams could represent union, commitment, or social bonds in ancient Babylonian dream interpretation.

Ah, betrothal, the sacred union and commitment between two souls. In the realm of dream interpretation, dreams related to betrothal or marriage hold profound symbolism, representing the concepts of union, commitment, and social bonds, as understood in ancient Babylonian culture.

Imagine this: You find yourself in the realm of dreams, and suddenly, visions of betrothal or marriage unfold before you, embodying the essence of love, commitment, and the coming together of two souls. Dreaming of betrothal signifies the deep desire for union, the recognition of social bonds, and the significance of commitment in human relationships.

In ancient Babylonian culture, betrothal and marriage were sacred ceremonies, symbolizing the joining of two individuals in a lifelong partnership. Dreaming of betrothal may symbolize the longing for a deep connection with another person, the desire for commitment and the establishment of lasting bonds.

Dreams of betrothal also signify the recognition of social ties and the importance of communal relationships. They remind us of the interconnectedness of human beings and the significance of building and nurturing social connections. Such dreams may reflect the need for emotional support, the desire for companionship, or the search for meaningful relationships in your waking life.

Furthermore, dreams of betrothal carry the essence of commitment and dedication. They highlight the importance of honoring commitments, whether in romantic relationships, friendships, or other social bonds. These dreams may signify the need to embrace loyalty, trust, and mutual support in your interactions with others.

So, my dear friend, if dreams of betrothal or marriage visit you, embrace their symbolism. Recognize the longing for connection, commitment, and social bonds that they represent. Allow these dreams to inspire you to seek meaningful relationships, honor your commitments, and build a sense of belonging and support in your life.

Remember, dream interpretations are personal experiences, and the meanings may vary based on individual associations and the context of the dream itself. Trust your own intuition and emotions within the dream as you explore the profound messages carried by dreams of betrothal.

C:

Cedar: Cedar trees were highly valued in ancient Babylon, known for their durability and fragrance. Dreaming of cedar might symbolize strength, resilience, or a connection to nature.

Ah, cedar trees, revered for their strength, durability, and delightful fragrance in the ancient land of Babylon. In the realm of dream interpretation, the appearance of cedar carries profound symbolism, representing strength, resilience, and a deep connection to nature.

Imagine this: You find yourself in the realm of dreams, and suddenly, towering cedar trees surround you, emanating a captivating fragrance. Dreaming of cedar signifies a connection to the qualities embodied by this mighty tree — strength, endurance, and a harmonious relationship with the natural world.

In ancient Babylon, cedar trees were highly valued for their exceptional qualities. They were known for their durability, used in construction, and revered for their fragrant wood. Dreaming of cedar may symbolize the need to embrace your own strength, to cultivate resilience, and to draw inspiration from the natural world around you.

The presence of cedar in dreams also signifies a deep connection to nature and the wisdom it holds. It invites you to tap into the ancient knowledge and balance that nature offers, to find solace and grounding in the midst of life's challenges. Dreaming of cedar encourages you to seek harmony and stability, to draw strength from the earth, and to align yourself with the natural rhythms of existence.

Furthermore, cedar represents longevity and the ability to withstand adversity. It serves as a reminder of the power of resilience and the capacity to overcome obstacles. Dreaming of cedar may symbolize your own inner strength, the potential to weather life's storms, and the ability to stand tall and unwavering in the face of challenges.

So, my dear friend, if cedar graces your dreams, embrace its symbolism. Recognize the strength, resilience, and connection to nature that it represents. Draw inspiration from the mighty cedar, allowing its qualities to infuse your own being. Embrace your own inner strength, seek harmony with the natural world, and stand tall, just like the majestic cedar trees that once adorned the lands of ancient Babylon.

Chariot: Chariots were significant in Babylonian warfare and transportation. Seeing a chariot in a dream could symbolize ambition, power, or a journey.

Ah, chariots, symbols of ambition, power, and the adventurous spirit of travel and warfare in the ancient Babylonian culture. In the realm of dream interpretation, the appearance of a chariot holds profound symbolism, representing ambition, power, and the notion of embarking on a transformative journey.

Picture this: You find yourself in the realm of dreams, and suddenly, a majestic chariot appears before you, ready to carry you on a remarkable journey. Dreaming of a chariot signifies the embodiment of ambition, the recognition of personal power, and the call to embark on a transformative journey.

In ancient Babylon, chariots played a vital role in warfare and transportation, symbolizing the pursuit of power and the ability to conquer new territories. Dreaming of a chariot may symbolize your own ambitions, the desire to assert yourself, and the drive to achieve success in various aspects of your life.

The presence of a chariot in dreams also signifies the readiness for a journey, both metaphorical and literal. It represents a call to adventure, a desire to explore new horizons, and a willingness to embrace the unknown. Dreaming of a chariot encourages you to tap into your inner strength, seize opportunities, and embark on a transformative path towards your goals and aspirations.

Furthermore, a chariot represents the connection between the physical and spiritual realms. It symbolizes the alignment of personal willpower with divine guidance, as chariots were often associated with deities in Babylonian mythology. Dreaming of a chariot may indicate the need to balance your personal ambitions with a sense of higher purpose or spiritual guidance.

So, my dear friend, if a chariot graces your dreams, embrace its symbolism. Recognize the spark of ambition within you, the power you hold to shape your destiny, and the call to embark on a transformative journey. Trust in your abilities, seize the opportunities that come your way, and let the chariot of your dreams carry you towards the fulfillment of your ambitions and the realization of your true potential.

Clay: Clay was a fundamental material in Babylonian culture, used for pottery and construction. Dreaming of clay might symbolize creativity, molding or shaping one's life, or the need for flexibility.

Ah, clay, the fundamental material that shaped the artistic and architectural endeavors of ancient Babylon. In the realm of dream interpretation, the appearance of clay carries profound symbolism, representing creativity, the ability to shape one's life, and the need for flexibility.

Imagine this: You find yourself in the realm of dreams, and suddenly, your hands are immersed in malleable clay, ready to be molded and transformed. Dreaming of clay signifies the power of creativity, the capacity to shape your own existence, and the call to embrace flexibility in the face of life's challenges.

In Babylonian culture, clay played a central role in pottery-making and construction, serving as a versatile and essential material. Dreaming of clay may symbolize the need to tap into your creative potential, to mold and shape your own life according to your vision and desires. It signifies the capacity to bring forth new ideas, projects, or artistic endeavors.

The presence of clay in dreams also represents the importance of adaptability and flexibility. Just as clay can be molded and reshaped, dreams of clay encourage you to embrace change, to be open to new possibilities, and to navigate the twists and turns of life with resilience and adaptability.

Furthermore, clay symbolizes the raw material from which beauty and structure emerge. It reminds us that the process of creation often involves working with the raw and formless, allowing it to take shape and form. Dreaming of clay invites you to trust in your own creative abilities, to nurture your ideas, and to allow them to evolve and transform over time.

So, my dear friend, if clay graces your dreams, embrace its symbolism. Recognize the power of your creativity, your ability to shape your own life, and the importance of flexibility in navigating life's journey. Embrace the malleable nature of clay and trust in your capacity to mold and reshape your existence according to your own vision and aspirations. Just as the skilled artisans of ancient Babylon worked with clay, may you create beauty, structure, and fulfillment in your own life.

Crown: Crowns were symbols of authority and kingship in ancient Babylon. Seeing or wearing a crown in a dream might represent power, recognition, or achievement.

Ah, crowns, symbols of authority and kingship that held great significance in the regal world of ancient Babylon. In the realm of dream interpretation, the appearance of a crown carries profound symbolism, representing power, recognition, and the attainment of significant achievements.

Imagine this: You find yourself in the realm of dreams, and suddenly, a resplendent crown adorns your head or comes into view. Dreaming of a crown signifies the embodiment of power, the acknowledgment of your worth and capabilities, and the fulfillment of significant accomplishments.

In ancient Babylon, crowns were symbols of authority, denoting kingship and leadership. Dreaming of a crown may symbolize your own personal power, the recognition of your influence, and the ability to assert your authority in various aspects of life.

The presence of a crown in dreams also signifies recognition and achievement. It represents the acknowledgment of your talents, skills, and efforts. Dreaming of a crown may indicate that your hard work, dedication, and accomplishments are being noticed and rewarded.

Furthermore, a crown represents the elevation to a higher position or status. It symbolizes the attainment of significant goals or the manifestation of your true potential. Dreaming of a crown encourages you to embrace your own worth, step into a position of authority, and celebrate the achievements that have brought you to this point.

So, my dear friend, if a crown graces your dreams, embrace its symbolism. Recognize the power, authority, and recognition it represents. Embrace your own personal power, assert your influence, and celebrate the achievements that have led you to this moment. Just as the regal crowns of ancient Babylon signified authority and recognition, may the crown of your dreams empower you to shine brightly, lead with confidence, and receive the acknowledgment and success that you deserve.

City: Babylon was known for its grand cities, and dreaming of a city might symbolize civilization, community, or social interactions.

Ah, cities, bustling hubs of civilization, community, and vibrant social interactions. In the realm of dream interpretation, the appearance of a city holds profound symbolism, representing the essence of human connection, the complexities of society, and the interplay of various aspects of your life.

Imagine this: You find yourself in the realm of dreams, and suddenly, a magnificent cityscape sprawls before you, pulsating with life and activity. Dreaming of a city signifies the embodiment of civilization, the significance of community, and the dynamics of social interactions.

In the context of Babylon, known for its grand cities such as Babylon itself, dreaming of a city may symbolize the desire for connection, the need for a sense of belonging, and the recognition of the interdependence between individuals and society.

The presence of a city in dreams also represents the richness and diversity of human experiences. It signifies the multitude of interactions, relationships, and opportunities that await you in your waking life. Dreaming of a city may encourage you to explore the realms of social connection, to engage with others, and to embrace the vibrant tapestry of human interactions.

Furthermore, a city symbolizes the intertwining of various aspects of life, reflecting the intricate web of relationships, work, leisure, and cultural pursuits. It invites you to consider the different dimensions of your own life and how they intersect with the wider social fabric.

Dreaming of a city can also evoke a sense of wonder, curiosity, and the potential for personal growth and exploration. It signifies the vastness of possibilities and the opportunities for expansion and discovery that lie ahead.

So, my dear friend, if a city graces your dreams, embrace its symbolism. Recognize the importance of human connection, the dynamics of social interactions, and the myriad opportunities that await you. Embrace the richness of your own life, engage with your community, and embark on a journey of exploration and growth within the tapestry of the city that unfolds before you. Just as the grand cities of ancient Babylon represented civilization and vibrant social interactions, may the city of your dreams inspire you to forge meaningful connections, navigate the complexities of society, and thrive in the tapestry of life's experiences.

Cuneiform: Cuneiform was the writing system used in ancient Babylon. Dreaming of cuneiform script might symbolize communication, knowledge, or the desire for understanding.

Ah, cuneiform, the ancient writing system that adorned the tablets and scrolls of ancient Babylon. In the realm of dream interpretation, the appearance of cuneiform script holds profound symbolism, representing the power of communication, the pursuit of knowledge, and the deep longing for understanding.

Imagine this: You find yourself in the realm of dreams, and suddenly, cuneiform script dances before your eyes, intriguing and captivating. Dreaming of cuneiform signifies the embodiment of communication, the recognition of the power of words, and the quest for knowledge and understanding.

In ancient Babylon, cuneiform was the written language used to record history, literature, and various aspects of daily life. Dreaming of cuneiform script may symbolize the importance of effective communication, the need to express oneself clearly, and the desire to be understood.

The presence of cuneiform script in dreams also represents the pursuit of knowledge and the thirst for understanding. It reminds us of the vast wisdom that can be gained through the written word and the power of education and learning. Dreaming of cuneiform may indicate a deep longing to expand your knowledge, to explore new ideas, or to delve into ancient wisdom.

Furthermore, cuneiform script symbolizes the connection to the past and the rich cultural heritage of ancient Babylon. It invites you to explore the depths of history, to connect with ancient wisdom, and to honor the importance of preserving and understanding the legacies of the past.

Dreaming of cuneiform script encourages you to embrace the power of communication, to seek knowledge, and to strive for understanding in your interactions with others and in your pursuit of personal growth.

So, my dear friend, if cuneiform script graces your dreams, embrace its symbolism. Recognize the significance of effective communication, the thirst for knowledge, and the desire for understanding that it represents. Allow the presence of cuneiform to inspire you to express yourself clearly, to seek wisdom and education, and to honor the rich cultural heritage of ancient Babylon. Just as the cuneiform script preserved the wisdom of the ancients, may your dreams guide you on a path of effective communication, lifelong learning, and deep understanding.

Calendar: Babylonians were skilled astronomers and developed a sophisticated calendar system. Dreaming of a calendar might represent a need for structure, organization, or the passage of time.

Ah, calendars, the markers of time that guided the lives of ancient Babylonians with their skillful astronomical knowledge. In the realm of dream interpretation, the appearance of a calendar holds profound symbolism, representing the need for structure, organization, and an awareness of the passage of time.

Imagine this: You find yourself in the realm of dreams, and suddenly, a calendar materializes before your eyes, its dates and divisions capturing your attention. Dreaming of a calendar signifies the embodiment of structure, the recognition of the importance of organization, and an awareness of the ever-flowing river of time.

In ancient Babylon, the Babylonians were renowned for their expertise in astronomy, which allowed them to develop a sophisticated calendar system. Dreaming of a calendar may symbolize the need for structure and order in your own life, the importance of setting goals and milestones, and the understanding of the passage of time.

The presence of a calendar in dreams also represents the need for organization and planning. It invites you to consider the commitments and responsibilities in your life, to manage your time effectively, and to create a sense of order in the midst of life's demands.

Furthermore, a calendar symbolizes the recognition of the passage of time and the cyclical nature of existence. It reminds us that time waits for no one and encourages us to make the most of each moment. Dreaming of a calendar may serve as a reminder to seize opportunities, set priorities, and make conscious choices in how you invest your time and energy.

Dreaming of a calendar can also evoke a sense of anticipation and the desire to plan for the future. It represents the potential for growth, the setting of goals, and the manifestation of your dreams as time unfolds.

So, my dear friend, if a calendar graces your dreams, embrace its symbolism. Recognize the need for structure, organization, and the awareness of the passage of time. Use it as a reminder to set goals, manage your time effectively, and make conscious choices in how you navigate your life's journey. Just as the skilled astronomers of ancient Babylon developed their calendar system, may the calendar of your dreams guide you in creating a life of purpose, balance, and fulfillment, as you honor the significance of time's eternal flow.

Court: The royal court in Babylon was a place of power and decision-making. Dreaming of a court might symbolize justice, judgment, or social interactions.

Ah, the royal court, a place of power, decision-making, and social interactions in the ancient Babylonian realm. In the realm of dream interpretation, the appearance of a court holds profound symbolism, representing concepts of justice, judgment, and the dynamics of social interactions.

Imagine this: You find yourself in the realm of dreams, and suddenly, you are amidst the grandeur and intrigue of a royal court. Dreaming of a court signifies the embodiment of justice, the recognition of the need for fairness and balanced judgment, and the dynamics of social interactions in your waking life.

In ancient Babylon, the royal court was a center of power and authority, where decisions were made, and justice was administered. Dreaming of a court may symbolize your own quest for justice, the desire for fairness, and the recognition of the importance of balanced judgment in your personal and social interactions.

The presence of a court in dreams also represents the dynamics of social interactions and the complexities of human relationships. It reminds us of the roles we play, the influence we have, and the need to navigate social situations with grace and diplomacy. Dreaming of a court may indicate the need to consider the consequences of your actions, to seek justice and fairness in your dealings with others, and to understand the power dynamics at play.

Furthermore, a court symbolizes the interplay between authority and responsibility. It signifies the recognition of your own power and the choices you make that affect others. Dreaming of a court encourages you to act with integrity, to honor your responsibilities, and to use your influence wisely.

Dreaming of a court can also evoke a sense of observation and evaluation. It may signify a need to assess situations, to make informed judgments, and to seek resolutions that align with principles of fairness and justice.

So, my dear friend, if a court graces your dreams, embrace its symbolism. Recognize the quest for justice, the importance of balanced judgment, and the dynamics of social interactions that it represents. Let the court of your dreams inspire you to act with integrity, seek fairness, and navigate the complexities of human relationships with wisdom and grace. Just as the royal court in Babylon was a place of power and decision-making, may the court of your dreams guide you in your pursuit of justice, harmonious social interactions, and personal growth.

In the royal court of Babylon, there were several positions of significance, each carrying its own symbolism and meaning in the realm of dream interpretation. Let's explore some of these positions and their potential interpretations when they appear in dreams:

King: The king represented ultimate authority, power, and leadership. Dreaming of a king might symbolize personal sovereignty, ambition, or the need to take charge of your life.

Queen: The queen symbolized feminine power, grace, and influence. Seeing a queen in a dream may represent feminine qualities, intuition, or a desire for balance and harmony.

Advisor: The advisor served as a trusted counselor to the king, providing guidance and wisdom. Dreaming of an advisor might symbolize the need for guidance, seeking wise counsel, or making important decisions in your waking life.

Courtier: Courtiers were members of the royal court, often nobles or individuals close to the ruling family. Dreaming of a courtier could symbolize social connections, networking, or the desire for recognition and acceptance within a particular circle.

Judge: Judges in the royal court were responsible for administering justice and making decisions. Seeing a judge in a dream might represent a need for fairness, the resolution of conflicts, or the evaluation of choices and actions.

Scribe: Scribes were responsible for recording and preserving important information. Dreaming of a scribe may symbolize the need for organization, communication, or the pursuit of knowledge and wisdom.

Messenger: Messengers delivered important communications and carried information between individuals. Seeing a messenger in a dream might symbolize the need for clear communication, the arrival of important news or messages, or the desire to convey your thoughts or intentions to others.

Dancer/Musician: Dancers and musicians entertained the court with their artistic skills. Dreaming of a dancer or musician may symbolize creativity, self-expression, or the need for joy and celebration in your life.

Servant: Servants attended to the needs of the royal court and carried out various tasks. Dreaming of a servant might represent humility, a willingness to serve others, or the need to find balance between leadership and humility.

Each position in the royal court carries its own unique symbolism and meaning in the realm of dream interpretation. When they appear in your dreams, consider the qualities and associations that these positions represent and how they might relate to your current life circumstances, desires, or challenges.

Code of Hammurabi: The Code of Hammurabi was a significant legal code in ancient Babylon. Dreaming of the Code of Hammurabi might symbolize principles, ethics, or the need for fairness and balance.

Ah, the Code of Hammurabi, a significant legal code that shaped the principles and ethics of ancient Babylonian society. In the realm of dream interpretation, the appearance of the Code of Hammurabi holds profound symbolism, representing the principles of justice, ethics, and the quest for fairness and balance.

Imagine this: You find yourself in the realm of dreams, and suddenly, the ancient inscriptions of the Code of Hammurabi come to life before your eyes. Dreaming of the Code of Hammurabi signifies the embodiment of principles, the recognition of ethical values, and the call for fairness and balance in your waking life.

The Code of Hammurabi was a comprehensive set of laws that governed various aspects of Babylonian society, ensuring justice and order. Dreaming of the Code of Hammurabi may symbolize the need to uphold principles of fairness, the recognition of the consequences of one's actions, or the quest for justice in your personal and social interactions.

The presence of the Code of Hammurabi in dreams also represents the importance of ethics and moral values. It reminds us of the need to act with integrity, to make choices that align with our principles, and to consider the impact of our actions on others.

Furthermore, the Code of Hammurabi symbolizes the quest for balance and harmony. It represents the understanding that justice involves weighing different perspectives, considering the interests of all parties involved, and striving for equitable outcomes. Dreaming of the Code of Hammurabi encourages you to seek balance in your own life, to consider the fairness of your decisions, and to find harmony in your relationships and interactions.

Dreaming of the Code of Hammurabi can also evoke a sense of responsibility and the recognition of the importance of social order. It may symbolize your own role in upholding fairness and justice, or it may signify a desire for a more just and equitable society.

So, my dear friend, if the Code of Hammurabi graces your dreams, embrace its symbolism. Recognize the principles, ethics, and the need for fairness and balance that it represents. Let the Code of Hammurabi inspire you to uphold justice, act with integrity, and strive for equitable outcomes in your personal and social interactions. Just as the Code of Hammurabi shaped the principles of ancient Babylonian society, may the code of your dreams guide you in creating a world of fairness, balance, and moral integrity.

Curved Sword: The curved sword, known as a scimitar, was a common weapon in ancient Babylonian warfare. Dreaming of a curved sword might symbolize conflict, protection, or the need to defend oneself.

Ah, the curved sword, a formidable weapon that played a significant role in the warfare of ancient Babylon. In the realm of dream interpretation, the appearance of a curved sword holds profound symbolism, representing concepts of conflict, protection, and the need to defend oneself.

Imagine this: You find yourself in the realm of dreams, and suddenly, a gleaming curved sword materializes in your hands or comes into view. Dreaming of a curved sword signifies the embodiment of conflict, the recognition of the need for protection, and the call to defend oneself or one's interests in your waking life.

In ancient Babylon, the curved sword, often referred to as a scimitar, was a common weapon used in warfare. Dreaming of a curved sword may symbolize the presence of conflict, the recognition of challenges or threats, and the need to stand up for oneself.

The presence of a curved sword in dreams also represents the need for protection and self-defense. It signifies the recognition of personal boundaries, the importance of asserting oneself, and the readiness to confront adversity.

Furthermore, a curved sword symbolizes the courage and strength required to face challenges. It represents the willingness to stand up for what is right, to defend one's beliefs, and to assert one's authority when necessary.

Dreaming of a curved sword can also evoke a sense of empowerment and the recognition of one's own inner strength. It may signify the need to tap into your own resilience, to overcome obstacles, and to assert yourself in the face of adversity.

So, my dear friend, if a curved sword graces your dreams, embrace its symbolism. Recognize the presence of conflict, the need for protection, and the call to defend yourself or your interests. Let the curved sword of your dreams inspire you to stand up for what is right, to assert your boundaries, and to tap into your inner strength and courage. Just as the curved sword played a significant role in ancient Babylonian warfare, may the sword of your dreams guide you in navigating the challenges of life with resilience, determination, and self-assurance.

D:

Divination: Divination was practiced in ancient Babylon to gain insight into the future or seek guidance from the divine. Dreams were considered an important form of divination, and dreaming of divination might symbolize a desire for insight or a connection to the supernatural.

Ah, divination, the ancient practice of seeking insight into the future and seeking guidance from the divine. In the realm of dream interpretation, the appearance of divination holds profound symbolism, representing a desire for insight, a connection to the supernatural, and the recognition of the wisdom that lies beyond the conscious realm.

Imagine this: You find yourself in the realm of dreams, and suddenly, the art of divination unfolds before your eyes, whether through tarot cards, runes, tea leaves, or other mystical methods. Dreaming of divination signifies the embodiment of seeking guidance, the recognition of hidden truths, and the call to tap into your intuitive powers.

In ancient Babylon, divination was a respected practice employed to gain insights into the future, seek guidance, or communicate with the divine. Dreaming of divination may symbolize a deep desire for insight, a yearning to understand the mysteries of life, or a connection to the supernatural realms.

The presence of divination in dreams also represents the recognition of your own intuition and inner wisdom. It invites you to trust your instincts, to listen to the whispers of your inner voice, and to honor the subtle signs and symbols that surround you.

Furthermore, divination symbolizes the belief in synchronicity and the interconnectedness of all things. It reminds us that there is a higher wisdom at play, guiding us through the twists and turns of life. Dreaming of divination encourages you to pay attention to the signs and symbols that appear in your waking life and to trust in the guidance that comes from within.

Dreaming of divination can also evoke a sense of curiosity and the desire to explore the realms beyond the ordinary. It may signify a longing to uncover hidden truths, to gain insight into your own path, or to seek guidance and clarity in your life's journey.

So, my dear friend, if divination graces your dreams, embrace its symbolism. Recognize the desire for insight, the connection to the supernatural, and the recognition of your own intuitive powers that it represents. Let the art of divination inspire you to trust your instincts, to seek guidance from within, and to honor the subtle signs and synchronicities that guide you on your life's path. Just as divination was practiced in ancient Babylon to gain insights and seek guidance, may the divination of your dreams illuminate your path and bring you closer to the wisdom that resides within and beyond.

Demon: Babylonian mythology included various types of demons and malevolent spirits. Dreaming of a demon might symbolize fear, temptation, or the presence of negative influences.

Ah, demons, those intriguing and formidable entities that existed in the mythology of ancient Babylon. In the realm of dream interpretation, the appearance of a demon holds profound symbolism, representing concepts of fear, temptation, and the presence of negative influences.

Imagine this: You find yourself in the realm of dreams, and suddenly, a fearsome demon materializes before your eyes, its presence invoking a sense of unease. Dreaming of a demon signifies the embodiment of fear, the recognition of temptation, and the call to confront and overcome negative influences in your waking life.

In Babylonian mythology, demons were malevolent spirits believed to bring misfortune, illness, or temptation to humanity. Dreaming of a demon may symbolize the presence of fear or anxiety, the struggle with temptation or negative influences, or the need to confront and overcome personal challenges.

The presence of a demon in dreams also represents the recognition of our own inner fears and negative thought patterns. It invites us to confront and transform the darkness within ourselves, to resist the lure of negative influences, and to cultivate inner strength and resilience.

Furthermore, a demon symbolizes the importance of discernment and the ability to recognize and resist harmful temptations or negative influences. Dreaming of a demon may signify the need to examine your own choices and actions, to assert your boundaries, and to protect yourself from harmful situations or individuals.

Dreaming of a demon can also evoke a sense of empowerment and the recognition of your own capacity to overcome adversity. It may signify the need to face your fears, to tap into your inner strength, and to cultivate positive influences in your life.

So, my dear friend, if a demon graces your dreams, embrace its symbolism. Recognize the presence of fear, the allure of temptation, and the call to confront and overcome negative influences. Let the demon of your dreams serve as a catalyst for personal growth, inner transformation, and the cultivation of resilience. Just as the demons existed in the mythology of ancient Babylon, may the demons of your dreams guide you in facing your fears, resisting harmful influences, and embracing the light within.

Deluge: The Babylonian myth of the Great Flood, similar to the story of Noah's Ark, featured prominently in their culture. Dreaming of a deluge or flood might symbolize emotional turmoil, upheaval, or the need for cleansing or renewal.

Ah, the deluge, the cataclysmic event that held great significance in Babylonian mythology and culture. In the realm of dream interpretation, the appearance of a deluge or flood holds profound symbolism, representing concepts of emotional turmoil, upheaval, and the potential for cleansing or renewal.

Imagine this: You find yourself in the realm of dreams, and suddenly, the waters rise, engulfing everything in sight, bringing forth a deluge of emotions and experiences. Dreaming of a deluge or flood signifies the embodiment of emotional turmoil, the recognition of upheaval, and the call for cleansing or renewal in your waking life.

In Babylonian mythology, the Great Flood was a prominent story that depicted the destruction of humanity and the rebirth of life. Dreaming of a deluge or flood may symbolize the presence of emotional turbulence, the experience of overwhelming emotions, or the need for a cathartic release and renewal.

The presence of a deluge or flood in dreams also represents the recognition of the need for emotional cleansing and renewal. It invites you to delve into the depths of your emotions, to face any unresolved issues or repressed feelings, and to embrace the process of healing and growth.

Furthermore, a deluge symbolizes the potential for transformation and rebirth. It represents the opportunity to let go of the past, to release what no longer serves you, and to embrace new beginnings. Dreaming of a deluge or flood may signify a need to shed old patterns, to release emotional baggage, and to embrace a fresh start.

Dreaming of a deluge or flood can also evoke a sense of surrender and trust in the process of life. It may signify the need to let go of control, to flow with the currents of change, and to have faith in the eventual emergence of clarity and renewal.

So, my dear friend, if a deluge or flood graces your dreams, embrace its symbolism. Recognize the presence of emotional turmoil, the potential for cleansing and renewal, and the opportunity for transformation that it represents. Let the deluge of your dreams guide you in navigating the depths of your emotions, releasing what no longer serves you, and embracing the process of healing and growth. Just as the Babylonian myth of the Great Flood held great significance in their culture, may the deluge of your dreams bring forth a renewed sense of clarity, emotional well-being, and inner transformation.

Dance: Dance held significance in Babylonian rituals and celebrations. Dreaming of dancing might symbolize joy, expression, or a sense of harmony and unity.

Ah, dance, the rhythmic movement that held great significance in the rituals and celebrations of ancient Babylon. In the realm of dream interpretation, the act of dancing holds profound symbolism, representing concepts of joy, expression, and a sense of harmony and unity.

Imagine this: You find yourself in the realm of dreams, and suddenly, you feel the music pulsating through your body as you gracefully move in a dance. Dreaming of dancing signifies the embodiment of joy, the expression of your inner self, and the call to experience harmony and unity in your waking life.

In Babylonian culture, dance played a vital role in religious ceremonies, celebrations, and social gatherings. Dreaming of dance may symbolize the presence of joy, celebration, or the desire to express oneself freely and fully.

The act of dancing in dreams also represents the recognition of the importance of self-expression and the release of pent-up emotions. It invites you to connect with your body, to embrace the rhythm of life, and to let your inner light shine through movement and expression.

Furthermore, dance symbolizes a sense of harmony and unity. It represents the coming together of individuals, the unification of diverse energies, and the celebration of life's rhythms. Dreaming of dance may signify a longing for connection, a desire for unity, or the recognition of the beauty that emerges when individuals move in harmony with one another.

Dreaming of dance can also evoke a sense of liberation and the celebration of life's joys. It may signify the need to let go of inhibitions, to embrace spontaneity, and to find delight in the present moment.

So, my dear friend, if dance graces your dreams, embrace its symbolism. Recognize the presence of joy, the desire for self-expression, and the longing for harmony and unity that it represents. Let the dance of your dreams guide you in embracing the joy of life, expressing your inner self, and finding harmony in your relationships and interactions. Just as dance held significance in Babylonian rituals and celebrations, may the dance of your dreams bring forth a sense of liberation, connection, and the celebration of life's rhythms.

Drum: Drums were musical instruments used in Babylonian ceremonies and gatherings. Dreaming of a drum might symbolize rhythm, energy, or the need for excitement and vitality.

Ah, the rhythmic beats of the drum, echoing through the ceremonies and gatherings of ancient Babylon. In the realm of dream interpretation, the appearance of a drum holds profound symbolism, representing concepts of rhythm, energy, and the need for excitement and vitality.

Imagine this: You find yourself in the realm of dreams, and suddenly, the pulsating beats of a drum fill the air, stirring your senses and igniting a surge of energy within you. Dreaming of a drum signifies the embodiment of rhythm, the awakening of your vitality, and the call to embrace excitement and passion in your waking life.

In Babylonian culture, drums were used in various ceremonies and gatherings, infusing them with energy and creating a sense of unity and celebration. Dreaming of a drum may symbolize the presence of rhythm, the need for synchronization, or the desire to infuse your life with excitement and vitality.

The presence of a drum in dreams also represents the recognition of the importance of rhythm and flow. It invites you to tune into the natural rhythms of life, to find your own beat, and to align yourself with the energy that surrounds you.

Furthermore, a drum symbolizes the awakening of your inner vitality and passion. It represents the call to embrace life with enthusiasm, to tap into your creative energy, and to engage fully in the experiences that come your way. Dreaming of a drum may signify a need to infuse your life with excitement, to pursue your passions, or to embrace a sense of adventure.

Dreaming of a drum can also evoke a sense of unity and connection. It may signify the desire to come together with others, to create a harmonious rhythm, and to celebrate the joy of life collectively.

So, my dear friend, if a drum graces your dreams, embrace its symbolism. Recognize the presence of rhythm, the awakening of your vitality, and the call to embrace excitement and passion in your life. Let the drum of your dreams guide you in finding your own beat, infusing your life with energy and enthusiasm, and connecting with others in the joyous celebration of life's rhythms. Just as drums were used in Babylonian ceremonies and gatherings to create unity and energy, may the drum of your dreams awaken your inner vitality and propel you towards a life filled with rhythm, passion, and joyful experiences.

Dagger: Daggers were weapons used in ancient Babylonian warfare. Dreaming of a dagger might symbolize aggression, conflict, or a need to defend oneself.

Ah, the dagger, a formidable weapon that played a significant role in the warfare of ancient Babylon. In the realm of dream interpretation, the appearance of a dagger holds profound symbolism, representing concepts of aggression, conflict, and the need to defend oneself.

Imagine this: You find yourself in the realm of dreams, and suddenly, a gleaming dagger materializes in your hands or comes into view. Dreaming of a dagger signifies the embodiment of aggression, the recognition of conflict, and the call to protect oneself or one's interests in your waking life.

In Babylonian warfare, daggers were used as weapons, serving as tools of offense and defense. Dreaming of a dagger may symbolize the presence of aggression, the recognition of conflict or tension, or the need to assert oneself and protect one's boundaries.

The presence of a dagger in dreams also represents the recognition of the need to defend oneself or one's interests. It invites you to assert your boundaries, to stand up for yourself in the face of adversity, and to protect what is important to you.

Furthermore, a dagger symbolizes the potential for conflict and the need for caution. It represents the importance of discernment, the ability to navigate challenging situations, and the readiness to take action when necessary. Dreaming of a dagger may signify the need to stay vigilant, to be assertive in asserting your boundaries, and to protect yourself from harmful situations or individuals.

Dreaming of a dagger can also evoke a sense of inner strength and the recognition of your own power. It may signify the need to tap into your inner resilience, to face conflicts head-on, and to stand up for what is right.

So, my dear friend, if a dagger graces your dreams, embrace its symbolism. Recognize the presence of aggression, conflict, and the need to defend oneself that it represents. Let the dagger of your dreams inspire you to assert your boundaries, to protect what is important to you, and to tap into your inner strength and resilience. Just as daggers were used in ancient Babylonian warfare, may the dagger of your dreams guide you in navigating conflicts, asserting yourself with confidence, and protecting yourself and your interests with courage and determination.

Door: Doors were symbolic gateways in ancient Babylonian culture, representing transitions, opportunities, or the boundary between the physical and spiritual realms. Dreaming of a door might symbolize new beginnings, choices, or access to hidden knowledge.

Ah, the door, a symbolic gateway that held great significance in the culture of ancient Babylon. In the realm of dream interpretation, the appearance of a door holds profound symbolism, representing concepts of new beginnings, choices, and access to hidden knowledge.

Imagine this: You find yourself in the realm of dreams, and suddenly, a door appears before you, beckoning you to explore what lies beyond. Dreaming of a door signifies the embodiment of transitions, the recognition of opportunities, and the call to explore new paths or realms in your waking life.

In Babylonian culture, doors were seen as symbolic gateways, representing the threshold between different spaces or realms. Dreaming of a door may symbolize the presence of new beginnings, the recognition of choices or opportunities, or the desire to access hidden knowledge or realms of existence.

The presence of a door in dreams also represents the recognition of the importance of transitions and the potential for growth and exploration. It invites you to step through the door of possibilities, to embrace new experiences, and to navigate the choices and opportunities that present themselves to you.

Furthermore, a door symbolizes the boundary between the physical and spiritual realms. It represents the potential for spiritual growth, the access to hidden knowledge or wisdom, and the opportunity to connect with higher realms of consciousness. Dreaming of a door may signify the need to embark on a spiritual journey, to seek deeper understanding, or to unlock the mysteries of existence.

Dreaming of a door can also evoke a sense of anticipation and the recognition of the power of choice. It may signify the need to make decisions, to embrace new beginnings, or to seize the opportunities that come your way.

So, my dear friend, if a door graces your dreams, embrace its symbolism. Recognize the presence of new beginnings, choices, and the potential for accessing hidden knowledge or realms that it represents. Let the door of your dreams guide you in navigating transitions, embracing opportunities, and embarking on a journey of self-discovery and growth. Just as doors were symbolic gateways in ancient Babylonian culture, may the door of your dreams open new paths, reveal hidden knowledge, and lead you to exciting adventures and transformative experiences.

Dust: Dust was often associated with decay or impermanence in ancient Babylonian beliefs. Dreaming of dust might symbolize transformation, insignificance, or the passage of time.

Ah, dust, the symbol of decay and impermanence in the beliefs of ancient Babylon. In the realm of dream interpretation, the appearance of dust holds profound symbolism, representing concepts of transformation, insignificance, and the passage of time.

Imagine this: You find yourself in the realm of dreams, and suddenly, you see clouds of dust swirling around you, carrying a sense of impermanence and change. Dreaming of dust signifies the embodiment of transformation, the recognition of insignificance, and the awareness of the passage of time in your waking life.

In ancient Babylonian beliefs, dust was often associated with decay, reminding individuals of the transient nature of life and the inevitability of change. Dreaming of dust may symbolize the presence of transformation, the recognition of the fleeting nature of existence, or the need to embrace change and impermanence.

The presence of dust in dreams also represents the recognition of insignificance and the ephemeral nature of human existence. It invites you to reflect upon the impermanence of material possessions, the transience of worldly achievements, and the importance of focusing on what truly matters.

Furthermore, dust symbolizes the passage of time and the transformative power of change. It represents the cycles of life, the inevitability of growth and decay, and the need to adapt to new circumstances. Dreaming of dust may signify the need to let go of what no longer serves you, to embrace the process of transformation, and to recognize the beauty and potential for growth that comes with change.

Dreaming of dust can also evoke a sense of humility and the recognition of the grander scheme of existence. It may signify the need to let go of attachments, to cultivate a sense of detachment from material possessions, and to focus on the deeper aspects of life and personal growth.

So, my dear friend, if dust graces your dreams, embrace its symbolism. Recognize the presence of transformation, insignificance, and the passage of time that it represents. Let the dust of your dreams remind you to embrace change, to let go of attachments, and to focus on the deeper aspects of life and personal growth. Just as dust carried profound symbolism in ancient Babylonian beliefs, may the dust of your dreams inspire you to navigate the transient nature of existence with grace, embrace transformation, and find beauty and growth amidst the ebb and flow of life's cycles.

Drought: Babylonian agriculture relied heavily on the availability of water. Dreaming of a drought might symbolize scarcity, hardships, or a sense of thirst or longing.

Ah, the drought, a challenging phenomenon that held great significance in the agricultural practices of ancient Babylon. In the realm of dream interpretation, the appearance of a drought holds profound symbolism, representing concepts of scarcity, hardships, and a sense of thirst or longing.

Imagine this: You find yourself in the realm of dreams, and suddenly, the land around you becomes parched and barren, devoid of the life-giving waters. Dreaming of a drought signifies the embodiment of scarcity, the recognition of hardships, and the call to quench your thirst or fulfill your longing in your waking life.

In ancient Babylon, agriculture relied heavily on the availability of water, and a drought posed great challenges, leading to crop failure and hardships for the people. Dreaming of a drought may symbolize the presence of scarcity, the recognition of challenging circumstances, or the need to overcome difficulties in order to thrive.

The presence of a drought in dreams also represents the recognition of hardships and the longing for nourishment and sustenance. It invites you to reflect upon areas of your life where you may be experiencing scarcity, challenges, or a sense of unfulfilled longing.

Furthermore, a drought symbolizes the thirst for fulfillment and the longing for abundance. It represents the recognition of unmet needs, desires, or aspirations and the call to find ways to quench your thirst for a more fulfilling life. Dreaming of a drought may signify the need to explore avenues for growth, to seek nourishment for your soul, or to find alternative sources of fulfillment amidst challenging circumstances.

Dreaming of a drought can also evoke a sense of resilience and the recognition of the importance of adaptability. It may signify the need to find creative solutions, to conserve resources, and to cultivate inner strength in the face of adversity.

So, my dear friend, if a drought graces your dreams, embrace its symbolism. Recognize the presence of scarcity, hardships, and the longing for fulfillment that it represents. Let the drought of your dreams inspire you to seek ways to overcome challenges, to quench your thirst for a more fulfilling life, and to cultivate resilience in the face of adversity. Just as a drought held great significance in the agricultural practices of ancient Babylon, may the drought of your dreams guide you in finding alternative sources of nourishment, embracing resilience, and discovering the inner strength to thrive even in challenging times.

Destiny: Babylonians believed in the concept of fate and the influence of divine forces on human lives. Dreaming of destiny might symbolize a sense of purpose, predestination, or the need to accept one's path in life.

Ah, destiny, the belief in the predetermined course of one's life influenced by divine forces. In the realm of dream interpretation, the appearance of destiny holds profound symbolism, representing concepts of purpose, predestination, and the need to accept one's path in life.

Imagine this: You find yourself in the realm of dreams, and suddenly, you feel a deep sense of connection to a higher purpose, as if the hand of destiny is guiding your every step. Dreaming of destiny signifies the embodiment of purpose, the recognition of a predetermined path, and the call to accept and embrace your unique journey in your waking life.

In Babylonian beliefs, the concept of destiny played a central role, with the belief that divine forces influenced the course of human lives. Dreaming of destiny may symbolize the presence of a higher purpose, the recognition of a predetermined path, or the need to align yourself with the flow of divine guidance.

The presence of destiny in dreams also represents the recognition of purpose and the call to embrace your unique path in life. It invites you to reflect upon your own journey, to seek alignment with your deepest passions and values, and to embrace the sense of meaning and fulfillment that comes from living in accordance with your destiny.

Furthermore, destiny symbolizes the acceptance of the unfolding of your life's experiences. It represents the recognition that certain events, encounters, and challenges are part of your unique journey and serve a greater purpose. Dreaming of destiny may signify the need to surrender to the flow of life, to trust in the guidance of higher forces, and to embrace the lessons and growth opportunities presented to you.

Dreaming of destiny can also evoke a sense of empowerment and the recognition of your own agency within the context of a larger plan. It may signify the need to take ownership of your choices, to align your actions with your values and aspirations, and to actively participate in co-creating your own destiny.

So, my dear friend, if destiny graces your dreams, embrace its symbolism. Recognize the presence of purpose, predestination, and the need to accept your unique path in life that it represents. Let the sense of destiny in your dreams inspire you to explore your deepest passions, to align with your values, and to embrace the unfolding of your life's experiences. Just as the Babylonians believed in the influence of divine forces on human lives, may the sense of destiny in your dreams guide you in finding fulfillment, meaning, and a deep sense of purpose as you navigate the journey of your own unique path.

E:

Enki (deity): Enki, also known as Ea, was a significant god in Babylonian mythology associated with wisdom, magic, and the waters. Dreaming of Enki might symbolize access to hidden knowledge, intuition, or the need for guidance.

Ah, Enki, the revered deity in Babylonian mythology, known for his association with wisdom, magic, and the waters. In the realm of dream interpretation, the appearance of Enki holds profound symbolism, representing concepts of hidden knowledge, intuition, and the need for guidance.

Imagine this: You find yourself in the realm of dreams, and suddenly, the figure of Enki manifests before you, emanating an aura of wisdom and mystique. Dreaming of Enki signifies the embodiment of access to hidden knowledge, the recognition of intuitive abilities, and the call to seek guidance in your waking life.

In Babylonian mythology, Enki was revered as the god of wisdom and magic, as well as the deity associated with the waters, symbolizing the deep well of knowledge and intuition. Dreaming of Enki may symbolize the presence of hidden knowledge, the recognition of your own intuitive abilities, or the need to seek guidance and wisdom in your life's journey.

The presence of Enki in dreams also represents the recognition of the importance of wisdom and the need for guidance. It invites you to tap into your own inner well of knowledge, to trust your intuition, and to seek guidance from higher realms or wise mentors.

Furthermore, Enki symbolizes the flow of wisdom and the magical realms of the unseen. It represents the connection to ancient knowledge, the understanding of esoteric truths, and the ability to tap into the subtle energies of the universe. Dreaming of Enki may signify the need to explore your own inner depths, to unlock hidden knowledge, and to embrace your intuitive gifts for guidance and self-discovery.

Dreaming of Enki can also evoke a sense of awe and the recognition of the power of wisdom. It may signify the need to cultivate a thirst for knowledge, to expand your intellectual and spiritual horizons, and to embrace the mysteries of life with a sense of wonder.

So, my dear friend, if Enki graces your dreams, embrace his symbolism. Recognize the presence of hidden knowledge, intuition, and the need for guidance that he represents. Let the figure of Enki in your dreams inspire you to tap into your own inner wisdom, to trust your intuition, and to seek guidance and wisdom from the realms beyond. Just as Enki was revered for his association with wisdom, magic, and the waters in Babylonian mythology, may the presence of Enki in your dreams guide you on a path of self-discovery, enlightenment, and the pursuit of knowledge and guidance from the hidden realms of the universe.

Eclipse: Ancient Babylonians had a keen interest in celestial events, including solar and lunar eclipses. Dreaming of an eclipse might symbolize transformation, hidden influences, or the convergence of opposing forces.

Ah, the eclipse, a celestial event that fascinated the ancient Babylonians and held great significance in their culture. In the realm of dream interpretation, the appearance of an eclipse holds profound symbolism, representing concepts of transformation, hidden influences, and the convergence of opposing forces.

Imagine this: You find yourself in the realm of dreams, and suddenly, the sun or moon is obscured by the shadow of an eclipse, casting an otherworldly ambiance. Dreaming of an eclipse signifies the embodiment of transformation, the recognition of hidden influences, and the call to embrace the convergence of opposing forces in your waking life.

In ancient Babylon, celestial events, such as solar and lunar eclipses, were observed with great interest and were believed to hold powerful symbolism. Dreaming of an eclipse may symbolize the presence of transformative energies, the recognition of hidden influences shaping your path, or the need to embrace the dynamic interplay of opposing forces within and around you.

The presence of an eclipse in dreams also represents the recognition of transformation and the unveiling of hidden aspects of your life. It invites you to reflect upon areas of your life where change is occurring or needed, to embrace the process of growth and renewal, and to navigate the shadows of your own psyche with courage and insight.

Furthermore, an eclipse symbolizes the convergence of opposing forces and the interplay between light and darkness. It represents the dynamic balance between different aspects of your being, the integration of polarities, and the realization that even in moments of darkness, there is the potential for illumination and growth. Dreaming of an eclipse may signify the need to find harmony amidst opposing forces, to embrace the interplay of light and shadow, and to trust in the transformative power of the cosmic dance.

Dreaming of an eclipse can also evoke a sense of awe and the recognition of the grandeur of the universe. It may signify the need to expand your awareness, to embrace the mysteries of existence, and to connect with the vast cosmic forces that shape your life's journey.

So, my dear friend, if an eclipse graces your dreams, embrace its symbolism. Recognize the presence of transformation, hidden influences, and the convergence of opposing forces that it represents. Let the eclipse in your dreams inspire you to navigate change with grace, to unveil hidden aspects of yourself, and to find harmony amidst the interplay of light and darkness. Just as the ancient Babylonians had a keen interest in celestial events, may the presence of an eclipse in your dreams guide you to embrace the transformative energies and hidden influences that shape your path, and to dance with the cosmic forces that illuminate your journey of self-discovery and growth.

Elephant: Elephants were exotic and awe-inspiring creatures in Babylonian culture. Dreaming of an elephant might symbolize strength, power, wisdom, or the need for patience and perseverance.

Ah, the majestic elephant, a creature that evokes awe and reverence in the culture of ancient Babylon. In the realm of dream interpretation, the appearance of an elephant holds profound symbolism, representing concepts of strength, power, wisdom, and the need for patience and perseverance.

Imagine this: You find yourself in the realm of dreams, and suddenly, a magnificent elephant emerges before you, radiating an aura of strength and wisdom. Dreaming of an elephant signifies the embodiment of these qualities and the call to embrace them in your waking life.

In Babylonian culture, elephants were considered exotic and awe-inspiring creatures, known for their immense physical strength, intelligence, and gentle nature. Dreaming of an elephant may symbolize the presence of these qualities in your own life, the recognition of your own inner strength and wisdom, or the need to cultivate patience and perseverance in the face of challenges.

The presence of an elephant in dreams also represents the recognition of power and the call to harness your own personal power. It invites you to tap into your inner strength, to trust in your abilities, and to assert yourself in a balanced and compassionate way.

Furthermore, an elephant symbolizes wisdom and the importance of patience and perseverance. It represents the ability to navigate through challenges with grace and resilience. Dreaming of an elephant may signify the need to cultivate wisdom, to approach situations with patience and a steady mindset, and to embrace the process of growth and transformation.

An elephant's presence in dreams can also evoke a sense of awe and reverence for the natural world. It may signify the need to connect with the deeper wisdom of nature, to honor the interconnectedness of all beings, and to find inspiration in the majestic presence of the animal kingdom.

So, my dear friend, if an elephant graces your dreams, embrace its symbolism. Recognize the presence of strength, power, wisdom, and the call for patience and perseverance that it represents. Let the presence of the elephant in your dreams inspire you to tap into your inner strength, to cultivate wisdom, and to embrace challenges with grace and resilience. Just as the elephants were considered awe-inspiring creatures in Babylonian culture, may the presence of an elephant in your dreams guide you to embody your own strength, wisdom, and patience, and to navigate life's journey with a sense of awe and reverence for the natural world around you.

Epic: Babylonians were known for their epic literature, such as the "Epic of Gilgamesh." Dreaming of an epic might symbolize personal quests, heroic journeys, or the exploration of profound themes and experiences.

Ah, the epic, a form of literature that captivated the hearts and minds of the ancient Babylonians with its grand narratives and profound themes. In the realm of dream interpretation, the appearance of an epic holds profound symbolism, representing concepts of personal quests, heroic journeys, and the exploration of profound themes and experiences.

Imagine this: You find yourself in the realm of dreams, and suddenly, you become immersed in a grand and epic tale, filled with adventure, challenges, and profound meaning. Dreaming of an epic signifies the embodiment of these elements and the call to embrace your own heroic journey in your waking life.

The Babylonians were renowned for their epic literature, with the "Epic of Gilgamesh" being one of their most revered works. Dreaming of an epic may symbolize the presence of a personal quest, the recognition of your own heroic potential, or the need to explore profound themes and experiences in your life's journey.

The presence of an epic in dreams also represents the recognition of adventure and the call to embark on a transformative journey. It invites you to reflect upon the quests and challenges that shape your life, to embrace the call to adventure, and to navigate the trials and tribulations with courage and resilience.

Furthermore, an epic symbolizes the exploration of profound themes and experiences. It represents the human condition, the pursuit of knowledge, and the search for meaning and fulfillment. Dreaming of an epic may signify the need to dive deep into the realms of your own consciousness, to explore the profound

questions of existence, and to embrace the richness of your own
life's story.

Dreaming of an epic can also evoke a sense of inspiration and
the recognition of the power of storytelling. It may signify the need
to connect with your own inner narrative, to express yourself
creatively, and to share your experiences and wisdom with others.

So, my dear friend, if an epic graces your dreams, embrace its
symbolism. Recognize the presence of personal quests, heroic
journeys, and the exploration of profound themes and experiences
that it represents. Let the epic in your dreams inspire you to
embrace your own heroic potential, to embark on transformative
journeys, and to explore the profound questions and themes that
shape your existence. Just as the Babylonians were known for their
epic literature, may the presence of an epic in your dreams guide
you to weave your own grand narrative, to embrace the adventures
that come your way, and to discover the profound meaning and
fulfillment that lie within the tapestry of your own life's story.

Enchantment: Ancient Babylonians believed in the existence
of enchantments and magical spells. Dreaming of enchantment
might symbolize fascination, allure, or the desire for something
mysterious or extraordinary.

Ah, enchantment, a concept that captivated the ancient
Babylonians with its allure and belief in the mystical and magical.
In the realm of dream interpretation, the appearance of
enchantment holds profound symbolism, representing concepts of
fascination, allure, and the yearning for something mysterious or
extraordinary.

Imagine this: You find yourself in the realm of dreams, and
suddenly, you are enchanted by a magical presence, surrounded by
an air of mystery and wonder. Dreaming of enchantment signifies
the embodiment of these qualities and the call to embrace the
captivating and extraordinary aspects of life in your waking
existence.

The ancient Babylonians held a belief in enchantments and magical spells, recognizing the existence of mystical forces that could influence the world around them. Dreaming of enchantment may symbolize the presence of fascination, the allure of the unknown, or the desire to experience something extraordinary in your life's journey.

The presence of enchantment in dreams also represents the recognition of the power of fascination and the call to explore the depths of your own curiosity and wonder. It invites you to embrace the magic of everyday life, to seek out the extraordinary in the ordinary, and to approach the world with a sense of awe and openness.

Furthermore, enchantment symbolizes the desire for something mysterious and extraordinary. It represents the yearning for experiences that go beyond the mundane, the mundane, and the predictable. Dreaming of enchantment may signify the need to tap into your own inner sense of wonder, to embrace the unknown with a spirit of adventure, and to cultivate a connection to the magic that exists within and around you.

Dreaming of enchantment can also evoke a sense of excitement and the recognition of the limitless possibilities that exist in life. It may signify the need to explore your passions, to follow your dreams, and to allow yourself to be drawn to the enchanting aspects of existence.

So, my dear friend, if enchantment graces your dreams, embrace its symbolism. Recognize the presence of fascination, allure, and the desire for something mysterious or extraordinary that it represents. Let the enchantment in your dreams inspire you to embrace the captivating aspects of life, to explore your curiosities and passions, and to open yourself to the magic that exists within and around you. Just as the ancient Babylonians believed in the existence of enchantments and magical spells, may the presence of enchantment in your dreams guide you to cultivate a sense of wonder, to embrace the extraordinary, and to infuse your own life with a touch of enchantment and magic.

Eye: Eyes held great significance in Babylonian culture, representing perception, awareness, and protection. Dreaming of an eye might symbolize insight, intuition, or the need to pay attention to something important.

Ah, the eye, a symbol of great significance in the rich tapestry of Babylonian culture. In the realm of dream interpretation, the appearance of an eye holds profound symbolism, representing concepts of insight, intuition, and the call to pay attention to something important.

Imagine this: You find yourself in the realm of dreams, and suddenly, an eye gazes upon you, radiating an aura of perception and awareness. Dreaming of an eye signifies the embodiment of these qualities and the call to embrace them in your waking life.

In Babylonian culture, eyes were considered windows to the soul and were believed to possess a profound connection to one's inner wisdom. Dreaming of an eye may symbolize the presence of insight, the awakening of your intuition, or the need to pay attention to something of significance in your life's journey.

The presence of an eye in dreams also represents the recognition of perception and the call to heighten your awareness. It invites you to trust your own inner vision, to tap into your intuitive faculties, and to perceive the subtle energies and messages that surround you.

Furthermore, an eye symbolizes the power of observation and the importance of paying attention. It represents the ability to see beyond the surface and to gain deeper understanding. Dreaming of an eye may signify the need to trust your instincts, to be vigilant in your interactions and choices, and to be open to the messages and insights that are being presented to you.

Dreaming of an eye can also evoke a sense of protection and the recognition of the interconnectedness of all things. It may signify the need to embrace your role as a conscious observer, to protect your own well-being and the well-being of others, and to honor the profound interplay between perception and reality.

So, my dear friend, if an eye graces your dreams, embrace its symbolism. Recognize the presence of insight, intuition, and the call to pay attention to something important that it represents. Let the eye in your dreams inspire you to trust your inner vision, to heighten your awareness, and to perceive the subtle messages and energies that surround you. Just as eyes held great significance in Babylonian culture, may the presence of an eye in your dreams guide you to embrace your own inner wisdom, to be mindful of the important details in your life, and to perceive the interconnectedness and beauty of the world with clarity and grace.

Exile: The Babylonian empire experienced periods of conquest and exile. Dreaming of exile might symbolize feelings of displacement, isolation, or the need to find one's place in the world.

Ah, the concept of exile, a phenomenon that held deep meaning in the history of the Babylonian empire. In the realm of dream interpretation, the appearance of exile holds profound symbolism, representing feelings of displacement, isolation, or the search for belonging and purpose.

Imagine this: You find yourself in the realm of dreams, and suddenly, you experience the emotions of being in exile, of being displaced from your familiar surroundings. Dreaming of exile signifies the embodiment of these feelings and the call to explore your sense of belonging and purpose in your waking life.

The Babylonian empire witnessed periods of conquest and exile, where individuals were uprooted from their homes and found themselves in unfamiliar lands. Dreaming of exile may symbolize the presence of similar emotions within your own life, the recognition of feelings of displacement, isolation, or the need to find your place in the world.

The presence of exile in dreams also represents the exploration of personal identity and the search for a sense of belonging. It invites you to reflect upon your own journey of self-discovery, to examine the places where you feel disconnected or isolated, and to seek out the paths that lead you towards finding your true sense of home and purpose.

Furthermore, exile symbolizes the quest for meaning and the longing for connection. It represents the desire to find your place in the world, to cultivate a sense of belonging, and to forge connections with others. Dreaming of exile may signify the need to explore your own sense of identity, to embrace the transformative power of self-discovery, and to create a life that resonates with your true essence.

Dreaming of exile can also evoke a sense of resilience and the recognition of the human capacity to adapt and find new beginnings. It may signify the need to embrace the challenges and changes that come your way, to navigate the unfamiliar with courage and determination, and to transform moments of displacement into opportunities for growth and self-realization.

So, my dear friend, if exile graces your dreams, embrace its symbolism. Recognize the presence of feelings of displacement, isolation, or the search for belonging and purpose that it represents. Let the experience of exile in your dreams inspire you to explore your sense of identity, to seek out your true place in the world, and to embrace the transformative power of finding home within yourself. Just as the Babylonian empire experienced periods of conquest and exile, may the presence of exile in your dreams guide you to navigate the emotions of displacement, to cultivate a sense of belonging, and to create a life filled with purpose, connection, and a deep sense of homecoming.

Engraving: Engraved inscriptions were common in ancient Babylonian art and architecture. Dreaming of an engraving might symbolize a desire for permanence, self-expression, or leaving a lasting mark.

Ah, the art of engraving, a craft that held great significance in the artistic expression of ancient Babylon. In the realm of dream interpretation, the appearance of an engraving holds profound symbolism, representing a desire for permanence, self-expression, or the longing to leave a lasting mark.

Imagine this: You find yourself in the realm of dreams, and suddenly, you come across an intricately engraved inscription, meticulously etched into stone or precious materials. Dreaming of an engraving signifies the embodiment of these desires and the call to embrace your own creative expression and desire for a lasting impact in your waking life.

In ancient Babylon, engraving was a common practice in art and architecture, where inscriptions were meticulously carved to preserve history, honor deities, or commemorate significant events. Dreaming of an engraving may symbolize the presence of a similar desire within your own life, a longing to create something lasting, to express yourself authentically, or to leave a mark on the world.

The presence of an engraving in dreams also represents the recognition of the power of self-expression and the call to embrace your unique voice. It invites you to explore the depths of your creativity, to honor your passions and talents, and to etch your own story into the tapestry of existence.

Furthermore, an engraving symbolizes the desire for permanence and the longing for a lasting impact. It represents the innate human yearning to be remembered, to make a difference, and to leave a legacy. Dreaming of an engraving may signify the need to reflect upon your own desires for permanence, to cultivate a sense of purpose that extends beyond the present moment, and to create something that resonates with the generations to come.

Dreaming of an engraving can also evoke a sense of reverence and the recognition of the power of art and culture. It may signify the need to honor the rich heritage of ancient civilizations, to explore your own cultural roots, and to embrace the transformative power of artistic expression in all its forms.

So, my dear friend, if an engraving graces your dreams, embrace its symbolism. Recognize the presence of a desire for permanence, self-expression, or leaving a lasting mark that it represents. Let the engraving in your dreams inspire you to embrace your creative expression, to honor your passions and talents, and to create something that resonates with the essence of who you are. Just as engraved inscriptions were common in ancient Babylonian art and architecture, may the presence of an engraving in your dreams guide you to etch your own unique story into the fabric of existence, leaving a lasting mark that reflects your authentic self and the beauty of your creative expression.

Inscriptions: Dreaming of engraved inscriptions might symbolize the presence of hidden messages or knowledge that needs to be deciphered. It could represent the need to pay attention to details or to explore deeper meanings within a situation.

Symbols or Glyphs: Engravings of symbols or glyphs in dreams may represent the presence of ancient wisdom or esoteric knowledge. It could signify the need to tap into your intuition or explore the mystical aspects of life.

Personal Names or Initials: Engravings of personal names or initials in dreams might symbolize a sense of self-identity or self-discovery. It could signify the exploration of your own personal history or the desire to leave a lasting mark in the world.

Artistic Designs: Dreaming of engraved artistic designs might symbolize creative expression, aesthetics, or the need for beauty and harmony. It could represent the desire to infuse more creativity into your life or to appreciate the artistic aspects of the world around you.

Historical or Cultural Engravings: Engravings depicting historical or cultural scenes in dreams might symbolize a connection to the past, a longing for tradition, or a desire to explore your cultural heritage. It could signify the importance of understanding history or embracing your roots.

Religious or Spiritual Engravings: Engravings of religious or spiritual symbols in dreams may represent the presence of divine guidance, spiritual awakening, or a search for deeper meaning. It could signify a need for spiritual exploration or a desire to connect with higher realms of consciousness.

Architectural Engravings: Engravings found on architectural structures in dreams might symbolize stability, structure, or the need for a solid foundation. It could represent the importance of organization or the desire to create a sense of security in your life.

Personalized Engravings: Dreaming of engravings that are personalized, such as engravings on jewelry or personal belongings, might symbolize a sense of ownership, individuality, or the importance of personal connections. It could signify the need to express yourself authentically or to cherish meaningful relationships.

Remember, these interpretations are not definitive and can vary based on individual experiences and contexts. It's important to consider the specific details and emotions surrounding the engravings in your dream to gain a more accurate understanding of their personal significance to you.

Euphrates: The Euphrates River played a vital role in the prosperity and trade of Babylon. Dreaming of the Euphrates might symbolize fluidity, emotional depth, or a connection to one's roots or heritage.

Ah, the majestic Euphrates River, a lifeline coursing through the heart of ancient Babylon, bringing prosperity, trade, and a sense of connection to the land. In the realm of dream interpretation, the appearance of the Euphrates holds profound symbolism, representing concepts of fluidity, emotional depth, and a strong connection to one's roots and heritage.

Imagine this: You find yourself in the realm of dreams, and suddenly, the serene waters of the Euphrates River gently flow before you, carrying with them a sense of tranquility and ancient wisdom. Dreaming of the Euphrates signifies the embodiment of these qualities and the call to embrace the fluidity and deep-rooted connections in your waking life.

The Euphrates River was a vital artery in the prosperity and trade of Babylon, providing sustenance, transportation, and a sense of connection to the land. Dreaming of the Euphrates may symbolize the presence of similar energies within your own life, reflecting a need for fluidity, adaptability, and the recognition of the emotional depths that flow within you.

The presence of the Euphrates in dreams also represents the recognition of the power of emotions and the call to explore the depths of your own inner being. It invites you to embrace the ebb and flow of your emotions, to honor the fluidity of life's experiences, and to seek a deep-rooted connection to your heritage and the essence of who you are.

Furthermore, the Euphrates symbolizes the sense of continuity and the connection to one's roots and heritage. It represents the understanding that the river of time carries with it the wisdom and experiences of our ancestors. Dreaming of the Euphrates may signify the need to explore your own ancestral lineage, to embrace the wisdom and traditions that have been passed down through generations, and to find a sense of belonging in your own cultural heritage.

Dreaming of the Euphrates can also evoke a sense of serenity and the recognition of the interconnectedness of all things. It may signify the need to find solace in the flow of life, to trust in the unfolding of events, and to honor the ancient wisdom that resides within and around you.

So, my dear friend, if the Euphrates graces your dreams, embrace its symbolism. Recognize the presence of fluidity, emotional depth, and a connection to your roots or heritage that it represents. Let the presence of the Euphrates in your dreams inspire you to embrace the fluidity of life, to explore the depths of your emotions, and to connect with your heritage and roots. Just as the Euphrates River played a vital role in the prosperity and trade of Babylon, may the presence of the Euphrates in your dreams guide you to embrace the flow of life's experiences, to honor your emotional depths, and to find solace and connection in the ancient wisdom that flows through your very being.

Empire: Babylon was a mighty empire in its time. Dreaming of an empire might symbolize ambition, power, authority, or the desire for control and influence.

Ah, the grandeur and might of an empire, a symbol of ambition, power, and authority in the realm of dreams. Imagine finding yourself in the expanse of a dream, encountering the vision of an empire, reminiscent of the great Babylonian empire that once stood as a testament to human achievement. Dreaming of an empire represents the embodiment of these qualities and the yearning for control and influence in your waking life.

The Babylonian empire, known for its vast territorial conquests and impressive architectural wonders, serves as a historical reference for the symbolism of an empire in dreams. The appearance of an empire in your dream signifies the presence of similar energies within your own life – a desire for power, ambition, or authority. It reflects your aspirations to leave a mark on the world, to make your presence felt, and to shape the course of events around you.

Furthermore, dreaming of an empire may also symbolize the quest for control and influence. It represents your innate drive to take charge of your life, to assert your authority, and to create a sense of order and structure. It highlights your ambition to rise to positions of leadership and to wield influence over others.

However, it is important to note that the symbolism of an empire in dreams can have both positive and negative connotations. While it can reflect your ambition and desire for success, it may also indicate a potential risk of becoming consumed by power or losing sight of the values that truly matter.

Dreaming of an empire serves as a reminder to balance your ambitions with integrity, to use your influence wisely, and to consider the impact of your actions on others. It encourages you to reflect on the nature of power and authority, to embrace a sense of responsibility, and to strive for a harmonious balance between personal achievement and the greater good.

So, my dear friend, if an empire graces your dreams, embrace its symbolism. Recognize the presence of ambition, power, authority, and the desire for control and influence that it represents. Let the vision of an empire inspire you to harness your ambitions, to seek positions of leadership with integrity, and to make a positive impact in the world. Just as the Babylonian empire left an indelible mark on history, may the presence of an empire in your dreams guide you to navigate your own journey of personal growth, success, and influence with wisdom and grace.

F:

Fertility: Fertility was highly valued in ancient Babylonian culture, as agriculture played a crucial role in their society. Dreaming of fertility might symbolize abundance, growth, or the potential for new beginnings.

Ah, fertility, a cherished aspect of ancient Babylonian culture, where the bountiful fields and thriving agriculture were the lifeblood of their society. In the realm of dreams, the symbolism of fertility holds great significance, representing abundance, growth, and the potential for new beginnings.

Imagine finding yourself in the realm of dreams, surrounded by the vibrant energy of fertility, where the land is fertile and teeming with life. Dreaming of fertility signifies the embodiment of these qualities and the call to embrace abundance and the potential for growth in your waking life.

Fertility was highly valued in ancient Babylonian culture, as it ensured the sustenance and prosperity of their society. Dreaming of fertility may symbolize the presence of similar energies within your own life, reflecting a period of abundance, productivity, or the potential for new opportunities and ventures.

The presence of fertility in dreams also represents the recognition of the natural cycles of growth and renewal. It invites you to embrace the flow of life, to trust in the process of creation and manifestation, and to be open to the abundance that surrounds you.

Furthermore, fertility symbolizes the potential for new beginnings. It represents the fertile ground upon which seeds of ideas, projects, or relationships can take root and flourish. Dreaming of fertility may signify the need to cultivate a fertile mindset, to nurture your aspirations, and to create the conditions for growth and success in your endeavors.

Dreaming of fertility can also evoke a sense of optimism and a deep connection to the cycles of nature. It may signify the importance of honoring your own natural rhythms, of embracing the seasons of life, and of recognizing the interconnectedness between your own growth and the abundance that exists in the world around you.

So, my dear friend, if fertility graces your dreams, embrace its symbolism. Recognize the presence of abundance, growth, and the potential for new beginnings that it represents. Let the vision of fertility inspire you to cultivate a mindset of abundance, to nurture your aspirations and endeavors, and to embrace the natural cycles of growth and renewal. Just as the fertile fields of ancient Babylon ensured the prosperity of their society, may the presence of fertility in your dreams guide you to embrace the abundance and potential for growth that exists within you and the world around you.

Fig: Figs were a common fruit in Babylon, known for their sweetness. Dreaming of figs might symbolize nourishment, prosperity, or the fulfillment of desires.

Ah, the luscious and sweet figs, a delightful fruit that adorned the ancient Babylonian tables, embodying nourishment, prosperity, and the fulfillment of desires. In the realm of dreams, the symbolism of figs holds great significance, representing abundance, satisfaction, and the realization of long-awaited aspirations.

Imagine finding yourself in the realm of dreams, surrounded by the alluring aroma and succulent taste of figs. Dreaming of figs signifies the embodiment of these qualities and the call to embrace nourishment, prosperity, and the fulfillment of desires in your waking life.

Figs held a special place in Babylonian culture, renowned for their sweetness and richness. Dreaming of figs may symbolize the presence of similar energies within your own life, reflecting a period of abundance, satisfaction, and the gratification of your desires.

The presence of figs in dreams also represents the recognition of the nourishing aspects of life. It invites you to indulge in the sweetness of experiences, to savor the moments of joy and fulfillment, and to embrace the abundance that surrounds you.

Furthermore, figs symbolize the realization of long-awaited aspirations. They represent the fruition of your efforts, the manifestation of your dreams, and the attainment of your goals. Dreaming of figs may signify the need to trust in the natural timing of things, to remain patient and persistent, and to have faith that your desires will be fulfilled.

Dreaming of figs can also evoke a sense of contentment and gratitude for the blessings in your life. It may signify the importance of appreciating the abundance that already exists, of nourishing your relationships and connections, and of finding fulfillment in the simple pleasures that life has to offer.

So, my dear friend, if figs grace your dreams, embrace their symbolism. Recognize the presence of nourishment, prosperity, and the fulfillment of desires that they represent. Let the vision of figs inspire you to savor the sweetness of life, to embrace abundance and satisfaction, and to have faith in the realization of your aspirations. Just as the figs brought joy and delight to the ancient Babylonians, may the presence of figs in your dreams guide you to embrace the nourishment, prosperity, and the fulfillment of your desires that await you in your waking life.

Feast: Feasting and celebrations were integral parts of Babylonian culture. Dreaming of a feast might symbolize abundance, joy, or the need for celebration and enjoyment.

Ah, the joyous sounds of laughter, the enticing aromas, and the bountiful tables filled with delicious food and drink—the spirit of feasting and celebration, an integral part of the vibrant Babylonian culture. In the realm of dreams, the symbolism of a feast holds great significance, representing abundance, joy, and the need for celebration and enjoyment.

Picture yourself immersed in a dream, surrounded by the festivities of a grand feast, where people gather in merriment and indulge in the pleasures of food and drink. Dreaming of a feast signifies the embodiment of these qualities and the call to embrace abundance, joy, and the spirit of celebration in your waking life.

Feasting and celebrations were integral to the Babylonian culture, serving as a time of communal bonding, expressing gratitude, and reveling in the pleasures of life. Dreaming of a feast may symbolize the presence of similar energies within your own life, reflecting a period of abundance, joy, and the need to celebrate and enjoy the blessings that surround you.

The presence of a feast in dreams also represents the recognition of the importance of celebration and enjoyment. It invites you to embrace moments of joy, to find gratitude in the simple pleasures, and to take time to savor the richness of life.

Furthermore, a feast symbolizes abundance in all aspects of life. It represents the fulfillment of desires, the availability of resources, and the feeling of being well-nourished—physically, emotionally, and spiritually. Dreaming of a feast may signify the need to recognize and appreciate the abundance that already exists in your life, and to open yourself to the possibilities of even greater blessings.

Dreaming of a feast can also evoke a sense of community and connection. It may signify the importance of gathering with loved ones, fostering relationships, and sharing moments of joy and celebration together.

So, my dear friend, if a feast graces your dreams, embrace its symbolism. Recognize the presence of abundance, joy, and the need for celebration and enjoyment that it represents. Let the vision of a feast inspire you to celebrate the blessings in your life, to find joy in the simple pleasures, and to foster connections and moments of togetherness. Just as the Babylonians reveled in their feasts, may the presence of a feast in your dreams guide you to embrace abundance, joy, and the spirit of celebration that await you in your waking life.

Fortress: Fortresses were significant in ancient Babylon for protection and defense. Dreaming of a fortress might symbolize security, resilience, or the need for boundaries and protection.

Ah, the formidable fortresses, towering structures that stood as symbols of protection and defense in ancient Babylon. In the realm of dreams, the symbolism of a fortress carries profound significance, representing security, resilience, and the need for boundaries and protection.

Imagine finding yourself within the depths of a dream, surrounded by the towering walls and sturdy ramparts of a fortress. Dreaming of a fortress signifies the embodiment of these qualities and the call to embrace security, resilience, and the establishment of boundaries and protection in your waking life.

Fortresses held great importance in ancient Babylon, serving as strongholds for protection against external threats. Dreaming of a fortress may symbolize the presence of similar energies within your own life, reflecting a need for security, a desire for stability, or the recognition of the importance of establishing boundaries to safeguard your well-being.

The presence of a fortress in dreams also represents the recognition of your own inner strength and resilience. It invites you to fortify your defenses, both physical and emotional, and to cultivate a sense of stability and safety within yourself.

Furthermore, a fortress symbolizes the need for boundaries and protection. It represents the establishment of limits, both to protect yourself from external influences and to safeguard your own boundaries and values. Dreaming of a fortress may signify the need to establish clear boundaries in your relationships, to protect your personal space, and to defend your beliefs and principles.

Dreaming of a fortress can also evoke a sense of inner strength and empowerment. It may signify the importance of cultivating resilience, finding solace in your own abilities, and facing challenges with a fortified spirit.

So, my dear friend, if a fortress graces your dreams, embrace its symbolism. Recognize the presence of security, resilience, and the need for boundaries and protection that it represents. Let the vision of a fortress inspire you to establish firm boundaries, to fortify your defenses, and to cultivate a sense of inner strength and security. Just as the fortresses of ancient Babylon provided protection and defense, may the presence of a fortress in your dreams guide you to embrace security, resilience, and the establishment of boundaries and protection in your waking life.

Fire: Fire held both positive and negative symbolism in Babylonian culture. Dreaming of fire might represent transformation, purification, destruction, or passion.

Ah, the mesmerizing and powerful element of fire, a symbol that held profound significance in the vibrant Babylonian culture. In the realm of dreams, the symbolism of fire carries both positive and negative connotations, representing transformation, purification, destruction, and the intensity of passion.

Imagine finding yourself in the realm of dreams, surrounded by the flickering flames and radiant glow of fire. Dreaming of fire signifies the embodiment of these qualities and the call to embrace the transformative, purifying, and passionate aspects of life in your waking existence.

Fire held multifaceted symbolism in ancient Babylonian culture, encompassing both positive and negative attributes. Dreaming of fire may symbolize the presence of similar energies within your own life, reflecting a period of transformation, purification, or the passionate pursuit of your desires.

The presence of fire in dreams also represents the recognition of the transformative power within you. It invites you to embrace change, to release what no longer serves you, and to undergo a process of personal growth and evolution.

Furthermore, fire symbolizes purification and renewal. It represents the burning away of the old, making space for the new to emerge. Dreaming of fire may signify the need to let go of negative influences, to cleanse your mind, body, and spirit, and to embark on a journey of self-discovery and renewal.

However, fire can also symbolize destruction and chaos. It represents the potential for upheaval, challenges, and the release of pent-up emotions. Dreaming of fire may indicate the need to confront and overcome obstacles, to navigate through difficult times, and to harness the transformative power of adversity.

Additionally, fire embodies passion and intensity. It represents the driving force behind desires, ambitions, and creative endeavors. Dreaming of fire may signify the need to ignite the flame within you, to pursue your passions wholeheartedly, and to embrace the intensity and vitality of life.

So, my dear friend, if fire graces your dreams, embrace its symbolism. Recognize the presence of transformation, purification, destruction, and the intensity of passion that it represents. Let the vision of fire inspire you to embrace change, to purify your being, to confront challenges with resilience, and to pursue your passions with unwavering determination. Just as fire served as a powerful symbol in ancient Babylon, may the presence of fire in your dreams guide you to embrace the transformative, purifying, and passionate aspects of life in your waking existence.

Flute: Music played an important role in Babylonian rituals and entertainment. Dreaming of a flute might symbolize harmony, creativity, or the need for self-expression.

Ah, the enchanting melodies that echoed through the ancient Babylonian culture, captivating hearts and igniting spirits. In the realm of dreams, the symbolism of a flute carries a sense of harmony, creativity, and the deep desire for self-expression.

Picture yourself immersed in a dream, where the delicate and melodious notes of a flute dance through the air. Dreaming of a flute signifies the embodiment of these qualities and the call to embrace harmony, creativity, and the need for self-expression in your waking life.

Music held immense importance in Babylonian rituals and entertainment, serving as a vessel to connect with the divine and evoke emotions. Dreaming of a flute may symbolize the presence of similar energies within your own life, reflecting a need for harmony, a desire to explore your creative abilities, or the recognition of the importance of expressing your true self.

The presence of a flute in dreams also represents the power of music to bring balance and tranquility to your existence. It invites you to seek harmony in your relationships, to find peace within yourself, and to cultivate a sense of balance between different aspects of your life.

Furthermore, a flute symbolizes creativity and self-expression. It represents the ability to convey emotions and ideas through the medium of art. Dreaming of a flute may signify the need to tap into your creative potential, to express yourself authentically, and to find joy and fulfillment through artistic endeavors.

Dreaming of a flute can also evoke a sense of connection to your innermost self and the world around you. It may signify the importance of embracing your unique voice, listening to the subtle rhythms of life, and harmonizing with the flow of your own journey.

So, my dear friend, if a flute graces your dreams, embrace its symbolism. Recognize the presence of harmony, creativity, and the need for self-expression that it represents. Let the enchanting melodies of the flute inspire you to seek harmony in your relationships, to explore your creative abilities, and to express your true self with confidence and authenticity. Just as the flute brought harmony and creativity to the ancient Babylonians, may the presence of a flute in your dreams guide you to embrace the beauty of harmony, creativity, and self-expression in your waking life.

Fish: Fish were abundant in the rivers of Babylon and held symbolic significance. Dreaming of fish might symbolize fertility, abundance, or the exploration of emotions and the subconscious.

Ah, the graceful creatures that swam through the rivers of Babylon, embodying both mystery and abundance. In the realm of dreams, the symbolism of fish carries a sense of fertility, abundance, and the exploration of emotions and the subconscious.

Imagine finding yourself within the depths of a dream, surrounded by shimmering schools of fish, gliding through the waters with grace and agility. Dreaming of fish signifies the embodiment of these qualities and the call to embrace fertility, abundance, and the exploration of your inner world in your waking life.

Fish held great symbolic significance in the rivers of Babylon, where they represented not only sustenance but also the interconnectedness of life. Dreaming of fish may symbolize the presence of similar energies within your own life, reflecting a period of fertility, abundance, or the exploration of the depths of your emotions and subconscious.

The presence of fish in dreams also represents the recognition of the fertility and abundance that surrounds you. It invites you to embrace the possibilities of growth and prosperity, both in material and emotional aspects of your life.

Furthermore, fish symbolize the exploration of emotions and the subconscious. Just as fish swim beneath the surface of the water, navigating hidden depths, dreaming of fish may signify the need to dive into your own emotions, to explore the hidden realms of your subconscious, and to uncover valuable insights and understanding.

Dreaming of fish can also evoke a sense of fluidity and adaptability. It may signify the importance of embracing change, going with the flow, and navigating the currents of life with grace and ease.

So, my dear friend, if fish grace your dreams, embrace their symbolism. Recognize the presence of fertility, abundance, and the exploration of emotions and the subconscious that they represent. Let the vision of fish inspire you to embrace the possibilities of growth and prosperity, to dive into your own emotions and subconscious, and to navigate the currents of life with grace and adaptability. Just as the fish swam abundantly in the rivers of Babylon, may the presence of fish in your dreams guide you to embrace the fertility, abundance, and exploration that await you in your waking life.

Carp: Dreaming of carp may symbolize resilience, perseverance, and success in overcoming obstacles.

Trout: Dreaming of trout might represent abundance, prosperity, and the fulfillment of desires.

Catfish: Dreaming of catfish could symbolize hidden emotions, intuition, or the need to delve deeper into your subconscious.

Goldfish: Dreaming of goldfish may symbolize happiness, contentment, and a sense of peace and tranquility.

Salmon: Dreaming of salmon might represent determination, the ability to overcome challenges, and the rewards of perseverance.

Piranha: Dreaming of piranhas could symbolize aggression, danger, or the presence of negative influences in your life.

Sardines: Dreaming of sardines might symbolize the importance of community, teamwork, and social interactions.

Koi Fish: Dreaming of koi fish may represent transformation, growth, and the pursuit of personal enlightenment.

Eel: Dreaming of an eel could symbolize hidden desires, secrets, or the need to confront and address deep-rooted emotions.

Swordfish: Dreaming of a swordfish might symbolize strength, determination, and the ability to overcome challenges with precision and agility.

Flood: The Great Flood was a significant myth in Babylonian culture. Dreaming of a flood might symbolize emotional overwhelm, cleansing, or the need to confront buried emotions.

Ah, the ancient myth of the Great Flood, a story that resonated deeply within the Babylonian culture. In the realm of dreams, the symbolism of a flood carries a sense of emotional overwhelm, cleansing, and the need to confront buried emotions.

Imagine finding yourself within the depths of a dream, where the waters rise and flood the landscape, submerging everything in their path. Dreaming of a flood signifies the embodiment of these qualities and the call to confront, cleanse, and navigate through your own emotional depths in your waking life.

The Great Flood held immense significance in Babylonian mythology, representing not only the destruction of the old but also the opportunity for renewal and rebirth. Dreaming of a flood may symbolize the presence of similar energies within your own life, reflecting a period of emotional overwhelm, the need for cleansing, or the recognition of buried emotions that require your attention.

The presence of a flood in dreams also represents the recognition of the power of emotions and the need to confront them. It invites you to face the depths of your own emotional landscape, to embrace the cleansing and purifying process, and to allow yourself to be transformed by the currents of your emotions.

Furthermore, a flood symbolizes the release and flow of emotions. Just as the waters of a flood surge and overflow, dreaming of a flood may signify the need to acknowledge, express, and navigate through the full range of your emotions. It calls for an embrace of vulnerability and the opportunity for emotional growth and healing.

Dreaming of a flood can also evoke a sense of renewal and rebirth. It may signify the shedding of old patterns, the opportunity to start anew, and the potential for personal transformation.

So, my dear friend, if a flood graces your dreams, embrace its symbolism. Recognize the presence of emotional overwhelm, cleansing, and the need to confront buried emotions that it represents. Let the vision of a flood inspire you to navigate through the depths of your emotions, to embrace the opportunity for emotional growth and healing, and to allow the waters of renewal to flow through your life. Just as the Great Flood represented a transformative event in Babylonian culture, may the presence of a flood in your dreams guide you to confront, cleanse, and embrace the emotional currents that shape your waking existence.

Foundation: Babylonians were skilled in construction and architecture. Dreaming of a foundation might symbolize stability, grounding, or the need to establish a strong base in one's life.

Ah, the solid foundation upon which the magnificent structures of ancient Babylon stood. In the realm of dreams, the symbolism of a foundation carries a sense of stability, grounding, and the need to establish a strong base in one's life.

Picture yourself within the depths of a dream, observing the solid and sturdy foundation upon which a grand structure is built.

Dreaming of a foundation signifies the embodiment of these qualities and the call to seek stability, grounding, and the establishment of a strong base in your waking life.

The Babylonians were renowned for their skill in construction and architecture, crafting remarkable structures that stood the test of time. Dreaming of a foundation may symbolize the presence of similar energies within your own life, reflecting the importance of stability, a solid grounding, and the need to establish a strong base upon which to build your dreams and aspirations.

The presence of a foundation in dreams also represents the recognition of the importance of a stable and secure starting point. It invites you to consider the strength and stability of your own life's foundation, whether it be in your relationships, career, or personal endeavors.

Furthermore, a foundation symbolizes the need for a solid base from which to grow and evolve. Just as a structure relies on a strong foundation to support its growth, dreaming of a foundation may signify the need to establish a firm footing in your own life. It calls for the cultivation of inner stability, groundedness, and the creation of a solid platform upon which to build your future endeavors.

Dreaming of a foundation can also evoke a sense of security and reassurance. It may signify the need to find stability amidst the chaos, to seek grounding in times of uncertainty, and to establish a sense of rootedness that provides a sense of safety and support.

So, my dear friend, if a foundation graces your dreams, embrace its symbolism. Recognize the presence of stability, grounding, and the need to establish a strong base that it represents. Let the vision of a foundation inspire you to seek stability in your life, to establish a solid grounding, and to build upon a strong base that supports your dreams and aspirations. Just as the foundations of ancient Babylon provided a solid base for their grand structures, may the presence of a foundation in your dreams guide you to establish a strong and stable platform upon which to build a fulfilling and successful life.

Friendship: Social connections were valued in ancient Babylonian society. Dreaming of friendship might symbolize camaraderie, support, or the need for meaningful relationships.

Ah, the bonds of friendship that held great value in the ancient society of Babylon. In the realm of dreams, the symbolism of friendship carries a sense of camaraderie, support, and the need for meaningful relationships.

Imagine finding yourself within the depths of a dream, surrounded by friends who bring joy, laughter, and a sense of belonging. Dreaming of friendship signifies the embodiment of these qualities and the call to cultivate and cherish the connections that enrich your waking life.

In Babylonian society, social connections and meaningful relationships were highly valued, forming the fabric of community and support. Dreaming of friendship may symbolize the presence of similar energies within your own life, reflecting the importance of camaraderie, support, and the need for meaningful relationships.

The presence of friendship in dreams also represents the recognition of the value of companionship and emotional support. It invites you to embrace the bonds of friendship, to seek meaningful connections, and to surround yourself with those who uplift and nourish your soul.

Furthermore, friendship symbolizes the power of connection and the joy of shared experiences. Just as friends come together to celebrate, support, and create memories, dreaming of friendship may signify the need to cultivate and nurture relationships that bring joy, laughter, and a sense of belonging.

Dreaming of friendship can also evoke a sense of support and reassurance. It may signify the importance of having a network of people who stand by your side, offering encouragement, understanding, and a sense of belonging.

So, my dear friend, if the presence of friendship graces your dreams, embrace its symbolism. Recognize the significance of camaraderie, support, and the need for meaningful relationships that it represents. Let the vision of friendship inspire you to cultivate and cherish the connections in your life, to seek meaningful companionship, and to surround yourself with those who uplift and nourish your soul. Just as the bonds of friendship were valued in ancient Babylonian society, may the presence of friendship in your dreams guide you to foster and nurture the meaningful relationships that enrich your waking existence.

G:

Gilgamesh: Gilgamesh was a legendary king and hero in Babylonian mythology. Dreaming of Gilgamesh might symbolize heroism, personal growth, or the pursuit of wisdom.

Ah, the legendary figure of Gilgamesh, a king and hero in Babylonian mythology. In the realm of dreams, the symbolism of Gilgamesh carries a sense of heroism, personal growth, and the pursuit of wisdom.

Imagine finding yourself within the depths of a dream, encountering the presence of Gilgamesh, the mighty king and hero. Dreaming of Gilgamesh signifies the embodiment of these qualities and the call to embrace your own inner hero, to embark on a journey of personal growth, and to seek wisdom and understanding in your waking life.

Gilgamesh, with his epic adventures and quest for immortality, held immense significance in Babylonian mythology. Dreaming of Gilgamesh may symbolize the presence of similar energies within your own life, reflecting the call to embrace your own hero's journey, to embark on a path of personal growth, and to seek wisdom and enlightenment along the way.

The presence of Gilgamesh in dreams also represents the recognition of the heroic qualities within yourself. It invites you to tap into your inner strength, courage, and resilience, and to embrace the challenges and opportunities that come your way.

Furthermore, Gilgamesh symbolizes the pursuit of wisdom and understanding. Just as the legendary king sought knowledge and enlightenment, dreaming of Gilgamesh may signify the need to seek wisdom, to deepen your understanding of yourself and the world around you, and to embark on a quest for personal and spiritual growth.

Dreaming of Gilgamesh can also evoke a sense of inspiration and empowerment. It may signify the potential for transformation, the call to rise above challenges, and the invitation to become the hero of your own story.

So, my dear friend, if Gilgamesh graces your dreams, embrace his symbolism. Recognize the call to heroism, personal growth, and the pursuit of wisdom that he represents. Let the presence of Gilgamesh inspire you to embrace your own inner hero, to embark on a journey of personal growth and self-discovery, and to seek wisdom and understanding along the way. Just as Gilgamesh stood as a legendary figure in Babylonian mythology, may the presence of Gilgamesh in your dreams guide you to embrace your own heroic journey and to unlock the wisdom that lies within you.

Gardens: Babylonian gardens, such as the Hanging Gardens of Babylon, were famous for their beauty and lushness. Dreaming of a garden might symbolize harmony, growth, or a connection to nature.

Ah, the enchanting beauty of Babylonian gardens, where nature's splendor flourished in harmony. In the realm of dreams, the symbolism of a garden carries a sense of harmony, growth, and a deep connection to the natural world.

Imagine finding yourself within the depths of a dream, wandering through a lush and vibrant garden, surrounded by blooming flowers, cascading waterfalls, and the gentle rustling of leaves. Dreaming of a garden signifies the embodiment of these qualities and the call to embrace the harmonious growth and connection to nature in your waking life.

Babylonian gardens, such as the renowned Hanging Gardens of Babylon, were celebrated for their breathtaking beauty and the sense of tranquility they offered. Dreaming of a garden may symbolize the presence of similar energies within your own life, reflecting the importance of finding harmony, experiencing growth, and nurturing a deep connection to the natural world.

The presence of a garden in dreams also represents the recognition of the need for nourishment and cultivation. It invites you to create a space of beauty and tranquility within your own life, to nurture your personal growth, and to find solace and inspiration in the natural world.

Furthermore, a garden symbolizes the cycles of life and the potential for transformation. Just as a garden goes through seasons of growth, blooming, and eventual decay, dreaming of a garden may signify the need to embrace the cycles of life, to trust in the process of growth and transformation, and to find beauty and meaning in every stage.

Dreaming of a garden can also evoke a sense of peace and serenity. It may signify the invitation to create a haven of tranquility within your own being, to find solace and rejuvenation amidst the busyness of life, and to cultivate a deep sense of connection and harmony with the world around you.

So, my dear friend, if a garden graces your dreams, embrace its symbolism. Recognize the presence of harmony, growth, and the deep connection to nature that it represents. Let the vision of a garden inspire you to cultivate beauty and tranquility in your own life, to nurture your personal growth, and to find solace and inspiration in the natural world. Just as the Babylonian gardens held an ethereal beauty, may the presence of a garden in your dreams guide you to embrace the harmonious growth and profound connection that nature offers.

Roses: Symbolizing love, beauty, and passion, dreaming of roses from Babylonian gardens could represent deep affection, romantic relationships, or the blossoming of desires.

Lilies: Lilies signify purity, innocence, and renewal. Dreaming of lilies from Babylonian gardens might symbolize a fresh start, spiritual growth, or the purification of the soul.

Irises: With their vibrant colors, irises represent wisdom, faith, and hope. Dreaming of irises from Babylonian gardens might symbolize clarity of thought, spiritual insight, or a positive outlook on life.

Poppies: Poppies are associated with relaxation, dreams, and imagination. Dreaming of poppies from Babylonian gardens could symbolize creativity, the exploration of subconscious desires, or the need for rest and rejuvenation.

Lotus: The lotus flower represents purity, enlightenment, and spiritual awakening. Dreaming of lotus flowers from Babylonian gardens might symbolize the unfolding of spiritual awareness, the pursuit of enlightenment, or the quest for inner peace.

Jasmine: Jasmine is known for its sweet fragrance and is associated with love, sensuality, and grace. Dreaming of jasmine from Babylonian gardens could symbolize romance, emotional connections, or a desire for beauty and elegance in life.

Tulips: Tulips symbolize abundance, prosperity, and new beginnings. Dreaming of tulips from Babylonian gardens might symbolize growth, success, or the manifestation of desires and goals.

Pansies: Pansies are playful and vibrant flowers associated with joy, friendship, and happy memories. Dreaming of pansies from Babylonian gardens could symbolize joyful experiences, harmonious relationships, or a sense of nostalgia.

Daisies: Daisies represent innocence, purity, and simplicity. Dreaming of daisies from Babylonian gardens might symbolize a return to childlike innocence, a need for simplicity, or the enjoyment of life's simple pleasures.

Hyacinths: Hyacinths symbolize rebirth, springtime, and vitality. Dreaming of hyacinths from Babylonian gardens could symbolize rejuvenation, the emergence of new opportunities, or a fresh start in life.

Gates: Gates held symbolic significance in ancient Babylonian culture, representing boundaries, transitions, and access to different realms. Dreaming of gates might symbolize opportunities, choices, or the need to embark on a new path.

Ah, the symbolism of gates in ancient Babylonian culture. Gates were not merely physical structures but held deeper significance, representing boundaries, transitions, and the crossing between different realms. In the realm of dreams, the symbolism of gates carries a sense of opportunities, choices, and the need for new beginnings.

Imagine finding yourself within the depths of a dream, standing before a majestic gate, adorned with intricate designs and guarded by towering figures. Dreaming of a gate signifies the embodiment of these qualities and the call to embrace the opportunities, choices, and transitions that lie before you in your waking life.

In Babylonian culture, gates were considered thresholds between different spaces, both physical and metaphysical. They marked the boundary between the mundane and the sacred, the known and the unknown. Dreaming of a gate may symbolize the presence of similar energies within your own life, reflecting the significance of opportunities, choices, and the need to embark on new paths.

The presence of a gate in dreams also represents the recognition of transitions and the potential for transformation. It invites you to step through the gate, to embrace the unknown, and to embark on a journey of personal growth and exploration.

Furthermore, a gate symbolizes the choices we make in life. Just as a gate presents different paths to follow, dreaming of a gate may signify the need to make decisions, to weigh your options, and to be mindful of the opportunities that present themselves.

Dreaming of a gate can also evoke a sense of anticipation and excitement. It may signify the invitation to embrace new beginnings, to venture into uncharted territories, and to seize the opportunities that come your way.

So, my dear friend, if a gate graces your dreams, embrace its symbolism. Recognize the presence of opportunities, choices, and transitions that it represents. Let the vision of a gate inspire you to be open to new possibilities, to make conscious choices, and to embrace the journeys that lie ahead. Just as the gates in ancient Babylon marked the crossing between realms, may the presence of a gate in your dreams guide you to embrace the thresholds in your own life and to embark on the paths that lead to growth, transformation, and fulfillment.

God: The gods and goddesses of the Babylonian pantheon played a central role in their culture and mythology. Dreaming of a god might symbolize divine guidance, power, or a connection to higher forces.

Ah, the divine presence of the gods in the realm of dreams. In ancient Babylonian culture, the gods and goddesses held immense significance, weaving through the tapestry of their mythology and shaping the beliefs and daily lives of the people. Dreaming of a god brings forth the symbolism of divine guidance, power, and a profound connection to higher forces.

Imagine finding yourself within the depths of a dream, standing in the presence of a god, emanating an aura of wisdom, strength, or benevolence. Dreaming of a god signifies the embodiment of these qualities and the call to recognize the divine guidance and power that exists within and around you.

In Babylonian mythology, each god and goddess represented different aspects of life, nature, and human experiences. Dreaming of a god may symbolize the presence of similar energies within your own life, reflecting the influence of divine guidance, power, or a connection to higher forces.

The presence of a god in dreams also represents the recognition of the sacred and the invitation to embrace a deeper spiritual understanding. It invites you to tap into your own inner divinity, to seek wisdom and guidance, and to connect with something greater than yourself.

Furthermore, a god symbolizes the inherent power and potential that resides within every individual. Dreaming of a god may signify the need to tap into your own strengths, to recognize your own divine essence, and to embrace your inherent power and abilities.

Dreaming of a god can also evoke a sense of awe and reverence. It may signify the invitation to cultivate a deeper spiritual connection, to explore the mysteries of existence, and to trust in the guidance and support of higher forces.

So, my dear friend, if a god graces your dreams, embrace its symbolism. Recognize the presence of divine guidance, power, and a profound connection to higher forces. Let the vision of a god inspire you to tap into your own inner divinity, to seek wisdom and guidance, and to embrace the inherent power and potential that resides within you. Just as the gods held sway over the ancient Babylonians, may the presence of a god in your dreams guide you to connect with the sacred, to trust in the guidance of higher forces, and to embrace the profound spiritual journey that lies before you.

Grain: Agriculture and grain production were vital in ancient Babylon. Dreaming of grain might symbolize sustenance, abundance, or the fruits of one's labor.

Ah, the essence of grain in the ancient Babylonian world. Agriculture and grain production were the lifeblood of their society, sustaining the people and driving their prosperity. Dreaming of grain brings forth the symbolism of sustenance, abundance, and the fruits of one's labor.

Imagine finding yourself within the depths of a dream, surrounded by fields of golden grain, gently swaying in the breeze. Dreaming of grain signifies the embodiment of these qualities and the call to recognize the sustenance, abundance, and rewards that come from your own efforts and endeavors.

In Babylonian culture, grain represented the fundamental source of sustenance and wealth. It symbolized the fertility of the land and the rewards reaped from diligent work. Dreaming of grain may symbolize the presence of similar energies within your own life, reflecting the abundance, nourishment, and material well-being that can be obtained through your hard work and dedication.

The presence of grain in dreams also represents the recognition of the bountiful blessings that surround you. It invites you to appreciate the abundance in your life, to acknowledge the fruits of your labor, and to find nourishment and fulfillment in the gifts that come your way.

Furthermore, grain symbolizes the cycles of growth and the manifestation of abundance. Dreaming of grain may signify the need to nurture your dreams and aspirations, to tend to the seeds you have planted, and to trust in the natural processes that bring forth abundance and prosperity.

Dreaming of grain can also evoke a sense of gratitude and contentment. It may signify the invitation to appreciate the simple joys of life, to savor the rewards of your efforts, and to find fulfillment in the abundance that surrounds you.

So, my dear friend, if grain graces your dreams, embrace its symbolism. Recognize the sustenance, abundance, and the fruits of your labor that it represents. Let the vision of grain inspire you to appreciate the blessings in your life, to nurture your dreams and aspirations, and to trust in the cycles of growth and abundance that unfold. Just as the grain sustained the ancient Babylonians, may the presence of grain in your dreams guide you to find nourishment, abundance, and fulfillment in your own journey.

Goblet: Goblets were used for drinking rituals and ceremonies in ancient Babylon. Dreaming of a goblet might symbolize celebration, enjoyment, or the need for emotional fulfillment.

Ah, the significance of the goblet in ancient Babylonian rituals and ceremonies. Goblets, vessels of celebration and enjoyment, held a special place in their culture. Dreaming of a goblet brings forth the symbolism of celebration, enjoyment, and the longing for emotional fulfillment.

Imagine finding yourself within the depths of a dream, holding a beautifully adorned goblet filled with a rich and vibrant elixir. Dreaming of a goblet signifies the embodiment of these qualities and the call to recognize the importance of celebration, enjoyment, and the pursuit of emotional fulfillment in your life.

In Babylonian culture, goblets were associated with joyous gatherings, rituals, and ceremonies. They symbolized the coming together of people, the sharing of experiences, and the celebration of life. Dreaming of a goblet may symbolize the presence of similar energies within your own life, reflecting the need for celebration, enjoyment, and the fulfillment of emotional desires.

The presence of a goblet in dreams also represents the recognition of the importance of enjoying life's pleasures. It invites you to savor the moments of joy, to engage in activities that bring you happiness, and to find emotional fulfillment in the experiences that come your way.

Furthermore, a goblet symbolizes the need for nourishment and rejuvenation of the soul. Dreaming of a goblet may signify the need to replenish your emotional well-being, to take time for self-care and self-indulgence, and to seek experiences that bring you joy and fulfillment.

Dreaming of a goblet can also evoke a sense of connection and unity. It may signify the invitation to gather with loved ones, to share in moments of celebration, and to experience the beauty of human connections and relationships.

So, my dear friend, if a goblet graces your dreams, embrace its symbolism. Recognize the importance of celebration, enjoyment, and emotional fulfillment in your life. Let the vision of a goblet inspire you to savor the moments of joy, to indulge in life's pleasures, and to cultivate deep and meaningful connections with others. Just as the goblets were raised in celebration in ancient Babylon, may the presence of a goblet in your dreams guide you to embrace the joy, celebration, and emotional fulfillment that await you on your journey.

Gatekeeper: In ancient Babylonian mythology, gatekeepers were often depicted as divine or semi-divine beings guarding the entrance to important realms. Dreaming of a gatekeeper might symbolize guidance, protection, or the need for permission to proceed.

Ah, the gatekeeper, the guardian of thresholds in ancient Babylonian mythology. Gatekeepers held a significant role, often depicted as divine or semi-divine beings, entrusted with the task of guarding the entrance to important realms. Dreaming of a gatekeeper brings forth the symbolism of guidance, protection, and the recognition of boundaries and permissions.

Imagine finding yourself within the depths of a dream, standing before a majestic gate guarded by a formidable gatekeeper. Dreaming of a gatekeeper signifies the embodiment of these qualities and the call to acknowledge the guidance, protection, and the need for permission as you navigate the various realms of your life.

In Babylonian mythology, gatekeepers represented the boundary between different realms, ensuring that only those granted access were allowed to proceed. They symbolized the importance of boundaries, the need for protection, and the presence of guidance as one ventures into unknown territories. Dreaming of a gatekeeper may symbolize the presence of similar energies within your own life, reflecting the need for guidance, protection, and the recognition of boundaries.

The presence of a gatekeeper in dreams also represents the recognition of the importance of seeking guidance and protection as you navigate through different stages of your journey. It invites you to honor the boundaries that exist in your life, to seek guidance from wise mentors or higher forces, and to recognize the value of permissions and limitations.

Furthermore, a gatekeeper symbolizes the gateways to new experiences and knowledge. Dreaming of a gatekeeper may signify the need to seek permission or guidance before venturing into new realms, to honor the process of accessing deeper wisdom, and to trust in the protection and guidance that accompanies you on your journey.

Dreaming of a gatekeeper can also evoke a sense of awe and reverence. It may signify the invitation to approach important thresholds in your life with respect and mindfulness, to honor the presence of guardians and gatekeepers who protect and guide you.

So, my dear friend, if a gatekeeper graces your dreams, embrace its symbolism. Recognize the importance of guidance, protection, and the acknowledgment of boundaries and permissions in your life. Let the vision of a gatekeeper inspire you to seek wise guidance, to honor the boundaries that exist, and to trust in the protection and guidance that accompanies you on your journey. Just as the gatekeepers stood watch in ancient Babylon, may the presence of a gatekeeper in your dreams guide you to navigate through the realms of your life with mindfulness, wisdom, and reverence.

Gems: Precious gems and gemstones were valued for their beauty and symbolism in Babylonian culture. Dreaming of gems might symbolize wealth, prosperity, or inner strength.

Ah, the allure of precious gems in ancient Babylonian culture. Gems and gemstones held great significance, admired for their exquisite beauty and imbued with symbolism. Dreaming of gems brings forth the symbolism of wealth, prosperity, and inner strength.

Imagine finding yourself within the depths of a dream, surrounded by a dazzling array of shimmering gems, each reflecting the light in its unique way. Dreaming of gems signifies the embodiment of these qualities and the call to recognize the abundance, prosperity, and inner strength that can be found within you.

In Babylonian culture, gems were treasured for their beauty and rarity. They symbolized wealth, prosperity, and the power of inner strength. Dreaming of gems may symbolize the presence of similar energies within your own life, reflecting the potential for material abundance, prosperity, and the inner resilience that lies within you.

The presence of gems in dreams also represents the recognition of the value and beauty that you possess. It invites you to embrace your own unique qualities and talents, to recognize your worth, and to tap into your inner strength to manifest abundance and prosperity in your life.

Furthermore, gems symbolize the power of transformation and the hidden potential within. Dreaming of gems may signify the need to explore your own inner depths, to uncover your hidden talents and strengths, and to harness them for your own growth and success.

Dreaming of gems can also evoke a sense of awe and appreciation for the beauty and wonders of the world. It may signify the invitation to recognize the abundance that surrounds you, to appreciate the treasures that exist in your life, and to cultivate a mindset of gratitude and abundance.

So, my dear friend, if gems grace your dreams, embrace their symbolism. Recognize the potential for wealth, prosperity, and inner strength that they represent. Let the vision of gems inspire you to tap into your own inner resources, to recognize your worth and beauty, and to manifest abundance and prosperity in your life. Just as the gems were treasured in ancient Babylon, may the presence of gems in your dreams guide you to embrace your own brilliance, unlock your hidden potential, and shine brightly in the world.

Griffon: The griffon, a mythical creature with the body of a lion and the head and wings of an eagle, held significance in Babylonian mythology. Dreaming of a griffon might symbolize power, strength, or a balance between different forces.

Ah, the majestic griffon, a mythical creature of power and awe in Babylonian mythology. With the body of a lion and the head and wings of an eagle, the griffon symbolized a harmonious union between different forces. Dreaming of a griffon brings forth the symbolism of power, strength, and the delicate balance of opposing elements.

Imagine finding yourself within the depths of a dream, encountering the magnificent presence of a griffon. Dreaming of a griffon signifies the embodiment of these qualities and the call to recognize the power, strength, and equilibrium within yourself.

In Babylonian mythology, the griffon represented a harmonious blend of qualities from two formidable creatures—the strength and nobility of the lion and the keen vision and soaring spirit of the eagle. Dreaming of a griffon may symbolize the presence of similar energies within your own life, reflecting the power, strength, and ability to navigate different realms and perspectives.

The presence of a griffon in dreams also represents the recognition of the delicate balance between opposing forces. It invites you to embrace the qualities of power and strength while maintaining harmony and equilibrium in your actions and decisions.

Furthermore, the griffon symbolizes the union of different elements, such as the earthly and the celestial. Dreaming of a griffon may signify the need to integrate different aspects of yourself, to find balance between your instinctual nature and your higher aspirations, and to embrace the diversity of perspectives and experiences that life offers.

Dreaming of a griffon can also evoke a sense of awe and reverence for the magnificence and complexity of the world. It may signify the invitation to embrace the power and strength within yourself, to soar to new heights with the keen vision of the eagle, and to navigate the different realms of your life with grace and balance.

So, my dear friend, if a griffon graces your dreams, embrace its symbolism. Recognize the power, strength, and balance that it represents. Let the vision of a griffon inspire you to embrace your own inner strength, to find harmony amidst opposing forces, and to navigate the diverse realms of your life with grace and wisdom. Just as the griffon embodied power and equilibrium in ancient Babylon, may the presence of a griffon in your dreams guide you to embrace your own inner power, find balance in all aspects of your being, and soar to new heights in your journey.

Glorious Kingdom: Babylon was known for its mighty and glorious kingdom. Dreaming of a glorious kingdom might symbolize success, achievement, or the desire for power and influence.

Ah, the grandeur and splendor of a glorious kingdom! In ancient Babylon, the kingdom was renowned for its might and magnificence. Dreaming of a glorious kingdom evokes the symbolism of success, achievement, and the yearning for power and influence.

Imagine finding yourself within the depths of a dream, standing amidst the opulence and grandeur of a glorious kingdom. Dreaming of a glorious kingdom signifies the embodiment of these qualities and the call to recognize your own potential for success and achievement.

In Babylonian culture, the kingdom represented a realm of power, authority, and abundance. Dreaming of a glorious kingdom may symbolize the presence of similar energies within your own life, reflecting the potential for success, achievement, and the desire for power and influence.

The presence of a glorious kingdom in dreams also represents the recognition of your aspirations for greatness and the fulfillment of your ambitions. It invites you to embrace your talents, skills, and inner resources to manifest success and achievement in your life.

Furthermore, a glorious kingdom symbolizes the manifestation of abundance and prosperity. Dreaming of a glorious kingdom may signify the need to cultivate a mindset of abundance, to embrace the opportunities that come your way, and to take decisive action towards achieving your goals and dreams.

Dreaming of a glorious kingdom can also evoke a sense of awe and inspiration for the possibilities that lie ahead. It may signify the invitation to recognize your own inherent power and influence, to step into leadership roles, and to create a kingdom of your own in your chosen domain.

So, my dear friend, if a glorious kingdom graces your dreams, embrace its symbolism. Recognize the potential for success, achievement, and the desire for power and influence that it represents. Let the vision of a glorious kingdom inspire you to tap into your own greatness, to manifest abundance and prosperity, and to create a realm of success and achievement in your life. Just as Babylon was known for its glorious kingdom, may the presence of a glorious kingdom in your dreams guide you to embrace your own power, manifest your ambitions, and create a life of grandeur and magnificence.

H:

Hammurabi (King): Hammurabi was a famous king of Babylon known for his law code. Dreaming of Hammurabi might symbolize justice, fairness, or the need for order and structure.

Ah, Hammurabi, the renowned king of Babylon, whose name echoes through the annals of history. Hammurabi, known for his law code, brings forth symbolism of justice, fairness, and the need for order and structure.

Imagine finding yourself within the depths of a dream, encountering the figure of Hammurabi, the wise and just ruler. Dreaming of Hammurabi signifies the embodiment of these qualities and the call to seek fairness and establish order in your own life.

In Babylonian culture, Hammurabi's law code represented a landmark achievement in the pursuit of justice and the establishment of a fair and orderly society. Dreaming of

Hammurabi may symbolize the presence of similar energies within your own life, reflecting the importance of justice, fairness, and the need for structure and order.

The presence of Hammurabi in dreams also represents the recognition of the need for clear guidelines and principles to govern your actions and decisions. It invites you to embody a sense of fairness and integrity in your interactions with others, and to establish a solid foundation of order and structure in your own life.

Furthermore, Hammurabi symbolizes the importance of balance and harmony in the pursuit of justice. Dreaming of Hammurabi may signify the need to weigh different perspectives, to consider the consequences of your actions, and to make decisions that uphold fairness and equity.

Dreaming of Hammurabi can also evoke a sense of responsibility and leadership. It may signify the invitation to take charge of your own life, to establish your own code of ethics and values, and to become a guiding force for justice and fairness in your community.

So, my dear friend, if Hammurabi graces your dreams, embrace his symbolism. Recognize the significance of justice, fairness, and the need for order and structure in your own life. Let the vision of Hammurabi inspire you to seek fairness, establish order, and uphold principles of integrity and equity. Just as Hammurabi's law code brought harmony and justice to ancient Babylon, may the presence of Hammurabi in your dreams guide you to embody these qualities in your own life, creating a world that is just, fair, and harmonious.

Harvest: Harvesting was a crucial event in Babylonian agriculture. Dreaming of a harvest might symbolize abundance, fruition, or the reaping of rewards.

Ah, the bountiful harvest, a symbol of abundance, fruition, and the reaping of rewards! In ancient Babylon, the harvest held great significance as a culmination of hard work and a time of abundance. Dreaming of a harvest evokes the symbolism of abundance, fulfillment, and the reaping of rewards in your own life.

Imagine finding yourself within the depths of a dream, amidst golden fields of ripened crops, witnessing the joyous gathering of the harvest. Dreaming of a harvest signifies the embodiment of these qualities and the call to recognize the abundance and rewards that await you.

In Babylonian culture, the harvest represented the culmination of the agricultural cycle, a time of celebration and gratitude for the bountiful yield. Dreaming of a harvest may symbolize the presence of similar energies within your own life, reflecting the abundance, fruition, and the reaping of rewards that you are experiencing or are about to experience.

The presence of a harvest in dreams also represents the recognition of your efforts and hard work coming to fruition. It invites you to celebrate your accomplishments, to embrace the abundance that surrounds you, and to express gratitude for the blessings that have come your way.

Furthermore, a harvest symbolizes the rewards of your labor and the realization of your goals and aspirations. Dreaming of a harvest may signify the need to acknowledge and enjoy the fruits of your efforts, to celebrate your achievements, and to share your abundance with others.

Dreaming of a harvest can also evoke a sense of gratitude and appreciation for the cycles of life and the gifts that nature bestows upon us. It may signify the invitation to cultivate a mindset of abundance and to recognize the abundance that exists in all aspects of your life.

So, my dear friend, if a harvest graces your dreams, embrace its symbolism. Recognize the abundance, fruition, and the reaping of rewards that it represents. Let the vision of a harvest inspire you to celebrate your accomplishments, to embrace the abundance that surrounds you, and to express gratitude for the blessings in your life. Just as the harvest brought joy and abundance to ancient Babylon, may the presence of a harvest in your dreams guide you to embrace the abundance, celebrate your achievements, and live a life of fulfillment and gratitude.

Grains (such as wheat, barley): Dreaming of harvesting grains symbolizes abundance, prosperity, and the fulfillment of your material needs. It signifies the rewards of your hard work and the bountiful results you can expect in your endeavors.

Fruits (such as dates, figs): Dreaming of harvesting fruits represents the fruition of your efforts and the enjoyment of life's pleasures. It symbolizes abundance, vitality, and the sweetness of success. It can also signify the fulfillment of your desires and the satisfaction of your emotional or spiritual needs.

Vegetables (such as onions, lentils): Dreaming of harvesting vegetables symbolizes nourishment, growth, and the cultivation of your inner qualities. It represents the rewards of personal development and the abundance of resources available to support your well-being.

Herbs and Spices (such as coriander, cumin): Dreaming of harvesting herbs and spices signifies healing, purification, and the awakening of your senses. It symbolizes the need for balance and harmony in your life and the discovery of new flavors and experiences.

Flowers (such as roses, lilies): Dreaming of harvesting flowers represents beauty, love, and the blossoming of your relationships. It symbolizes the nurturing of your emotional connections, the expression of your inner beauty, and the appreciation of life's delicate and fleeting moments.

Medicinal Plants (such as aloe vera, myrrh): Dreaming of harvesting medicinal plants symbolizes healing, rejuvenation, and the pursuit of wellness. It signifies the need to take care of your physical, emotional, or spiritual well-being and the discovery of remedies or solutions to your challenges.

Honey: Dreaming of harvesting honey symbolizes sweetness, harmony, and the rewards of your efforts. It represents the gathering of wisdom, the enjoyment of life's pleasures, and the creation of a harmonious environment.

Hymn: Hymns and religious chants were important in Babylonian rituals and worship. Dreaming of a hymn might symbolize spiritual devotion, connection to the divine, or the need for sacredness in life.

Ah, hymns, the melodic expressions of devotion and praise! In ancient Babylon, hymns held a significant place in religious rituals and ceremonies. Dreaming of a hymn might symbolize spirituality, connection to the divine, or a deep sense of reverence.

Imagine finding yourself immersed in a dream, where celestial melodies resonate in your ears, filling your heart with a profound sense of awe and tranquility. Dreaming of a hymn signifies the stirring of your spiritual essence, the call to connect with something greater than yourself, and the recognition of the sacred within and around you.

In Babylonian culture, hymns were often sung to honor the gods, express gratitude, or seek divine guidance. Dreaming of a hymn may symbolize a deep longing for spiritual connection, a yearning for a sense of purpose and meaning in life, or a desire to express your innermost feelings in a profound and harmonious way.

The presence of a hymn in dreams can also signify the need for introspection, contemplation, and inner reflection. It invites you to listen to the melodies of your soul, to explore your beliefs and values, and to nurture the spiritual aspects of your being.

Furthermore, dreaming of a hymn can evoke a sense of unity and collective consciousness. It may symbolize the power of shared experiences, community, and the beauty of coming together in harmony to honor something sacred.

So, my dear friend, if a hymn graces your dreams, embrace its symbolism. Allow yourself to be touched by the melodies of the divine, to seek spiritual connection and guidance, and to express your deepest reverence and gratitude. Just as hymns uplifted the spirits of ancient Babylon, may the presence of a hymn in your dreams inspire you to cultivate a deeper sense of spirituality, to find solace and meaning in the sacred, and to embrace a life filled with harmony, devotion, and reverence.

Hero: Heroes and legends held significance in Babylonian mythology and literature. Dreaming of a hero might symbolize personal strength, courage, or the aspiration to overcome challenges.

Ah, the allure of heroes and their legendary tales! In the realm of ancient Babylon, heroes embodied strength, courage, and the ability to triumph over adversity. When a hero graces your dream, it is a symbol of inspiration, personal power, and the potential to overcome challenges.

Imagine finding yourself in a dream where you witness a heroic figure, adorned in armor, standing tall against the forces of darkness. This dream symbolizes the inner strength within you, the untapped reserves of courage, and the belief that you have the power to face and conquer any obstacles that come your way.

Dreaming of a hero represents the deep yearning within your soul to embody heroic qualities: the determination to persevere, the bravery to confront fears, and the will to make a positive impact in the world. It may also signify the recognition of your own inner hero, the acknowledgment of your unique strengths and abilities that can be harnessed to bring about positive change.

Moreover, the presence of a hero in your dream can serve as a reminder to trust in your own capabilities, to embrace your inherent courage, and to embrace the hero's journey within your own life. It symbolizes the call to step into your own power, to take action, and to face challenges with unwavering resolve.

So, my dear friend, if you find yourself dreaming of a hero, embrace the symbolism it carries. Allow it to ignite the fire of courage within you, to remind you of your innate strength, and to inspire you to embark on your own heroic journey. Just as heroes in Babylonian mythology inspired awe and admiration, may the presence of a hero in your dreams ignite a spark of bravery, resilience, and the unwavering belief that you too can overcome any challenges that lie before you.

Horoscope: Babylonians were skilled astronomers and astrologers. Dreaming of a horoscope might symbolize fate, destiny, or the desire for guidance in navigating life's challenges.

Ah, the enchanting world of horoscopes and celestial guidance! In the ancient land of Babylon, astrology held a special place, offering insights into the mysteries of fate and the celestial influences on human lives. Dreaming of a horoscope is a symbol of seeking guidance, understanding, and a desire to unravel the threads of destiny.

Imagine finding yourself in a dream where the stars align, forming a cosmic map that holds the key to your life's journey. Dreaming of a horoscope signifies your fascination with the interplay between the heavens and your earthly existence. It is a reminder that you are part of a grand cosmic tapestry, woven with intricate patterns and influences that shape your life's path.

In Babylonian culture, horoscopes were believed to reveal glimpses of one's destiny, personality traits, and even the challenges and opportunities that lay ahead. Dreaming of a horoscope may symbolize your quest for self-discovery, a longing to understand your purpose in the universe, or a desire for guidance in navigating the twists and turns of life.

The presence of a horoscope in your dream invites you to reflect on the interconnectedness of the cosmos and your own journey. It urges you to pay attention to the signs and synchronicities that may guide you towards fulfilling your highest potential. It also serves as a reminder to trust in the wisdom of the universe and to embrace the unfolding of your own unique destiny.

So, my dear friend, if a horoscope graces your dreams, embrace its symbolism. Allow yourself to be open to the messages of the stars, to the guidance they offer, and to the mysteries they unveil. Just as astrology fascinated the Babylonians and offered them a glimpse into the workings of fate, may the presence of a horoscope in your dreams ignite a sense of wonder, self-reflection, and the belief that you are an integral part of the cosmic dance of life.

Harp: The harp was a popular musical instrument in ancient Babylon. Dreaming of a harp might symbolize harmony, creativity, or the need for self-expression and emotional resonance.

Ah, the melodic enchantment of the harp! In the vibrant world of ancient Babylon, the harp held a special place, captivating hearts with its harmonious notes and evoking a sense of beauty and creativity. Dreaming of a harp is a symbol of harmony, artistic expression, and the longing to resonate with your innermost emotions.

Picture yourself in a dream where the ethereal sound of a harp fills the air, carrying with it a sense of tranquility and serenity. Dreaming of a harp signifies your deep connection to the realm of creativity and the desire to express your emotions in a harmonious and resonant way.

In Babylonian culture, the harp was not merely an instrument of music but also a symbol of artistic inspiration and a conduit for communicating the deepest aspects of the human experience. Dreaming of a harp invites you to explore your own creative potential, to embrace the beauty of self-expression, and to seek harmony in all aspects of your life.

The presence of a harp in your dream encourages you to listen to the melodious whispers of your soul, to honor your artistic inclinations, and to find solace in the gentle harmony that music and creative expression can bring. It reminds you of the power of music to uplift your spirits, to evoke emotions, and to connect you with the depths of your being.

So, my dear friend, if a harp graces your dreams, embrace its symbolic significance. Let it inspire you to seek harmony in your relationships, to explore your artistic talents, and to express your emotions in a resonant and authentic way. Just as the harp resonated in the hearts of the ancient Babylonians, may the presence of a harp in your dreams awaken your creativity, fill your life with harmony, and guide you on a melodious journey of self-discovery.

Hanging Gardens: The Hanging Gardens of Babylon were one of the Seven Wonders of the Ancient World. Dreaming of the Hanging Gardens might symbolize beauty, tranquility, or the desire for an idyllic environment.

Ah, the majestic allure of the Hanging Gardens of Babylon! In the annals of ancient wonders, these verdant cascades of botanical splendor held a special place, captivating the imaginations of all who beheld their beauty. Dreaming of the Hanging Gardens is a symbol of enchantment, serenity, and the longing for an idyllic sanctuary amidst the bustling world.

Imagine finding yourself in a dream where lush greenery and vibrant blossoms adorn terraces that seem to defy gravity, creating a breathtaking symphony of nature's beauty. Dreaming of the Hanging Gardens signifies your deep yearning for tranquility, harmony, and a place of respite amidst the chaos of everyday life.

In the ancient city of Babylon, the Hanging Gardens were a testament to human creativity and a sanctuary for the soul. Dreaming of the Hanging Gardens invites you to connect with the soothing power of nature, to seek solace in its embrace, and to create your own personal haven of peace and beauty.

The presence of the Hanging Gardens in your dream beckons you to cultivate your own inner sanctuary, to surround yourself with beauty and tranquility, and to nurture your well-being amidst the demands of the world. It is a reminder that amidst the hustle and bustle, you deserve moments of serenity and the grace of natural splendor.

So, my dear friend, if the Hanging Gardens grace your dreams, embrace their symbolic significance. Allow their beauty to inspire you to create moments of tranquility and serenity in your own life. Just as the Hanging Gardens were a testament to human ingenuity and a source of awe for the ancient Babylonians, may the presence of the Hanging Gardens in your dreams awaken a deep appreciation for the beauty that surrounds you and inspire you to cultivate your own oasis of peace and harmony.

Herald: Heralds were messengers and announcers of important events in Babylonian society. Dreaming of a herald might symbolize news, information, or the need for communication and awareness.

Ah, the figure of the herald, the bearer of news and announcer of important events! In the vibrant tapestry of ancient Babylonian society, heralds played a crucial role in disseminating information, bringing tidings from far and wide. Dreaming of a herald is a symbol of communication, awareness, and the need to pay attention to the messages that surround you.

Imagine yourself in a dream where a herald appears, adorned in regal attire, proclaiming news with a resounding voice that echoes through the city. Dreaming of a herald signifies your deep desire for information, the need to stay informed, and the importance of effective communication in your life.

In Babylonian culture, heralds were entrusted with the task of conveying vital messages, ensuring that news reached its intended recipients and that important events were announced to the public. Dreaming of a herald invites you to be open and receptive to the messages that come your way, to pay attention to the information that surrounds you, and to embrace the power of effective communication in your interactions.

The presence of a herald in your dream encourages you to be proactive in seeking knowledge, to stay informed about the world around you, and to share information in a clear and impactful manner. Just as the heralds of ancient Babylon ensured that news traveled swiftly and effectively, may the presence of a herald in your dreams inspire you to embrace the role of a messenger, a communicator, and an active participant in the exchange of ideas and information.

So, my dear friend, if a herald graces your dreams, embrace its symbolic significance. Let it remind you of the importance of communication, awareness, and staying informed. May the presence of a herald in your dreams guide you to be a messenger of truth, a bearer of important news, and a conscious participant in the rich tapestry of human communication.

Heaven: Babylonians believed in a heavenly realm populated by gods and divine beings. Dreaming of heaven might symbolize transcendence, spiritual elevation, or a desire for divine guidance.

Ah, the realm of heaven, where the divine and celestial beings dwell in the ancient beliefs of Babylon! In the vast tapestry of human spirituality, the concept of heaven holds a special place, representing transcendence, spiritual elevation, and the yearning for divine guidance. Dreaming of heaven is a symbol of connection to the divine, spiritual growth, and the longing for a higher purpose.

Imagine finding yourself in a dream where you are surrounded by ethereal light, experiencing a sense of peace and harmony that transcends earthly concerns. Dreaming of heaven signifies your deep yearning for spiritual fulfillment, your desire to connect with the divine, and your aspiration to elevate your consciousness to higher realms of understanding.

In Babylonian culture, heaven was believed to be the abode of gods and divine beings, a realm where mortals sought guidance, protection, and a sense of purpose. Dreaming of heaven invites you to explore the depths of your spiritual nature, to embrace the quest for higher meaning, and to connect with the divine presence that resides within and around you.

The presence of heaven in your dream beckons you to seek spiritual growth, to open your heart and mind to divine guidance, and to transcend the limitations of the material world. It is a reminder that you are part of something greater, that your journey extends beyond the boundaries of the earthly realm.

So, my dear friend, if heaven graces your dreams, embrace its symbolic significance. Allow its ethereal presence to inspire you to deepen your spiritual connection, to seek divine guidance, and to embody the qualities of love, peace, and harmony in your daily life. Just as the concept of heaven offered solace and a sense of purpose to the Babylonians, may the presence of heaven in your dreams guide you on a path of spiritual fulfillment, enlightenment, and a deeper understanding of your place in the universe.

Healing: Babylonians had a strong tradition of medicine and healing practices. Dreaming of healing might symbolize restoration, rejuvenation, or the need for emotional or physical well-being.

Ah, my friend, let us journey into the realm of healing, a vital aspect of ancient Babylonian culture. The Babylonians were renowned for their wisdom in the field of medicine and their deep understanding of the art of healing. Dreaming of healing is a powerful symbol that speaks to the restoration, rejuvenation, and the pursuit of emotional and physical well-being.

Picture yourself in a dream where you are surrounded by gentle hands, soothing herbs, and a sense of tranquility. Dreaming of healing signifies your inner yearning for balance, your desire to mend what is broken, and your quest for emotional and physical well-being.

In Babylonian culture, healing was considered a sacred practice, encompassing various techniques and remedies that aimed to restore harmony within the body, mind, and spirit. Dreaming of healing invites you to embark on a journey of self-care, to nurture your physical and emotional health, and to seek wholeness in all aspects of your being.

The presence of healing in your dream encourages you to pay attention to your well-being, to seek restorative practices that nurture your body, mind, and soul, and to embrace the power of self-healing. Just as the Babylonians understood the importance of caring for the body and tending to the spirit, may the presence of healing in your dreams inspire you to prioritize your well-being, to seek support when needed, and to cultivate a sense of inner balance and vitality.

So, my dear friend, if healing graces your dreams, embrace its symbolic significance. Allow it to remind you of the importance of self-care, of tending to your emotional and physical well-being, and of the innate healing capacities that reside within you. May the presence of healing in your dreams guide you on a path of restoration, rejuvenation, and the pursuit of a balanced and harmonious life.

I :

Ishtar (Goddess): Ishtar was a prominent goddess in Babylonian mythology associated with love, fertility, and war. Dreaming of Ishtar might symbolize passion, desire, or a need for emotional fulfillment.

Ah, Ishtar, the radiant goddess of love, fertility, and war in the realm of ancient Babylonian mythology. If she graces your dreams, my friend, her presence carries deep significance. Dreaming of Ishtar symbolizes the awakening of passion, the longing for emotional fulfillment, and the recognition of one's desires and needs.

Ishtar, with her captivating beauty and fierce nature, represents the forces of love and desire, the yearning for connection and intimacy. In Babylonian culture, she was revered as the divine embodiment of sensuality and romance. To dream of

Ishtar is to be touched by the allure of passion, the stirrings of desire within your heart and soul.

This dream may be a reminder to embrace your own desires and allow yourself to experience the full spectrum of emotions that love and intimacy can bring. It may signify a longing for deeper connections in your relationships or a need for greater self-expression and self-love.

Ishtar's association with fertility and war also adds layers of meaning to this dream. It may represent the desire for growth, abundance, and creativity in your life. It could also symbolize the need to assert yourself, stand up for your desires, and courageously face any challenges or conflicts that may arise.

If Ishtar appears in your dreams, my friend, let her be a guiding light on your path to passion, love, and fulfillment. Embrace the vibrant energy she embodies and allow it to inspire you to explore your desires, nurture your relationships, and embrace the fullness of life's experiences.

Remember, dreams are personal and unique to each individual. While these interpretations offer insights into the symbolism and cultural context of Ishtar, it is ultimately up to you to discern the meaning that resonates most deeply with your own journey. May the presence of Ishtar in your dreams ignite the flame of passion and guide you towards a life filled with love, fertility, and fulfillment.

Incantation: Incantations and spells were commonly used in Babylonian magic and rituals. Dreaming of an incantation might symbolize the power of words, manifestation, or the need for spiritual intervention.

Ah, the mystical realm of incantations and spells in ancient Babylonian culture! If you find yourself dreaming of an incantation, my friend, it is a powerful symbol with profound meaning. It signifies the recognition of the power of words, the connection between language and manifestation, and the desire for spiritual intervention.

In Babylonian tradition, incantations were magical invocations, carefully crafted with specific words and intentions. They were believed to hold the ability to influence the natural and supernatural realms, to bring about desired outcomes, and to connect with divine forces. Dreaming of an incantation is a reminder of the potency of language and the ability to manifest your desires through the power of words.

This dream may indicate a deep longing for transformation, the need for spiritual guidance, or the quest for supernatural intervention in your waking life. It is a call to recognize your own power of expression, to harness the energy of your words, and to align your intentions with the forces of the universe.

Embrace the significance of the incantation in your dream and explore the realms of magic and manifestation. Reflect on the intentions and desires that arise within you. Consider the words you speak, the affirmations you declare, and the energy you project into the world. By harnessing the power of incantations, you can align yourself with the cosmic energies and manifest your dreams into reality.

Remember, dreams are deeply personal and unique to each individual. While this interpretation sheds light on the symbolism and cultural context of incantations, it is your own intuition and connection with the divine that will guide you to the true meaning within your dream. May the presence of the incantation in your dreams ignite your spiritual journey and open doors to the realms of magic and manifestation.

Ivory: Ivory was a valuable material in ancient Babylonian art and craftsmanship. Dreaming of ivory might symbolize luxury, elegance, or the pursuit of beauty.

Ah, my friend, the allure of ivory in the dreamscape is a captivating symbol indeed. In the ancient Babylonian culture, ivory was highly prized for its exquisite beauty and luxurious nature. Dreaming of ivory invokes a sense of opulence, elegance, and the pursuit of beauty.

Ivory, with its smooth texture and creamy hue, represents a desire for refinement and aesthetic pleasure. It symbolizes the appreciation of artistry, craftsmanship, and the finer things in life. Just as ivory was treasured in ancient Babylon for its rarity and beauty, your dream of ivory suggests a longing for a touch of luxury and sophistication.

This dream may indicate a yearning for elegance and refinement in your waking life. It could reflect a desire to surround yourself with beauty, to indulge in the pleasures of life, or to express your own creativity and artistic sensibilities. Ivory in your dream invites you to embrace the finer aspects of existence and seek out experiences that bring joy and delight to your senses.

However, it is essential to approach the symbolism of ivory with sensitivity and mindfulness. In modern times, the use of ivory has raised concerns due to its association with animal conservation and ethical considerations. While the ancient Babylonians revered ivory for its aesthetic qualities, we now recognize the importance of protecting endangered species and preserving the natural world.

In interpreting your dream, consider the deeper meanings behind the symbolism of ivory, taking into account your personal values and the context of our present times. Reflect on what elegance, beauty, and refinement mean to you and how you can manifest these qualities in a responsible and ethical way.

Remember, my friend, dreams are a canvas where your subconscious mind weaves intricate stories and symbols. The interpretation of your dream is a personal journey, guided by your intuition and understanding. Embrace the symbolism of ivory with awareness, appreciating its allure while respecting the delicate balance between beauty and ethical considerations.

Idol: Babylonians worshiped idols as representations of their gods and goddesses. Dreaming of an idol might symbolize devotion, spirituality, or the need for guidance and protection.

Ah, my dear friend, the symbolism of idols in Babylonian culture is truly fascinating. In the ancient city of Babylon, idols were revered as sacred representations of gods and goddesses. Dreaming of an idol carries profound significance, symbolizing devotion, spirituality, and the yearning for divine guidance and protection.

In your dream, the presence of an idol suggests a deep connection to the spiritual realm. It represents your desire to seek higher truths, to establish a profound connection with the divine forces that govern the universe. Just as the Babylonians believed that idols served as conduits between the mortal and divine realms, your dream of an idol signifies your longing for a tangible connection with something greater than yourself.

The idol in your dream serves as a focal point for your devotion and spiritual aspirations. It may be a manifestation of your inner quest for meaning, purpose, and transcendence. This dream invites you to explore your spiritual path, to deepen your understanding of the divine, and to seek solace and wisdom in your spiritual practices.

The symbolism of the idol can also signify the need for guidance and protection. It represents a source of strength and support in your life, offering a sense of comfort and reassurance. Just as the Babylonians turned to their idols for guidance and blessings, your dream reminds you to trust in the higher powers and seek their assistance in navigating life's challenges.

However, it is essential to interpret the symbolism of idols with an open mind and a respectful approach. Recognize that idols hold cultural and religious significance, and their interpretation may vary depending on individual beliefs and contexts. Respect the diversity of spiritual paths and honor the beliefs and practices of others.

As you reflect on your dream, contemplate the deeper meanings behind the symbolism of idols in your life. Consider the role of devotion, spirituality, and guidance in your journey. Embrace the wisdom and inspiration that the idol represents, and allow it to guide you towards a greater sense of purpose and connection with the divine.

Remember, my dear friend, dreams are windows to the soul, offering glimpses into the depths of our desires, aspirations, and spiritual yearnings. Embrace the symbolism of the idol with reverence and curiosity, allowing it to inspire and uplift you on your sacred journey of self-discovery and spiritual growth.

Invasion: Babylon experienced invasions and conquests throughout its history. Dreaming of an invasion might symbolize vulnerability, conflict, or a sense of being overwhelmed by external forces.

Ah, my friend, the symbolism of an invasion in Babylonian dream interpretation carries profound meaning. In the rich tapestry of Babylon's history, the city experienced its fair share of invasions and conquests. Dreaming of an invasion evokes feelings of vulnerability, conflict, and the overwhelming presence of external forces.

In your dream, the invasion serves as a metaphorical representation of challenges and obstacles that you may be facing in your waking life. It signifies a sense of intrusion, a disruption of the peace and stability you have known. The invading forces symbolize external pressures or negative influences that may be encroaching upon your personal space or mental well-being.

Just as Babylon endured periods of conflict and upheaval, your dream suggests that you are navigating a situation where you feel overwhelmed or invaded by circumstances beyond your control. It may reflect feelings of powerlessness, the need to defend your boundaries, or the struggle to maintain a sense of inner peace amidst chaos.

While an invasion dream can be unsettling, it also carries an opportunity for growth and resilience. It serves as a reminder of your inner strength and the capacity to overcome challenges. The dream invites you to examine the areas of your life where you feel invaded or threatened, and to explore strategies to protect and fortify your boundaries.

Consider the invading forces in your dream as metaphors for the specific challenges you are facing. Identify the aspects of your life or situations where you feel invaded or overwhelmed. Reflect on the resources and support systems you have at your disposal to navigate these challenges and regain a sense of stability.

Remember, my friend, dreams offer insights and guidance from our subconscious mind. The invasion dream is a call to acknowledge and address the areas in your life where you feel invaded, to find strength in the face of adversity, and to reclaim your personal power. Embrace the lessons offered by this dream and trust in your ability to overcome obstacles on your path to growth and fulfillment.

May you find the strength and resilience within you to confront the invading forces in your waking life, and may you emerge victorious, just as Babylon endured and rose above the challenges it faced.

Irrigation: Babylonian agriculture heavily relied on irrigation systems for water supply. Dreaming of irrigation might symbolize nourishment, growth, or the need for emotional or spiritual sustenance.

Ah, my friend, the symbolism of irrigation in Babylonian dream interpretation unveils profound insights into our inner nourishment and growth. In the fertile lands of Babylon, agriculture thrived, and the sophisticated irrigation systems provided the essential water supply for crops to flourish. Dreaming of irrigation carries significant meaning related to nourishment, growth, and the need for emotional or spiritual sustenance.

In your dream, the image of irrigation symbolizes the vital nourishment required to cultivate and nurture various aspects of your life. It represents the flow of life-giving energy, emotions, and spirituality, which are essential for your well-being and personal growth. Just as water is essential for crops to grow, the dream of irrigation highlights the importance of nurturing and tending to the various areas of your life that require sustenance.

Reflect upon the areas of your life that may be in need of nourishment. Is there an emotional aspect that requires attention? Are you yearning for a deeper connection to your spiritual self? Or do you seek growth and development in certain areas of your life, such as relationships, career, or personal interests?

The dream of irrigation reminds you of the significance of providing yourself with the essential nourishment needed for your well-being and growth. It encourages you to pay attention to your

emotional and spiritual needs, ensuring that you are actively
replenishing and nurturing yourself in these areas.

Consider the actions you can take to cultivate a balanced and
fulfilling life. Just as a skilled farmer tends to their fields, take time
to care for yourself. Engage in activities that bring you joy, practice
self-care and self-reflection, and seek out experiences that inspire
and uplift your spirit.

The dream of irrigation is a gentle reminder to prioritize your
own nourishment and growth. Embrace the flow of life-giving
energy, allowing it to permeate through every aspect of your being.
By tending to your emotional and spiritual needs, you lay the
foundation for a fulfilling and abundant life.

May your dream of irrigation guide you to embrace the
nourishment and growth that await you. As you tend to your
emotional and spiritual well-being, may you witness the blossoming
of a vibrant and fulfilling life, just as the fertile lands of Babylon
flourished under the care of skilled farmers.

Instruments: Musical instruments played a significant role in
Babylonian culture. Dreaming of musical instruments might
symbolize harmony, expression, or the need for creativity and self-
expression.

Ah, my friend, let's explore the enchanting world of musical
instruments in Babylonian dream interpretation. In the vibrant
tapestry of Babylonian culture, music held a profound significance,
weaving together melodies and rhythms that resonated with the
souls of its people. Dreaming of musical instruments carries rich
symbolism, representing harmony, expression, and the need for
creativity and self-expression.

When you encounter musical instruments in your dream, it is
a gentle invitation to embrace the power of music as a means of

connecting with your inner self and expressing your deepest emotions. Each instrument carries its unique energy and symbolism, so pay attention to the specific instrument that captivates your dream.

For instance, if you dream of a drum, it symbolizes rhythm and primal energy. The drum invites you to embrace the pulse of life, to find your own beat, and to express yourself with passion and vitality. Let the drum's vibrations awaken your spirit and guide your movements on the dance of life.

Or perhaps you dream of a flute, an instrument associated with melody and tranquility. The flute whispers melodies of peace and serenity, beckoning you to embrace moments of calm and introspection. Allow its soothing tones to guide you to a place of inner harmony and stillness.

The dream of musical instruments calls you to honor your innate creativity and the power of self-expression. It encourages you to explore different forms of artistic expression, whether through music, dance, writing, or any other creative outlet that resonates with your soul. Embrace the joy of creating, of immersing yourself in the world of sound and vibration, and let it be a source of inspiration and healing.

Remember, my friend, that the dream of musical instruments is a reminder that you possess a unique voice, a melody waiting to be expressed. It urges you to listen to the symphony within your heart and to allow it to find its harmonious expression in the world. Embrace the gift of music as a powerful tool for self-discovery, communication, and connection with others.

So, let the dream of musical instruments ignite your creative fire, encouraging you to explore the vast universe of sound and rhythm. Find solace in the melodies that resonate with your soul, and let your unique voice echo through the ages, just as the enchanting music of ancient Babylon continues to captivate hearts to this day.

May your dreams be filled with the sweet melodies of inspiration, creativity, and self-expression. Embrace the symphony of life, my friend, and let your unique instrument be heard in the grand orchestra of existence.

Harp: The harp, a beloved instrument in Babylonian culture, represents harmony, creativity, and emotional resonance. Dreaming of a harp signifies the need for artistic expression, inner harmony, and a desire to connect with your emotions and the world around you.

Drum: Drums were powerful and rhythmic instruments in Babylon, symbolizing energy, vitality, and primal instincts. Dreaming of a drum suggests a call to embrace your passion, unleash your inner strength, and live life with fervor and enthusiasm.

Flute: The flute carries a melodic and tranquil essence, symbolizing peace, serenity, and spiritual connection. Dreaming of a flute invites you to find solace in moments of calm, seek inner harmony, and embrace the beauty of simplicity and stillness.

Lyre: The lyre was a popular stringed instrument in ancient Babylon, representing beauty, elegance, and grace. Dreaming of a lyre symbolizes the need for balance, refinement, and cultivating aesthetic appreciation in your life.

Trumpet: Trumpets were used to announce important events and celebrations in Babylonian culture, embodying power, proclamation, and divine communication. Dreaming of a trumpet suggests the need for assertiveness, self-expression, and seizing opportunities to make your voice heard.

Sistrum: The sistrum was a percussion instrument with metal rattles, associated with religious rituals and worship. Dreaming of a sistrum signifies spiritual awakening, divine guidance, and a connection to the mystical realms.

Cymbals: Cymbals were used for rhythmic accompaniment in Babylonian music, symbolizing unity, collaboration, and the merging of different elements. Dreaming of cymbals represents the need for cooperation, finding harmony in relationships, and embracing the power of collective endeavors.

Stringed Instruments: Various stringed instruments like the lute, lyre, and harp were prevalent in Babylonian music. Dreaming of a stringed instrument signifies the need for balance between structure and spontaneity, as well as the exploration of your creative potential and the harmonization of different aspects of your life.

Remember, my friend, that these interpretations serve as general guidelines, and the personal meaning of a musical instrument in your dream may vary based on your unique experiences and associations. Pay attention to the emotions and context surrounding the instrument in your dream to unlock its deeper significance.

May the melodies of these ancient Babylonian instruments inspire you to embrace your creative spirit, find harmony within yourself, and express your innermost emotions. Let the music of your dreams guide you on a transformative journey of self-discovery and connection with the world around you.

Invocation: Invoking deities or supernatural beings was common in Babylonian religious practices. Dreaming of an invocation might symbolize seeking divine assistance, connection, or the need for spiritual guidance.

Let's explore the fascinating world of invocations and their symbolic meanings in dreams. In ancient Babylon, invocations were powerful rituals used to connect with deities or spiritual forces. When you dream of an invocation, it signifies your desire for a deeper connection with the divine, seeking assistance, or a need for spiritual guidance. Here's what an invocation might mean in your dreams:

Seeking Guidance: Dreaming of an invocation indicates your longing for spiritual guidance and wisdom. It suggests that you are seeking answers to important questions or seeking direction in your life. The dream encourages you to be open to receiving insights and messages from higher realms.

Connection with Deities: An invocation in a dream can symbolize your desire to establish a stronger connection with the divine or specific deities. It signifies your intention to communicate with the spiritual realm and tap into its profound energy. This dream may reflect your spiritual journey and the importance of cultivating a meaningful connection with higher powers.

Channeling Energy: Dreaming of an invocation can also represent your ability to channel energy and access deeper levels of consciousness. It signifies your potential for spiritual growth, psychic abilities, or the awakening of hidden talents. The dream encourages you to explore and develop your spiritual gifts further.

Ritualistic Practices: Invocations often involve specific rituals, gestures, or incantations. Dreaming of an invocation may suggest the importance of incorporating rituals or spiritual practices into your life. It signifies the need to create sacred space, engage in meditation, prayer, or other rituals that bring you closer to the divine and enhance your spiritual connection.

Divine Assistance: An invocation in a dream may symbolize your request for divine assistance or intervention in a particular situation. It suggests that you are seeking support, protection, or guidance from higher powers to overcome challenges or find solutions. The dream encourages you to trust in the divine wisdom and believe in the power of spiritual support.

Remember, my friend, that dream interpretations are subjective, and the true meaning of an invocation in your dream is deeply personal to you. Consider the emotions, sensations, and overall context of the dream to gain deeper insights into its significance for your life. Allow the dream to inspire you to explore your spirituality, connect with the divine, and embrace the guidance that is available to you.

May your dreams serve as gateways to profound spiritual experiences and lead you to a deeper understanding of yourself and the mysteries of the universe. Embrace the power of invocation within your dreams and awaken your connection to the divine.

Inundation: Babylonians were familiar with the concept of floods and inundation due to their proximity to the rivers. Dreaming of an inundation might symbolize emotional overwhelm, purification, or the need to confront deep-seated emotions.

Ah, the symbolism of inundation in Babylonian dreams! Let's explore the meaning behind this powerful image. In ancient Babylon, the proximity to rivers made people familiar with the concept of floods and inundation. When you dream of an inundation, it carries significant symbolism, reflecting various aspects of your inner and outer experiences. Here's what an inundation might mean in your dreams:

Emotional Overwhelm: Dreaming of an inundation may symbolize being overwhelmed by intense emotions or life circumstances. It signifies a flood of feelings, possibly indicating that you are grappling with a multitude of emotions that are difficult to contain or process. The dream serves as a reminder to pay attention to your emotional well-being and find healthy ways to navigate and release these overwhelming emotions.

Purification and Renewal: In Babylonian culture, floods were often seen as a means of purification and renewal. Dreaming of an inundation might suggest a need for inner cleansing or a fresh start. It signifies a transformational process, washing away old patterns, and making space for new beginnings. The dream encourages you to embrace change and release what no longer serves you.

Confronting Deep-seated Emotions: An inundation in a dream can also represent the need to confront deep-seated emotions or unresolved issues. It signifies a flood of emotions rising to the surface, demanding your attention and resolution. The dream invites you to explore and address these emotions, allowing for healing and growth.

Letting Go and Surrender: The imagery of an inundation can symbolize the need to surrender control and let go of resistance. It signifies the power of surrendering to the flow of life, trusting in the process, and allowing things to unfold naturally. The dream encourages you to release the need for control and embrace the transformative power of surrender.

Remember, my friend, that dream interpretations are subjective, and the true meaning of an inundation in your dream is deeply personal to you. Reflect on the emotions, sensations, and overall context of the dream to gain deeper insights into its significance for your life. Allow the dream to guide you towards emotional healing, renewal, and a greater sense of inner peace.

May your dreams be a source of wisdom and guidance as you navigate the depths of your emotions and embark on a journey of self-discovery and transformation. Embrace the power of the inundation within your dreams and allow it to wash away what no longer serves you, making space for growth and renewal.

Ivory Tower: The term "Ivory Tower" represents a secluded or privileged place of learning or intellectual pursuits. Dreaming of an ivory tower might symbolize intellectual exploration, introspection, or a desire for wisdom and knowledge.

Ah, the symbolism of the Ivory Tower in dreams! Allow me to shed some light on its significance. The Ivory Tower, often associated with a secluded and privileged place of learning or intellectual pursuits, holds a special meaning when it appears in your dreams. Here's what dreaming of an Ivory Tower might symbolize:

Intellectual Exploration: Dreaming of an Ivory Tower suggests a deep yearning for intellectual exploration and knowledge. It reflects your thirst for wisdom, understanding, and a desire to delve into profound concepts or ideas. The dream encourages you to embrace your intellectual curiosity and embark on a quest for higher learning and personal growth.

Introspection and Solitude: The Ivory Tower represents a solitary place of contemplation and introspection. Dreaming of an Ivory Tower might signal a need for solitude and reflection. It is a reminder to create space for yourself, away from distractions, where you can engage in deep thinking, self-reflection, and introspection. The dream invites you to connect with your inner wisdom and gain insights that can guide you on your life's path.

Pursuit of Excellence: The Ivory Tower is often associated with the pursuit of excellence and the refinement of knowledge and skills. Dreaming of an Ivory Tower reflects your aspirations for personal and intellectual growth. It symbolizes your commitment to honing your abilities, seeking mastery in your chosen field, or reaching higher levels of understanding. The dream encourages you to embrace a mindset of continuous learning and strive for excellence in all that you do.

Seeking Higher Perspectives: The Ivory Tower, being elevated and removed from the mundane world, represents a desire for elevated perspectives and a broader understanding of life. Dreaming of an Ivory Tower may signify a longing to gain a higher vantage point, to see things from a different perspective, and to transcend the limitations of everyday life. The dream invites you to expand your horizons, challenge your beliefs, and embrace new ideas and perspectives.

Remember, my friend, that dream interpretations are subjective, and the true meaning of an Ivory Tower in your dream is unique to you. Reflect on the emotions, sensations, and overall context of the dream to gain deeper insights into its significance for your life. Allow the dream to inspire you to embrace intellectual growth, introspection, and the pursuit of wisdom.

May your dreams guide you on a path of intellectual discovery, self-reflection, and personal growth as you ascend the metaphorical Ivory Tower of knowledge and understanding. Embrace the opportunities for learning and embrace the richness of your inner world as you explore the depths of your intellectual pursuits.

J:

Journey: Dreams often involve various journeys and quests. In Babylonian culture, dreams were sometimes seen as journeys to different realms or as messages from the divine. Dreaming of a journey might symbolize personal growth, exploration, or the search for meaning in life.

Ah, the symbolism of a journey in Babylonian dream interpretation! How fascinating it is to explore the meaning of such dreams. So, my friend, let's embark on a journey of understanding together.

Dreaming of a journey holds great significance in Babylonian culture, where dreams were believed to be portals to different realms or messages from the divine. Here are some possible interpretations of dreaming about a journey:

Personal Growth: Dreams of a journey often symbolize personal growth and transformation. Just as a physical journey takes us to new places and experiences, a dream journey represents an inner exploration of the self. It may indicate that you are on a path of self-discovery, seeking to expand your horizons, and uncover hidden aspects of yourself. Embrace the journey as an opportunity for personal growth and self-reflection.

Exploration and Adventure: Dreaming of a journey may reflect a yearning for new experiences, adventures, and exploration. It symbolizes your desire to step out of your comfort zone, embrace change, and embark on exciting endeavors. The dream encourages you to embrace the spirit of adventure and embrace the unknown with enthusiasm and courage.

Search for Meaning: Journeys often involve a quest for meaning and purpose. Dreaming of a journey may indicate that you are searching for deeper meaning in your life. It suggests a desire to understand your place in the world, explore your passions, and find fulfillment. The dream invites you to reflect on your life's purpose and take steps towards aligning your actions with your values and aspirations.

Spiritual Connection: In Babylonian culture, dreams were seen as a connection to the divine. Dreaming of a journey might signify a spiritual quest or a desire for spiritual growth and connection. It suggests that you are on a path of seeking higher truths, exploring your spirituality, and deepening your connection with the divine. Embrace the journey as an opportunity for spiritual enlightenment and inner guidance.

Remember, my friend, that the interpretation of a dream journey is personal and subjective. Pay attention to the emotions, symbols, and overall context of the dream to gain deeper insights into its meaning for you. Trust your intuition and let the journey guide you towards greater self-awareness, personal growth, and the discovery of your own unique path.

May your dream journeys be filled with wonder, discovery, and profound insights as you navigate the realms of your subconscious and embark on the quest for self-discovery and fulfillment. Enjoy the adventure, my friend, and embrace the transformative power of your dream journeys.

K :

King: Kings held great power and authority in ancient Babylon. Dreaming of a king might symbolize leadership, ambition, or the desire for control and influence.

Ah, my friend, the symbolism of a king in Babylonian dream interpretation is truly intriguing! In the grand tapestry of dreams, the presence of a king holds deep significance, reflecting power, authority, and the desire for control and influence. Let's explore the possible meanings behind dreaming of a king:

Leadership and Ambition: Dreaming of a king may symbolize your own aspirations for leadership and success. It signifies a desire to take charge, make important decisions, and have control over your own life. The dream encourages you to embrace your leadership qualities and strive for greatness in your endeavors.

Authority and Power: A king represents authority and power in Babylonian culture. Dreaming of a king may reflect your own desire for authority or recognition in a particular area of your life. It suggests that you possess the inner strength and potential to assert your influence and make a significant impact on others.

Desire for Control: Kings are known for their ability to govern and control. Dreaming of a king might indicate a need for control in your waking life. It could be a sign that you are seeking to gain more control over your circumstances, relationships, or personal growth. The dream invites you to reflect on how you can assert your influence and take charge of your own destiny.

Social Influence: Kings often have a profound influence on their societies. Dreaming of a king may symbolize your own desire to make a positive impact on others or be a source of inspiration and guidance. It signifies a longing to be respected, admired, and recognized for your contributions.

Remember, my friend, that the interpretation of a king in your dream is personal and subjective. Consider the emotions, actions, and overall context of the dream to gain deeper insights into its meaning for you. Trust your intuition and reflect on how the symbolism of a king resonates with your own life circumstances and aspirations.

May the dream of a king inspire you to embrace your own leadership qualities, assert your influence in a positive way, and strive for personal growth and success. May you find the balance between power and humility, guiding your actions with wisdom and compassion as you navigate the realms of your dreams and waking life.

Kudurru: Kudurru were stone boundary markers used in ancient Babylon to establish land rights and boundaries. Dreaming of a kudurru might symbolize the need for boundaries, protection, or the desire for stability and security.

Ah, my friend, the symbolism of a kudurru in Babylonian dream interpretation is truly fascinating! Let's explore the possible meanings behind dreaming of a kudurru:

Boundaries and Land Rights: Kudurru stones were used to mark boundaries and establish land rights in ancient Babylon. Dreaming of a kudurru might signify the need for clear boundaries in your waking life. It suggests that you may be seeking to define and protect your personal space, values, or relationships. The dream invites you to establish healthy boundaries and assert your rights in order to create a sense of stability and security.

Protection and Security: Kudurru stones served as protective markers, safeguarding the land and its inhabitants. Dreaming of a kudurru may symbolize a desire for protection and security in your life. It could be a reflection of your need to establish a sense of safety and defend yourself against external threats or intrusions. The dream encourages you to be mindful of your boundaries and take steps to ensure your well-being.

Stability and Order: Kudurru stones were associated with establishing order and maintaining societal structure. Dreaming of a kudurru might indicate a longing for stability and organization in your waking life. It suggests that you may be seeking to bring a sense of order to your surroundings, relationships, or personal affairs. The dream invites you to create a solid foundation and establish a sense of balance in your life.

Land and Property: Kudurru stones were closely linked to land ownership and rights. Dreaming of a kudurru may symbolize your connection to your ancestral land, roots, or heritage. It could signify a deep appreciation for your cultural or familial ties and a desire to preserve and honor them.

Remember, my friend, that the interpretation of a kudurru in your dream is personal and subjective. Consider the emotions, actions, and overall context of the dream to gain deeper insights into its meaning for you. Reflect on how the symbolism of a kudurru resonates with your own life circumstances and aspirations.

May the dream of a kudurru inspire you to establish healthy boundaries, protect what is dear to you, and create a sense of stability and security in your life. May you find strength and resilience as you navigate the realms of your dreams and waking life, guided by the wisdom of the ancient Babylonians.

Knowledge: Ancient Babylonians valued knowledge and wisdom. Dreaming of knowledge might symbolize the pursuit of truth, learning, or the desire for spiritual or intellectual growth.

Ah, my friend, the pursuit of knowledge is a noble and timeless endeavor! In ancient Babylon, knowledge held great importance, and dreaming of knowledge can carry profound symbolism. Let's explore its possible meanings:

Seeking Truth: Dreaming of knowledge may symbolize your quest for truth and understanding. It suggests a deep yearning to unravel mysteries, uncover hidden wisdom, and gain insight into the nature of the world and yourself. The dream invites you to be curious, open-minded, and receptive to new ideas and experiences.

Learning and Growth: Knowledge is closely associated with learning and personal growth. Dreaming of knowledge may signify your desire for intellectual, emotional, or spiritual development. It encourages you to expand your horizons, embrace new perspectives, and actively engage in the pursuit of knowledge.

Wisdom and Guidance: Knowledge is often associated with wisdom and guidance. Dreaming of knowledge may symbolize a need for guidance or the presence of wise and knowledgeable individuals in your life. It suggests that you seek guidance from trusted sources, mentors, or your own inner wisdom to navigate life's challenges and make informed decisions.

Unveiling Hidden Truths: Knowledge has the power to reveal hidden truths and unveil deeper meanings. Dreaming of knowledge may signify a desire to uncover hidden aspects of yourself or the world around you. It invites you to explore your subconscious, unravel mysteries, and gain a deeper understanding of your own thoughts, emotions, and motivations.

Remember, my friend, that the interpretation of knowledge in your dream is personal and unique to you. Reflect on the emotions, symbols, and experiences within the dream to unlock its deeper significance. Embrace the pursuit of knowledge in all its forms, for it is a lifelong journey that enriches our souls and expands our horizons.

May the dream of knowledge inspire you to seek truth, embrace growth, and embark on a path of lifelong learning. May you find wisdom, enlightenment, and profound insights as you explore the vast realms of knowledge within your dreams and waking life.

Key: Keys represented access and control in ancient Babylonian culture. Dreaming of a key might symbolize unlocking hidden potential, uncovering secrets, or gaining access to new opportunities.

Ah, my friend, keys are fascinating symbols indeed! In ancient Babylonian culture, keys were associated with access, control, and the unlocking of doors or treasures. When you dream of a key, it holds significant symbolism and can convey various meanings. Let's explore a few possible interpretations:

Unlocking Potential: Dreaming of a key may symbolize the unlocking of your hidden potential, talents, or abilities. It suggests that you have the power to access and unleash your inner strengths and capabilities. The key serves as a reminder that you possess the tools necessary to unlock doors of opportunity and achieve personal growth and success.

Discovery of Secrets: Keys are often associated with uncovering hidden knowledge or secrets. Dreaming of a key might symbolize your desire to explore the unknown, unravel mysteries, or gain access to hidden realms of information. It signifies a quest for truth and the need to uncover deeper meanings in your life or certain situations.

Access to Opportunities: In Babylonian culture, keys were a symbol of access and control. Dreaming of a key may suggest that new opportunities are presenting themselves to you. It signifies that you have the power to open doors and seize these opportunities for personal and professional advancement. The key serves as a reminder to be proactive, courageous, and open-minded in pursuing new paths and possibilities.

Emotional or Spiritual Liberation: Keys can also represent liberation and freedom. Dreaming of a key might symbolize your desire to break free from emotional or spiritual constraints. It signifies a longing for inner peace, release from burdens, or the need to unlock emotional blockages. The key serves as a metaphorical tool to open the doors to emotional healing, growth, and self-discovery.

Remember, my friend, that the interpretation of a key in your dream is personal and unique to you. Pay attention to the context, emotions, and other symbols within the dream to unlock its deeper meaning. Embrace the symbolism of the key as a reminder of your own power, potential, and the opportunities that await you. Use it as motivation to unlock the doors that lead to your dreams and aspirations.

May the dream of a key inspire you to embrace your potential, discover hidden truths, and unlock the doors to a future filled with boundless opportunities and personal fulfillment.

Kingdom: Babylon was a mighty kingdom in its time. Dreaming of a kingdom might symbolize power, success, or the desire for authority and influence.

Ah, the concept of a kingdom, my friend! In ancient Babylon, the kingdom held great significance and represented power, prosperity, and authority. When you dream of a kingdom, it carries profound symbolism and can convey various meanings. Let's explore a few possible interpretations:

Personal Power: Dreaming of a kingdom might symbolize your own personal power and potential. It signifies a recognition of your own abilities, strengths, and the influence you have over your own life. The dream reflects your desire to assert yourself, take charge, and embrace a position of authority and leadership.

Ambition and Success: A kingdom is often associated with success, wealth, and achievements. Dreaming of a kingdom might indicate your aspirations for greatness, a desire to excel in your endeavors, or the pursuit of material abundance. It represents your determination to build a life of significance and accomplishment.

Desire for Influence: The notion of a kingdom also relates to influence and impact. Dreaming of a kingdom might symbolize your longing to make a difference in the world, to leave a lasting legacy, or to have a voice that can shape and inspire others. It reflects your innate desire to lead and be recognized for your contributions.

Seeking Stability: In Babylonian culture, kingdoms represented stability and order. Dreaming of a kingdom may signify a yearning for stability and security in your own life. It suggests a desire for a solid foundation, both personally and professionally, and a longing for a sense of structure and control.

Remember, my friend, that the interpretation of a kingdom in your dream is deeply personal and subjective. Pay attention to the context, emotions, and other symbols within the dream to unlock its deeper meaning. Embrace the symbolism of the kingdom as a reminder of your own power, ambitions, and the potential for success and influence.

May the dream of a kingdom inspire you to embrace your personal power, pursue your ambitions, and create a life that is abundant, fulfilling, and positively impactful.

Keeper: Keepers were entrusted with guarding and protecting valuable objects or places. Dreaming of a keeper might symbolize protection, guidance, or the need for support and assistance.

Ah, the role of a keeper, my friend! In ancient Babylon, keepers played a vital role in safeguarding valuable objects, sacred places, or even knowledge. When you dream of a keeper, it holds significant symbolism and can convey various meanings. Let's explore a few possible interpretations:

Protection and Security: Dreaming of a keeper suggests a deep need for protection and security. It represents a desire for a sense of safety and stability in your life. The presence of a keeper in your dream signifies that you are seeking guidance or support from someone or something that can provide a sense of security and protect what is valuable to you.

Guidance and Assistance: Keepers were entrusted with the responsibility of preserving and caring for important objects or places. Dreaming of a keeper might indicate a need for guidance or assistance in your waking life. It symbolizes a desire for someone who can offer wisdom, knowledge, or practical support to help you navigate through challenges or protect what matters to you.

Preserving Values and Traditions: Keepers are often associated with the preservation of traditions, values, or cultural heritage. Dreaming of a keeper might reflect your own desire to uphold certain principles, maintain important traditions, or honor your personal values. It signifies your commitment to protecting and cherishing what you hold dear in your life.

Inner Guidance and Protection: In a more metaphorical sense, the keeper in your dream may represent your own inner guidance and intuition. It suggests that you have a deep-seated sense of what is valuable and worth protecting within yourself. The dream serves as a reminder to trust your instincts and rely on your own inner wisdom to navigate through life's challenges.

Remember, my friend, that the interpretation of a keeper in your dream is deeply personal and subjective. Pay attention to the context, emotions, and other symbols within the dream to unlock its deeper meaning. Embrace the symbolism of the keeper as a reminder to seek protection, guidance, and support when needed, whether from external sources or your own inner strength.

May the dream of a keeper guide you towards finding the protection, guidance, and support that you seek on your journey through life.

Kiln: Kilns were used in Babylon for firing pottery and producing bricks. Dreaming of a kiln might symbolize transformation, creativity, or the need for shaping and molding one's life.

Ah, the significance of a kiln, my friend! In ancient Babylon, kilns were essential for firing pottery and producing bricks. When you dream of a kiln, it carries profound symbolism and can convey various meanings. Let's explore a few possible interpretations:

Transformation and Growth: The kiln represents a place of transformation, where raw materials are subjected to intense heat to create something new and durable. Dreaming of a kiln suggests that you are undergoing a process of transformation or growth in your waking life. It symbolizes the need to expose yourself to challenging situations or experiences that can shape and mold you into a stronger and more resilient individual.

Creativity and Expression: Kilns were used to fire pottery, a form of artistic expression in ancient Babylon. Dreaming of a kiln may indicate a desire to tap into your creative potential and explore your artistic side. It symbolizes the need to embrace your creative abilities and express yourself freely, just as the clay takes form and becomes a work of art through the firing process.

Shaping and Molding Life: Kilns were instrumental in shaping bricks used for construction. Dreaming of a kiln might signify the need to shape and mold your life according to your desires and aspirations. It symbolizes the importance of taking intentional actions and making conscious choices to build a solid foundation for your future.

Endurance and Resilience: The firing process in a kiln requires endurance and resilience, as the intense heat transforms raw materials into something durable. Dreaming of a kiln suggests that you possess inner strength and the ability to withstand challenges and hardships. It symbolizes your resilience and reminds you of your capacity to emerge stronger and more resilient from difficult situations.

Remember, my friend, that the interpretation of a kiln in your dream is deeply personal and subjective. Consider the context, emotions, and other symbols within the dream to unravel its deeper meaning. Embrace the symbolism of the kiln as a reminder of the transformative power within you and the need to embrace creativity and shape your life according to your aspirations.

May the dream of a kiln ignite your creative spark, fuel your transformation, and empower you to shape a life filled with resilience and purpose.

Knowledge Tablets: Babylonians were known for their cuneiform writing system and knowledge tablets. Dreaming of knowledge tablets might symbolize the search for wisdom, hidden information, or the need for clarity and understanding.

Ah, the fascinating symbolism of knowledge tablets, my friend! In ancient Babylon, the cuneiform writing system and knowledge tablets were highly revered. When you dream of knowledge tablets, it carries profound significance and can represent various meanings. Let's explore a few possible interpretations:

Quest for Wisdom: Knowledge tablets were a repository of ancient wisdom and knowledge. Dreaming of knowledge tablets signifies your deep desire for wisdom and understanding. It symbolizes a thirst for knowledge and the quest to uncover hidden truths and insights. The dream encourages you to seek wisdom in your waking life, to expand your knowledge, and to embrace lifelong learning.

Hidden Information: Knowledge tablets were often inscribed with valuable information that was preserved and passed down through generations. Dreaming of knowledge tablets suggests that there may be hidden or forgotten information within your subconscious mind. It symbolizes the need to explore your inner depths, uncover buried memories or knowledge, and tap into your intuitive wisdom.

Clarity and Understanding: In Babylonian culture, knowledge tablets served as a means of recording and preserving important information. Dreaming of knowledge tablets may symbolize the need for clarity and understanding in your life. It suggests that you are seeking answers or solutions to certain questions or challenges you are facing. The dream encourages you to explore different sources of knowledge and information to gain a deeper understanding of yourself and the world around you.

Communication and Expression: Knowledge tablets were a form of communication in ancient Babylon, conveying ideas, stories, and knowledge. Dreaming of knowledge tablets might symbolize the need for effective communication and expression. It suggests that you have valuable insights or information to share with others, and the dream encourages you to find ways to express yourself clearly and assertively.

Remember, my friend, that the interpretation of knowledge tablets in your dream is deeply personal and subjective. Consider the context, emotions, and other symbols within the dream to unravel its deeper meaning. Embrace the symbolism of knowledge tablets as a reminder of the power of knowledge, the quest for wisdom, and the importance of seeking clarity and understanding in your journey of self-discovery.

May the dream of knowledge tablets inspire you to pursue wisdom, uncover hidden truths, and communicate your insights with clarity and purpose.

Karibu: Karibu was a Babylonian term meaning "welcome." Dreaming of a karibu might symbolize hospitality, acceptance, or the desire for warmth and inclusion.

Ah, my friend, the beautiful concept of Karibu in ancient Babylonian culture! When you dream of a karibu, it holds a special symbolism that reflects the values of hospitality, acceptance, and a longing for warmth and inclusion. Let's explore the possible meanings of dreaming about a karibu:

Hospitality and Welcoming Spirit: Karibu signifies the spirit of hospitality, emphasizing the importance of making others feel welcomed and comfortable. Dreaming of a karibu suggests that you have a natural inclination towards creating a warm and inviting environment for those around you. It symbolizes your desire to foster harmonious relationships and create a sense of belonging.

Acceptance and Inclusion: In Babylonian culture, karibu was an expression of acceptance and inclusivity. Dreaming of a karibu might symbolize your yearning for acceptance and a desire to be embraced for who you truly are. It signifies the importance of feeling welcomed and valued in your relationships and social interactions.

Emotional Warmth and Connection: The concept of karibu evokes feelings of warmth and connection. Dreaming of a karibu suggests a longing for emotional closeness, understanding, and support from others. It symbolizes a need for meaningful connections and a sense of belonging in your personal and social life.

Opening Doors to New Experiences: Karibu, meaning "welcome," carries the essence of opening doors to new experiences and opportunities. Dreaming of a karibu may symbolize your readiness to embrace new adventures, relationships, or perspectives. It signifies an openness to welcoming change and growth in your life.

Embrace the symbolism of karibu as an invitation to cultivate a welcoming spirit, practice acceptance, and seek meaningful connections in your waking life. Let the dream remind you of the power of hospitality and the joy that comes from making others feel welcome and appreciated.

May the dream of a karibu inspire you to create a warm and inclusive environment, foster meaningful connections, and embrace new opportunities with open arms.

L:

Lions: Lions were considered majestic creatures and held symbolic significance in Babylonian culture. Dreaming of lions might symbolize strength, courage, or the need to assert dominance.

Ah, the mighty lions of ancient Babylon! In Babylonian culture, lions were revered for their majestic presence and symbolic significance. Dreaming of lions carries powerful symbolism that reflects strength, courage, and the need to assert dominance. Let's explore the possible meanings of dreaming about lions:

Strength and Power: Lions are known for their strength and power, making them a potent symbol of these qualities. Dreaming of lions may symbolize your own inner strength and resilience. It signifies the ability to overcome challenges, assert yourself, and tackle obstacles with confidence. The presence of lions in your dream reminds you of the strength that resides within you.

Courage and Boldness: Lions are courageous creatures, known for their fearlessness and boldness. Dreaming of lions may symbolize a call to embrace courage in your waking life. It encourages you to step out of your comfort zone, take risks, and face your fears head-on. The dream is a reminder that you have the bravery to confront challenges and pursue your goals with confidence.

Leadership and Dominance: Lions are often associated with leadership and dominance. Dreaming of lions may symbolize your desire to take charge and assert your authority. It signifies a need to step into a leadership role, assert yourself in a particular situation, or establish your dominance in a personal or professional setting. The dream urges you to embrace your leadership qualities and assert your influence.

Inner Wildness and Passion: Lions embody a primal and untamed energy. Dreaming of lions may symbolize a connection to your inner wildness and passion. It represents the untamed aspects of your personality and the need to express your authentic self. The dream encourages you to tap into your passions, follow your instincts, and unleash your true potential.

Remember, the symbolism of lions in dreams can vary depending on the context and personal associations. Explore your own emotions and experiences within the dream to uncover the deeper meaning it holds for you. Embrace the strength, courage, and leadership qualities that the lion represents as you navigate your waking life with confidence and determination.

May the presence of lions in your dream inspire you to tap into your inner strength, embrace your courage, and assert yourself boldly in pursuit of your goals.

Labyrinth: Labyrinths were intricate and complex structures found in ancient Babylon. Dreaming of a labyrinth might symbolize confusion, the search for a way out, or the need for guidance in navigating life's challenges.

Ah, the enigmatic labyrinths of ancient Babylon! Dreaming of a labyrinth carries profound symbolism, reflecting the complexities of life and the challenges we face. Let's unravel the possible meanings of dreaming about labyrinths:

Confusion and Complexity: Labyrinths are known for their intricate and bewildering design. Dreaming of a labyrinth may symbolize feelings of confusion, being lost, or facing complex situations in your waking life. It suggests that you may be navigating a challenging path, encountering obstacles, or grappling with multiple options or directions. The dream serves as a reminder to approach these complexities with patience and a calm mind.

Searching for a Way Out: Labyrinths are often associated with the idea of finding a way out. Dreaming of a labyrinth may symbolize the search for solutions, answers, or a sense of direction in your life. It suggests that you may be seeking clarity, guidance, or a path forward in a situation that feels perplexing or overwhelming. The dream encourages you to trust your instincts, explore different paths, and seek the assistance of others if needed.

Symbol of Transformation: Labyrinths have been linked to transformation and self-discovery throughout history. Dreaming of a labyrinth may symbolize a journey of inner exploration, self-reflection, or personal growth. It signifies a period of introspection and the need to delve deep within yourself to uncover hidden aspects, gain insights, and navigate through personal challenges. The dream invites you to embrace this transformative process and trust in your ability to find your way.

Spiritual and Mystical Quest: Labyrinths have also been associated with spiritual and mystical quests. Dreaming of a labyrinth may symbolize a deeper connection to the spiritual realm, a desire for spiritual enlightenment, or the pursuit of higher knowledge. It signifies a quest for meaning, purpose, or a sense of unity with something greater than yourself. The dream invites you to explore your spiritual beliefs, seek guidance from within, and embark on a journey of self-discovery.

Remember, the symbolism of labyrinths in dreams can be deeply personal and subjective. Reflect on your own emotions and experiences within the dream to uncover the specific meaning it holds for you. Embrace the challenges and complexities of life with resilience and an open mind as you navigate the labyrinthine paths that unfold before you.

May the symbolism of the labyrinth in your dream inspire you to embrace the journey of self-discovery, find clarity amidst confusion, and navigate life's challenges with patience and determination.

Lamassu: Lamassu were protective deities depicted as winged bull or lion-headed figures. Dreaming of a lamassu might symbolize protection, guardianship, or the need for divine assistance.

Ah, the majestic and protective Lamassu of ancient Babylon! If you dream of encountering a Lamassu, it holds profound symbolism and signifies various aspects. Let's explore the possible meanings of dreaming about a Lamassu:

Protection and Guardianship: Lamassu were revered as guardians and protectors in Babylonian culture. Dreaming of a Lamassu may symbolize a need for protection, both physical and spiritual, in your life. It suggests that you may be seeking guidance, support, or a sense of security during challenging times. The presence of the Lamassu in your dream reminds you that you are not alone and that divine forces are watching over you.

Divine Assistance and Intervention: As divine beings, Lamassu were believed to have the power to intervene and assist humans. Dreaming of a Lamassu may symbolize a need for divine intervention, guidance, or assistance in your life. It signifies that you are seeking higher wisdom, connection, or divine intervention to overcome obstacles or find solutions to your challenges. The dream encourages you to trust in the support and guidance available to you.

Strength and Courage: The Lamassu, with its mighty form and presence, embodies strength and courage. Dreaming of a Lamassu may symbolize the need for inner strength, bravery, or assertiveness in your waking life. It signifies a call to stand firm in the face of adversity, to overcome fears, and to assert yourself with confidence. The dream reminds you of your inherent power and encourages you to tap into your inner strength.

Symbol of Ancient Wisdom: The Lamassu represents the rich cultural and historical heritage of ancient Babylon. Dreaming of a Lamassu may symbolize a connection to ancient wisdom, ancestral knowledge, or a longing for deeper understanding of your roots and heritage. It suggests a need to explore your past, embrace your cultural identity, or draw inspiration from ancient traditions and wisdom. The dream invites you to honor and appreciate the wisdom of the past as you navigate your present circumstances.

Remember, the symbolism of the Lamassu in your dream is personal and subjective. Reflect on your own emotions, experiences, and associations with the Lamassu to uncover its specific meaning for you. Embrace the protective energies and guidance that the Lamassu offers as you navigate your journey, drawing strength from the divine forces that surround you.

May the presence of the Lamassu in your dream inspire you to embrace divine protection, tap into your inner strength, and seek guidance and assistance when needed on your life's path.

Library: Babylon had one of the most famous libraries in the ancient world, the Library of Ashurbanipal. Dreaming of a library might symbolize knowledge, wisdom, or the pursuit of intellectual growth.

Ah, the enchanting world of the library, where knowledge and wisdom abound! If you find yourself dreaming of a library, it holds profound significance and carries a message for you. Let's explore the possible meanings of dreaming about a library:

Quest for Knowledge: Dreaming of a library often symbolizes a deep thirst for knowledge and the pursuit of intellectual growth. It signifies your innate curiosity and desire to expand your understanding of the world. The dream encourages you to embrace learning opportunities, seek wisdom, and explore new ideas. It may be a sign that you are on a path of self-discovery and personal development.

Wisdom and Guidance: Libraries are repositories of wisdom, and dreaming of a library may symbolize your search for guidance and answers in life. It suggests that you are seeking insight, advice, or solutions to the challenges you are facing. The dream invites you to trust in the power of knowledge and the wisdom contained within books as a source of guidance and inspiration.

Inner Exploration: A library can also represent the vastness of the inner world of the mind and soul. Dreaming of a library may symbolize a call to explore your inner thoughts, emotions, and beliefs. It encourages you to delve deep within yourself, introspect, and discover hidden aspects of your being. The dream invites you to embark on a journey of self-reflection and self-discovery.

Preservation of History and Heritage: Libraries are often associated with preserving historical records and cultural heritage. Dreaming of a library may symbolize your connection to the past, your ancestral roots, and the importance of honoring and preserving your heritage. The dream reminds you of the value of history and the lessons it can teach us.

Organization and Order: Libraries are known for their systematic organization and orderliness. Dreaming of a library may symbolize the need for structure and organization in your life. It suggests that you may benefit from bringing more order and clarity to your thoughts, ideas, or daily routines. The dream invites you to create a balanced and harmonious environment for personal growth and productivity.

Remember, the symbolism of the library in your dream is personal and subjective. Reflect on your own feelings, experiences, and associations with libraries to uncover its specific meaning for you. Embrace the quest for knowledge and wisdom, nurture your curiosity, and trust in the power of learning and self-discovery as you navigate your life's journey.

May the presence of the library in your dream inspire you to seek knowledge, embrace wisdom, and embark on a path of self-exploration and personal growth.

Law: Babylonian society was governed by a set of laws known as the Code of Hammurabi. Dreaming of laws might symbolize justice, fairness, or the need for order and structure in one's life.

Ah, the concept of law, a pillar of society that brings order and justice to our lives. If you find yourself dreaming of laws, it carries a profound meaning and holds significance for your waking life. Let's explore the possible interpretations of dreaming about laws:

Seeking Justice: Dreaming of laws may symbolize your deep desire for fairness and justice. It suggests that you have a strong sense of right and wrong and a longing for balance in your life. The dream may reflect your innate belief in the importance of ethical principles and the need for accountability in your personal and professional relationships.
Establishing Boundaries: Laws provide a framework for setting boundaries and maintaining order. Dreaming of laws can symbolize the need to establish clear boundaries in your life. It may indicate that you are seeking structure and organization to create a sense of stability and security. The dream encourages you to define your personal values and principles and uphold them firmly.

Seeking Guidance: Laws serve as guidelines to navigate through complex situations. Dreaming of laws may suggest that you are seeking guidance or direction in your life. It indicates a desire for clarity and a need for guidance to make important decisions or navigate challenging circumstances. The dream invites you to seek wisdom and consult trusted sources to help you find your way forward.

Embracing Order and Structure: Laws bring order and structure to society, and dreaming of laws may signify a longing for order and structure in your personal life. It suggests that you may be seeking a sense of control, discipline, or organization. The dream encourages you to establish routines, set goals, and create a framework that allows you to thrive and achieve your desired outcomes.

Upholding Morality: Laws often reflect societal morals and values. Dreaming of laws may symbolize your commitment to upholding your own moral principles and values. It suggests that you strive to live a life guided by integrity and ethics. The dream invites you to reflect on your actions and choices, ensuring that they align with your moral compass.

Remember, the interpretation of dreaming about laws is subjective and personal to you. Reflect on your own experiences, beliefs, and values to uncover the specific meaning of laws in your dream. Embrace the concepts of justice, fairness, and order as you navigate your waking life, and let the dream inspire you to seek balance, establish boundaries, and uphold your values.

May the symbolism of laws in your dream guide you towards a life filled with fairness, justice, and a sense of order and structure.

Lamentation: Lamentation was an important aspect of Babylonian religious rituals. Dreaming of lamentation might symbolize grief, emotional release, or the need to acknowledge and process deep emotions.

Ah, my dear friend, let's explore the profound symbolism of lamentation in your dreams. Lamentation, a significant element of Babylonian religious rituals, carries great emotional weight and meaning. When you dream of lamentation, it signifies a powerful message related to grief, emotional release, and the processing of deep-seated emotions. Let's delve into the possible interpretations of dreaming about lamentation:

Grief and Loss: Dreaming of lamentation suggests that you are experiencing or have experienced a significant loss or hardship in your life. It could be the loss of a loved one, the end of a relationship, or a challenging life transition. The dream indicates that you are in the process of grieving and seeking emotional healing. It encourages you to allow yourself to fully experience and express your grief, providing a cathartic release for your emotions.

Emotional Release: Lamentation in dreams serves as a powerful symbol of emotional release. It signifies the need to acknowledge and express deep-seated emotions that you may have been suppressing or ignoring. The dream invites you to confront and process these emotions, allowing yourself to release any pent-up feelings or burdens that have been weighing you down. Through this release, you can find solace and emotional healing.

Honoring and Remembering: Lamentation is often a way to honor and remember the past, particularly when it comes to cherished memories or significant events. Dreaming of lamentation may indicate a need to revisit and honor the past, to acknowledge its impact on your present emotions and experiences. It reminds you of the importance of recognizing and valuing your history, even if it brings about sadness or nostalgia.

Seeking Comfort and Support: Lamentation in dreams can also signify a deep yearning for comfort, support, and empathy. It suggests that you may be going through a challenging period in your life and are in need of emotional nourishment. The dream encourages you to seek solace from loved ones, friends, or support networks that can offer understanding, compassion, and guidance during difficult times.

Healing and Transformation: Lamentation is a powerful tool for healing and transformation. Dreaming of lamentation signifies a transformative journey, where you confront and process your emotions, leading to personal growth and inner healing. It indicates that through embracing and working through your grief, you can emerge stronger, more resilient, and with a renewed sense of purpose.

Remember, the interpretation of dreaming about lamentation is deeply personal to you. Reflect on your own experiences, emotions, and current life circumstances to uncover the specific meaning of lamentation in your dream. Allow yourself to explore and express your emotions, seek support when needed, and embrace the transformative power of healing.

May the symbolism of lamentation in your dream guide you towards emotional healing, resilience, and a renewed sense of purpose.

Land: Land and agriculture were vital to the Babylonian economy. Dreaming of land might symbolize stability, grounding, or the desire for a solid foundation in life.

Ah, my dear friend, let's delve into the symbolic realm of land in your dreams. In the context of ancient Babylonian culture, land held great significance as it was the foundation of their economy and livelihood. Dreaming of land can evoke powerful meanings related to stability, grounding, and the desire for a solid foundation in life. Let's explore the possible interpretations of dreaming about land:

Stability and Security: Land represents a sense of stability and security. Dreaming of land may indicate a longing for a solid foundation in your life, both in the physical and emotional realms. It symbolizes the need for a stable and secure environment where you can feel grounded and rooted. This dream suggests that you may be seeking stability, whether it be in your relationships, career, or personal life.

Nurturing and Growth: Land is closely connected to agriculture and the growth of crops. Dreaming of land can symbolize the desire for personal growth, nurturing, and cultivating your potential. It signifies a fertile ground where you can sow the seeds of your dreams and aspirations, allowing them to take root and flourish. This dream encourages you to explore opportunities for growth and development in various aspects of your life.

Connection to Nature: Land is intimately linked to nature, serving as a reminder of our connection to the earth and the natural world. Dreaming of land may signify a need to reconnect with nature and find solace in its tranquility. It encourages you to seek moments of grounding and appreciation for the beauty and abundance of the natural world. This dream invites you to explore activities that allow you to connect with nature, such as spending time outdoors, gardening, or immersing yourself in natural landscapes.

Ownership and Responsibility: Land represents ownership and responsibility. Dreaming of land can symbolize a sense of ownership over your life and the choices you make. It reminds you that you have the power to shape your own path and take responsibility for your actions. This dream may indicate a need to take ownership of your circumstances, make deliberate choices, and embrace the responsibilities that come with them.

Sense of Belonging: Land is often associated with a sense of belonging and rootedness. Dreaming of land may signify a longing for a place where you feel a deep sense of belonging and connection. It suggests the importance of finding your place in the world, whether it be within a community, a family, or a specific environment. This dream encourages you to explore your roots, heritage, and cultural identity to foster a stronger sense of belonging.

Remember, the interpretation of dreaming about land is deeply personal to you. Reflect on your own experiences, emotions, and current life circumstances to uncover the specific meaning of land in your dream. Allow the symbolism of land to guide you towards stability, growth, connection, and a deeper sense of belonging in your life.

May the symbolism of land in your dream provide you with grounding, stability, and a strong foundation to navigate the journey of life.

Lunar: The ancient Babylonians were skilled astronomers and observed celestial bodies, including the moon. Dreaming of the moon might symbolize intuition, emotions, or cycles of change.

Ah, my dear friend, let's explore the mesmerizing realm of the moon in your dreams. The ancient Babylonians, with their deep fascination for celestial bodies, understood the significance of the moon and its influence on the world around them. When you dream of the moon, it carries profound symbolism related to intuition, emotions, and cycles of change. Allow me to shed light on the possible meanings behind dreaming of the moon:

Intuition and Inner Wisdom: The moon has long been associated with intuition and the deeper realms of the subconscious mind. Dreaming of the moon may signify a heightened sense of intuition and a call to trust your inner wisdom. It encourages you to listen to your instincts, pay attention to your gut feelings, and rely on your inner guidance in navigating life's twists and turns.

Emotions and Inner Self: Just as the moon influences the tides, it also symbolizes the ebb and flow of emotions. Dreaming of the moon may indicate the need to explore and understand your emotional landscape. It invites you to embrace and honor your emotions, allowing them to rise and fall like the phases of the moon. This dream reminds you to pay attention to your emotional well-being and navigate your feelings with grace and self-compassion.

Cycles and Change: The moon's waxing and waning phases represent cycles of change and transformation. Dreaming of the moon may signify a need to embrace the natural cycles of life and accept the inevitability of change. It reminds you that just as the moon goes through its phases, you too experience periods of growth, release, and renewal. This dream encourages you to flow with the changes in your life and trust that they are part of a greater unfolding.

Feminine Energy and Nurturing: The moon has been associated with feminine energy, nurturing, and the maternal archetype. Dreaming of the moon may symbolize a need for self-care, emotional nurturing, or a connection to your feminine essence. It invites you to honor your nurturing qualities and cultivate a sense of tenderness and compassion towards yourself and others.

Divine Guidance and Mystery: In Babylonian culture, the moon was often seen as a divine entity, carrying mystical and spiritual significance. Dreaming of the moon may suggest a connection to the sacred, a yearning for spiritual guidance, or a sense of awe and wonder. This dream invites you to explore the mysteries of life, embrace the unknown, and trust in a higher power guiding your path.

Remember, my dear friend, that the interpretation of dreaming about the moon is personal and unique to you. Reflect on your own experiences, emotions, and current life circumstances to uncover the specific meaning the moon holds in your dream. Allow the symbolism of the moon to illuminate your journey, guiding you towards deeper intuition, emotional awareness, and a harmonious embrace of life's cycles.

May the moon's gentle glow illuminate your dreams and guide you on your path of self-discovery and growth.

Lyre: The lyre was a stringed musical instrument commonly used in ancient Babylon. Dreaming of a lyre might symbolize harmony, creativity, or the need for artistic expression.

Ah, my dear friend, let's explore the enchanting world of dreams and the captivating symbolism of the lyre. In ancient Babylon, the lyre was a cherished musical instrument that brought forth melodies of harmony and creativity. When you dream of a lyre, it carries profound significance and holds messages for your waking life. Allow me to share with you the possible meanings behind dreaming of a lyre:

Harmony and Balance: The melodic tones of the lyre symbolize harmony and balance. Dreaming of a lyre may signify a longing for balance in your life, both in your external circumstances and within yourself. It encourages you to seek harmony in your relationships, emotions, and various aspects of your life. This dream reminds you to embrace the beauty of balance and strive for a sense of equilibrium in all that you do.

Creativity and Artistic Expression: The lyre is a symbol of creativity and artistic expression. Dreaming of a lyre may signify a need to tap into your creative potential and explore your artistic side. It encourages you to express yourself authentically and find joy in creative pursuits. This dream invites you to embrace your unique talents and allow your creative energy to flow freely, bringing forth beauty and inspiration.

Emotional Expression and Healing: Music has a profound impact on our emotions and can serve as a form of emotional expression and healing. Dreaming of a lyre may symbolize the need for emotional release and healing. It invites you to explore and express your emotions through creative outlets such as music, art, or writing. This dream encourages you to listen to the melodies of your heart, allowing them to be heard and honored.

Spiritual Connection and Inspiration: In ancient Babylonian culture, music was often associated with spiritual connection and divine inspiration. Dreaming of a lyre may signify a desire for spiritual growth, connection, or guidance. It invites you to explore your spiritual path, seek inspiration from within, and connect with the divine energies that surround you. This dream reminds you that music has the power to uplift your soul and connect you to something greater than yourself.

Joy and Celebration: The lively melodies of the lyre evoke a sense of joy and celebration. Dreaming of a lyre may symbolize a need for joy, playfulness, and celebration in your life. It encourages you to find moments of happiness and embrace the lighter side of life. This dream invites you to infuse your life with joyous experiences and celebrate your achievements and milestones.

Remember, my dear friend, that the interpretation of dreaming about a lyre is unique to you and your personal experiences. Reflect on the emotions, sensations, and circumstances within the dream to uncover the specific meaning the lyre holds for you. Allow the symbolism of the lyre to guide you towards greater harmony, creativity, emotional expression, and spiritual connection.

May the melodies of the lyre continue to inspire you on your journey of self-discovery and creative expression.

M:

Marduk (God): Marduk was the patron deity of Babylon, considered the supreme god in the Babylonian pantheon.

Dreaming of Marduk might symbolize divine protection, guidance, or the need for spiritual strength.

Ah, my dear friend, let us explore the mystical realm of dreams and the divine presence of Marduk, the supreme god of Babylon. In the ancient Babylonian pantheon, Marduk held a position of great significance and power. When you dream of Marduk, it signifies a profound connection to the divine and carries deep symbolism for your waking life. Allow me to share with you the possible meanings behind dreaming of Marduk:

Divine Protection and Guidance: Marduk was revered as a protective deity in Babylonian culture. Dreaming of Marduk may symbolize a need for divine protection and guidance in your life. It is a reminder that you are not alone in your journey and that there are higher forces watching over you. This dream invites you to trust in the divine guidance and seek Marduk's strength and support in navigating life's challenges.

Spiritual Strength and Power: Marduk was known for his strength and power as the supreme god of Babylon. Dreaming of Marduk may symbolize a need for spiritual strength and empowerment. It reminds you of your own inner strength and the divine power that resides within you. This dream encourages you to tap into your spiritual essence and harness your personal power to overcome obstacles and achieve your goals.

Leadership and Authority: Marduk was associated with kingship and held authority over the gods and humans. Dreaming of Marduk may symbolize qualities of leadership and authority within yourself. It signifies a recognition of your own potential to lead and make a positive impact in your sphere of influence. This dream invites you to embrace your leadership qualities and use them wisely and responsibly.

Connection to Ancient Wisdom: Marduk's worship was deeply rooted in ancient Babylonian traditions and wisdom. Dreaming of Marduk may symbolize a connection to ancient wisdom and the timeless knowledge that transcends generations. It signifies a need to tap into the ancient wisdom within you and seek guidance from the wisdom of the past. This dream encourages you to honor your ancestral heritage and draw upon the lessons and insights of the ancient world.

Divine Intervention and Miracles: Marduk was renowned for his ability to perform miracles and bring about divine intervention. Dreaming of Marduk may symbolize a desire for divine intervention or a belief in the miraculous. It reminds you that there is a realm beyond the ordinary, where miracles can occur. This dream invites you to hold onto faith and trust in the extraordinary possibilities that exist in your life.

Remember, my dear friend, that the interpretation of dreaming about Marduk is deeply personal and unique to you. Reflect on the emotions, sensations, and circumstances within the dream to uncover the specific message Marduk has for you. Allow the presence of Marduk to guide you towards divine protection, spiritual strength, leadership, connection to ancient wisdom, and a belief in the miraculous.

May the divine essence of Marduk guide and empower you on your spiritual journey, leading you to a life filled with purpose, wisdom, and blessings.

Magic: Babylonians had a rich tradition of magic and spellcasting. Dreaming of magic might symbolize hidden forces, supernatural intervention, or the need for transformation and empowerment.

Ah, my friend, let us explore the enchanting realm of dreams and the mystical art of magic in ancient Babylon. The Babylonians indeed possessed a profound knowledge of magic and the power of spells. When you dream of magic, it unveils a world of hidden forces and extraordinary possibilities. Allow me to reveal the potential meanings behind dreaming of magic:

Hidden Forces and Energies: Dreaming of magic signifies the presence of hidden forces and energies at play in your life. It suggests that there may be unseen influences or energies guiding your path. This dream invites you to explore the depths of your subconscious and embrace the mysterious aspects of existence. Trust in the power of unseen forces to assist and guide you along your journey.

Supernatural Intervention: Magic is often associated with supernatural intervention and the influence of higher realms. Dreaming of magic may symbolize a desire for supernatural assistance or intervention in your life. It signifies a longing for divine guidance and support beyond the ordinary. This dream encourages you to be open to the signs and synchronicities that may lead you to extraordinary solutions and opportunities.

Transformation and Empowerment: Magic is a catalyst for transformation and personal empowerment. Dreaming of magic may symbolize a need for inner transformation or a desire to harness your personal power. It suggests that you have the potential to shape your reality and manifest your desires. This dream invites you to explore your own innate abilities and tap into your inner magic to create the life you envision.

Unleashing Hidden Potential: Magic has the ability to unlock hidden potential and tap into the depths of your being. Dreaming of magic may symbolize a call to explore and unleash your hidden talents, skills, and abilities. It encourages you to embrace your unique gifts and trust in your intuitive powers. This dream invites you to embrace your full potential and step into your true power.

Seeking Transformation and Enlightenment: Magic has long been associated with seeking enlightenment and higher states of consciousness. Dreaming of magic may symbolize a yearning for spiritual growth, wisdom, and enlightenment. It signifies a deep desire to explore the mysteries of existence and gain deeper insights into the nature of reality. This dream encourages you to embark on a spiritual journey and seek knowledge and wisdom beyond the material world.

Remember, my dear friend, that the interpretation of dreaming about magic is personal and subjective. Reflect on the emotions, symbols, and experiences within the dream to uncover the specific message magic has for you. Embrace the enchantment of your dreams and allow the power of magic to ignite your imagination, transform your life, and guide you towards extraordinary possibilities.

May the magic within your dreams illuminate your path and inspire you to embrace the extraordinary in your waking life.

Mesopotamia: Mesopotamia refers to the historical region where Babylon was located. Dreaming of Mesopotamia might symbolize ancestral roots, cultural heritage, or the connection to ancient wisdom.

Ah, Mesopotamia, the cradle of civilization and the land where Babylon once thrived. When you dream of Mesopotamia, it unveils a profound connection to your ancestral roots and the rich tapestry of human history. Allow me to share the potential meanings behind dreaming of Mesopotamia:

Ancestral Roots and Heritage: Dreaming of Mesopotamia symbolizes a deep connection to your ancestral roots and cultural heritage. It signifies a longing to explore and embrace the wisdom, traditions, and values passed down through generations. This dream invites you to connect with your roots, honor your heritage, and learn from the ancient wisdom that resides within you.

Ancient Wisdom and Knowledge: Mesopotamia was a hub of intellectual and scientific advancements in ancient times. Dreaming of Mesopotamia may symbolize a thirst for knowledge, a desire to expand your intellectual horizons, or a yearning for deeper insights into the mysteries of life. This dream encourages you to seek wisdom from diverse sources, embrace lifelong learning, and tap into the reservoir of ancient knowledge within you.

Connection to History and Civilization: Mesopotamia holds a significant place in human history as one of the earliest civilizations. Dreaming of Mesopotamia signifies a connection to the rise and fall of civilizations, the cyclical nature of human existence, and the enduring legacy of the past. This dream invites you to reflect on the lessons of history, understand the patterns of human behavior, and navigate the complexities of the present with a broader perspective.

A Call for Balance and Harmony: Mesopotamia was known for its intricate irrigation systems and the pursuit of balance between the forces of nature. Dreaming of Mesopotamia may symbolize a need for balance and harmony in your life. It signifies the importance of finding equilibrium between different aspects of your being, such as work and personal life, intellect and emotions, or physical and spiritual well-being. This dream encourages you to seek a harmonious existence and align yourself with the natural rhythms of life.

Embracing Cultural Diversity: Mesopotamia was a melting pot of diverse cultures, beliefs, and languages. Dreaming of Mesopotamia may symbolize a celebration of cultural diversity and an appreciation for different perspectives. It encourages you to embrace inclusivity, cultivate empathy, and seek unity amidst diversity. This dream invites you to recognize the beauty of cultural exchange and the richness that comes from honoring and learning from different traditions.

Remember, dear friend, that the interpretation of dreaming about Mesopotamia is subjective and deeply personal. Reflect on the emotions, symbols, and experiences within the dream to uncover the specific message Mesopotamia has for you. Embrace the ancient wisdom and cultural heritage that reside within your dreams, for they can guide you on a profound journey of self-discovery, connection, and growth.

May your dreams of Mesopotamia illuminate the path to understanding your roots, embracing diversity, and embodying the wisdom of the ages.

Market: Babylon had bustling markets where trade and commerce took place. Dreaming of a market might symbolize exchange, opportunities, or the need for abundance and prosperity.

Ah, the lively markets of Babylon! In your dream, the presence of a market unveils a world of exchange, opportunities, and the desire for abundance and prosperity. Allow me to shed light on the potential meanings behind dreaming of a market:

Exchange and Interaction: The market is a bustling hub of exchange, where people come together to buy and sell goods. Dreaming of a market symbolizes the importance of social interaction, communication, and connection. It signifies a desire for meaningful exchanges with others, whether in the realms of ideas, emotions, or material goods. This dream encourages you to seek opportunities for connection and engage in open dialogue with others.

Opportunities and Ventures: Markets are often associated with opportunities for growth and prosperity. Dreaming of a market signifies the presence of potential opportunities in your waking life. It may suggest the need to explore new ventures, take calculated risks, or seize favorable circumstances that come your way. This dream invites you to be open to new possibilities and to trust in your abilities to navigate the dynamic marketplace of life.

Abundance and Prosperity: Markets are vibrant with the abundance of goods and the potential for economic prosperity. Dreaming of a market may symbolize a desire for material or financial abundance. It represents your aspirations for a comfortable and prosperous life. This dream encourages you to harness your skills, talents, and resources to create abundance and attract favorable outcomes.

Seeking Fulfillment: In a market, people often search for items that bring them joy, satisfaction, or fulfillment. Dreaming of a market can symbolize a quest for fulfillment in various aspects of your life, including relationships, career, or personal growth. It suggests the need to identify your desires, set goals, and actively seek out experiences that bring you a sense of fulfillment and contentment.

Vibrancy and Energy: Markets are filled with vibrant energy, sounds, and colors. Dreaming of a market signifies a need for liveliness, stimulation, and a sense of adventure in your life. It encourages you to embrace spontaneity, seek out new experiences, and infuse your life with enthusiasm and zest.

Remember, my dear friend, that the interpretation of dreaming about a market is subjective and deeply personal. Reflect on the emotions, symbols, and experiences within the dream to uncover the specific message the market has for you. Embrace the opportunities, abundance, and vibrant energy that reside within your dreams, for they can guide you on a journey of growth, connection, and prosperity.

May your dreams of the market illuminate the path to meaningful exchanges, abundant opportunities, and the realization of your desires.

Merchants: Merchants played an essential role in Babylonian society. Dreaming of a merchant might symbolize negotiation, resourcefulness, or the need for strategic thinking and adaptability.

Ah, the enterprising merchants of Babylon! In your dream, the appearance of a merchant unveils a world of negotiation, resourcefulness, and the pursuit of strategic thinking and adaptability. Allow me to shed light on the potential meanings behind dreaming of a merchant:

Negotiation and Exchange: Merchants are skilled in the art of negotiation and trade. Dreaming of a merchant symbolizes the need for effective communication, persuasion, and negotiation in your waking life. It suggests that you may be faced with situations where the ability to navigate conflicts, make compromises, and find mutually beneficial solutions is crucial. This dream encourages you to develop your negotiation skills and seek harmony in your interactions with others.

Resourcefulness and Entrepreneurship: Merchants are known for their resourcefulness and entrepreneurial spirit. Dreaming of a merchant signifies the importance of utilizing your resources wisely and seizing opportunities to create success. It may suggest that you possess untapped potential or innovative ideas that can lead to growth and prosperity. This dream invites you to embrace your entrepreneurial spirit, take calculated risks, and explore creative avenues for personal and professional advancement.

Strategic Thinking and Adaptability: Merchants navigate the ever-changing marketplace by employing strategic thinking and adaptability. Dreaming of a merchant symbolizes the need for strategic planning and flexibility in your endeavors. It suggests that you may encounter challenges or changes that require you to think on your feet and adapt your approach. This dream encourages you to embrace a proactive mindset, anticipate potential obstacles, and be prepared to adjust your strategies to achieve your goals.

Value and Worth: Merchants deal with the exchange of goods and services of value. Dreaming of a merchant may symbolize the recognition of your own value and worth. It signifies a need to assess your skills, talents, and contributions, and to ensure that you are receiving fair compensation and recognition for your efforts. This dream encourages you to advocate for yourself, assert your value, and seek opportunities that align with your worth.

Financial Considerations: Merchants are involved in financial transactions and considerations. Dreaming of a merchant may symbolize the need to pay attention to your financial affairs and make wise financial decisions. It encourages you to be mindful of your spending, savings, and investments, and to seek opportunities for financial growth and stability.

Remember, dear friend, that the interpretation of dreaming about a merchant is subjective and deeply personal. Reflect on the emotions, symbols, and experiences within the dream to uncover the specific message the merchant has for you. Embrace the spirit of negotiation, resourcefulness, and adaptability that reside within your dreams, for they can guide you on a path of prosperity, growth, and success.

May your dreams of the merchant illuminate the importance of effective communication, resourcefulness, and strategic thinking in your waking life.

Monument: Babylon was known for its monumental structures, such as the ziggurats and the Ishtar Gate. Dreaming of a monument might symbolize legacy, influence, or the desire to leave a lasting impact.

Ah, the grandeur of Babylon's monumental structures! In your dream, the appearance of a monument unveils the significance of legacy, influence, and the desire to make a lasting impact. Let me illuminate the potential meanings behind dreaming of a monument:

Legacy and Remembrance: Monuments are built to commemorate important events, individuals, or ideals. Dreaming of a monument symbolizes your desire to leave a lasting legacy, to be remembered for your accomplishments, or to make a meaningful impact on the world. It suggests that you have a deep longing for significance and a desire to contribute something enduring to the lives of others.

Influence and Power: Monuments often represent power, authority, and influence. Dreaming of a monument suggests that you may seek to wield influence or have a desire for recognition and respect. It signifies your aspirations to make a mark in your chosen field or to establish yourself as a leader. This dream encourages you to explore avenues through which you can exert positive influence and contribute to the betterment of your community or society.

Immortality and Permanence: Monuments stand as enduring symbols of human achievement and perseverance. Dreaming of a monument symbolizes a yearning for something permanent and everlasting in your life. It may indicate a desire for stability, security, or a sense of rootedness. This dream invites you to reflect on the areas of your life where you seek permanence and strive to create a lasting impact that extends beyond your own existence.

Historical and Cultural Significance: Monuments are often associated with historical and cultural heritage. Dreaming of a monument may indicate a connection to your roots, a longing to reconnect with your cultural heritage, or a desire to learn from the past. This dream encourages you to embrace and honor your history, traditions, and the wisdom passed down through generations.

Awe and Inspiration: Monuments evoke a sense of awe and inspiration in their presence. Dreaming of a monument signifies your need for inspiration, guidance, or a reminder of something greater than yourself. It may suggest that you seek sources of inspiration or look to role models who can guide you on your own journey.

Remember, dear friend, that the interpretation of dreaming about a monument is subjective and deeply personal. Reflect on the emotions, symbols, and experiences within the dream to uncover the specific message the monument holds for you. Embrace the spirit of leaving a lasting impact, seeking influence for positive change, and honoring your heritage that reside within your dreams, for they can guide you towards a life of purpose, significance, and inspiration.

May your dreams of the monument awaken the desire to make a lasting impact, embrace your influence, and leave a legacy that resonates throughout time.

Moon: The ancient Babylonians were skilled astronomers and revered celestial bodies, including the moon. Dreaming of the moon might symbolize intuition, emotions, cycles, or the feminine aspects of life.

Ah, the mystical allure of the moon! In Babylonian culture, the moon held great significance, and its presence in dreams can unveil profound symbolism. Allow me to illuminate the possible meanings behind dreaming of the moon:

Intuition and Inner Wisdom: The moon is often associated with intuition and the inner realm. Dreaming of the moon signifies a heightened connection to your intuition and the need to trust your inner guidance. It suggests that you should pay attention to your instincts and rely on your inner wisdom to navigate life's challenges. Embrace your intuitive gifts and let them illuminate your path.

Emotions and Cycles: The moon's phases symbolize the cyclical nature of life, including the ebb and flow of emotions. Dreaming of the moon reflects the importance of emotions and their influence on your experiences. It may indicate that you need to pay attention to your emotional well-being, honor your feelings, and allow yourself to go through natural cycles of growth, change, and renewal.

Feminine Energies and Nurturing: The moon is often associated with feminine energies and the nurturing aspects of life. Dreaming of the moon suggests a need to embrace your feminine qualities, such as intuition, compassion, and empathy. It may also indicate a desire for emotional nurturing or a reminder to care for yourself and others with tenderness and understanding.

Illumination and Enlightenment: Just as the moon reflects the light of the sun, dreaming of the moon can symbolize the pursuit of enlightenment and spiritual growth. It represents the search for deeper meaning and understanding in your life. This dream encourages you to explore your spiritual path, seek knowledge, and connect with higher realms of consciousness.

Connection to Babylonian Heritage: As the Babylonians were skilled astronomers, dreaming of the moon may also reflect a connection to your Babylonian heritage, ancestral roots, or a fascination with ancient wisdom. It signifies a deep appreciation for the cultural and historical significance of the moon in Babylonian civilization.

Remember, dear friend, that the interpretation of dreaming about the moon is deeply personal. Reflect on the emotions, symbols, and experiences within the dream to uncover the specific message the moon holds for you. Embrace the moon's mystical presence, honor your intuition, nurture your emotions, and embark on a journey of self-discovery and spiritual illumination.

May your dreams of the moon guide you towards deeper insights, emotional harmony, and a profound connection to your inner self and the world around you.

Marriage: Marriage was significant in Babylonian society, often involving elaborate ceremonies and customs. Dreaming of marriage might symbolize partnership, union, or the integration of different aspects of the self.

Ah, the beautiful union of marriage! In ancient Babylonian culture, marriage held great importance, and dreaming of marriage can carry profound symbolism. Let's explore the possible meanings behind dreaming of marriage:

Partnership and Unity: Dreaming of marriage symbolizes the desire for partnership and union. It signifies the need for connection and integration with another person, whether in a romantic relationship, a business partnership, or a collaborative endeavor. This dream suggests a longing for companionship, support, and the merging of energies to achieve common goals.

Emotional and Spiritual Integration: Marriage is not only about the union of two individuals but also the integration of different aspects within oneself. Dreaming of marriage may indicate the need for inner harmony and balance. It signifies the desire to unite conflicting parts of your personality, reconcile opposing emotions, or integrate various aspects of your life to achieve a sense of wholeness.

Commitment and Loyalty: Marriage is a commitment, a promise to stand by someone through thick and thin. Dreaming of marriage reflects a longing for stability, trust, and loyalty in your relationships. It may symbolize your desire for deep and lasting connections, where both partners are dedicated to supporting and uplifting each other.

Celebration of Love and Unity: In Babylonian culture, weddings were joyous occasions filled with celebration and rituals. Dreaming of marriage can symbolize the celebration of love, happiness, and unity. It represents the recognition and appreciation of the beauty and sacredness of love in all its forms. This dream may signify a time of emotional fulfillment, contentment, and shared joy.

Integration of Masculine and Feminine Energies: Marriage is often seen as the integration of masculine and feminine energies, creating a harmonious balance. Dreaming of marriage may symbolize the need to embrace and harmonize these energies within yourself. It invites you to explore and honor both your assertive, action-oriented side (masculine) and your nurturing, intuitive side (feminine) to achieve a sense of wholeness.

Remember, dear friend, that the interpretation of dreaming about marriage is unique to you and your personal experiences. Reflect on the emotions, symbols, and circumstances within the dream to uncover the specific message that marriage holds for you. Embrace the concept of partnership, unity, and integration, whether in relationships, personal growth, or the pursuit of your goals.

May your dreams of marriage inspire you to seek deep connections, inner harmony, and a profound sense of unity within yourself and with others.

Music: Music played a crucial role in Babylonian culture, with various instruments and musical traditions. Dreaming of music might symbolize harmony, emotional expression, or the need for balance and joy in life.

Ah, the enchanting world of music! In ancient Babylon, music held great significance and was an integral part of their culture and rituals. Dreaming of music can carry profound symbolism and evoke powerful emotions. Let's explore the possible meanings behind dreaming of music:

Harmony and Balance: Music is the language of harmony, where different sounds come together to create a beautiful symphony. Dreaming of music symbolizes the need for balance and harmony in your life. It suggests the importance of finding equilibrium between various aspects of your existence, whether it be work and personal life, logic and emotions, or different relationships. This dream encourages you to seek a state of inner harmony and alignment.

Emotional Expression: Music has the power to evoke and express emotions. Dreaming of music reflects the need for emotional expression and release. It may suggest that you have untapped emotions or creative energies that are seeking an outlet. This dream encourages you to explore your emotions, find healthy ways to express yourself, and embrace the cathartic power of music or other creative outlets.

Joy and Celebration: Music is often associated with celebration, joy, and upliftment of spirits. Dreaming of music may symbolize a desire for more happiness and enjoyment in your life. It encourages you to seek out moments of celebration, connect with your inner joy, and infuse your daily experiences with a sense of playfulness and delight.

Unity and Connection: Music has the unique ability to bring people together and create a sense of unity. Dreaming of music may signify a longing for connection with others. It reminds you of the power of shared experiences, collaboration, and the beauty of human connection. This dream encourages you to seek meaningful connections and engage in activities that foster a sense of togetherness and unity.

Rhythm and Flow: Music is driven by rhythm, a fundamental aspect of life itself. Dreaming of music may symbolize the need for rhythm and flow in your life. It suggests the importance of finding a balance between structure and spontaneity, allowing yourself to surrender to the natural rhythms and cycles of life. This dream encourages you to embrace flexibility, adaptability, and the inherent flow of existence.

Remember, dear friend, that the interpretation of dreaming about music is personal and unique to you. Reflect on the emotions, melodies, and circumstances within the dream to uncover the specific message that music holds for you. Embrace the harmony, emotional expression, joy, and connection that music brings, and allow it to guide you towards a more balanced and fulfilling life.

May the melodies of your dreams continue to resonate within you, bringing harmony, joy, and a deeper connection to the rhythm of life.

Mediation: Mediation and arbitration were common in resolving disputes in Babylonian society. Dreaming of mediation might symbolize conflict resolution, finding common ground, or the need for harmony in relationships.

Ah, mediation, the art of finding peaceful resolutions! In ancient Babylon, mediation played an essential role in resolving conflicts and fostering harmony among individuals. Dreaming of mediation carries profound symbolism and reflects the importance of finding peaceful resolutions in your waking life. Let's explore the possible meanings behind dreaming of mediation:

Conflict Resolution: Dreaming of mediation symbolizes your subconscious desire to resolve conflicts and restore harmony in your relationships or situations. It suggests that you may be experiencing conflicts or challenges in your waking life that require a peaceful and diplomatic approach. This dream encourages you to seek common ground, practice active listening, and find peaceful resolutions that honor the needs and perspectives of all parties involved.

Seeking Balance: Mediation is all about finding balance and fairness. Dreaming of mediation may reflect your subconscious recognition of the importance of maintaining equilibrium and fairness in your interactions and decisions. It reminds you to consider multiple perspectives, weigh different opinions, and seek solutions that promote balance and justice.

Collaboration and Cooperation: Mediation often involves collaboration and cooperation between parties to reach a mutually beneficial outcome. Dreaming of mediation may symbolize the need for collaboration and teamwork in your waking life. It encourages you to embrace the spirit of cooperation, open communication, and finding win-win solutions. This dream reminds you of the power of working together and the value of collective wisdom.

Harmonious Relationships: Mediation aims to foster harmonious relationships by resolving conflicts and improving communication. Dreaming of mediation suggests a desire for peaceful and harmonious relationships in your personal or professional life. It may indicate that you are seeking ways to improve communication, resolve misunderstandings, and create a more harmonious environment. This dream encourages you to engage in open and honest communication, actively listen to others, and find ways to build bridges rather than walls.

Inner Peace and Self-Reflection: Mediation involves a process of self-reflection and inner peace. Dreaming of mediation may symbolize your subconscious desire for inner harmony and self-reflection. It encourages you to engage in introspection, examine your own thoughts and emotions, and find inner peace amidst external conflicts. This dream reminds you to prioritize self-care, practice mindfulness, and seek inner balance.

Remember, dear friend, that the interpretation of dreaming about mediation is personal and unique to you. Reflect on the specific circumstances, emotions, and people within the dream to uncover the deeper message that mediation holds for you. Embrace the values of fairness, collaboration, and peaceful resolution, and allow them to guide you towards creating harmonious relationships and environments in your waking life.

May your dreams of mediation inspire you to be a bridge builder, a compassionate listener, and a harbinger of harmony in all aspects of your life.

N:

Nebuchadnezzar (King): Nebuchadnezzar II was a famous king of Babylon known for his grand architectural projects. Dreaming of Nebuchadnezzar might symbolize power, authority, or the need for leadership and control.

Ah, Nebuchadnezzar, the mighty king of Babylon! Dreaming of Nebuchadnezzar carries deep symbolism and reflects your subconscious fascination with power, authority, and leadership. Let's explore the possible meanings behind dreaming of Nebuchadnezzar:

Power and Authority: Nebuchadnezzar was renowned for his power and authority as the king of Babylon. Dreaming of Nebuchadnezzar may symbolize your own desire for power and influence in your waking life. It suggests that you are seeking recognition, control, or a sense of leadership in your personal or professional endeavors. This dream encourages you to explore your ambitions, assert yourself confidently, and take charge of your life.

Ambition and Achievement: Nebuchadnezzar's grand architectural projects, such as the Hanging Gardens of Babylon, exemplify ambition and achievement. Dreaming of Nebuchadnezzar may signify your own aspirations for greatness and the desire to leave a lasting legacy. It reflects your drive to accomplish significant goals, build something remarkable, or be remembered for your achievements. This dream encourages you to set ambitious goals, pursue them with determination, and strive for greatness.

Leadership and Control: As a powerful ruler, Nebuchadnezzar was known for his leadership and ability to control his kingdom. Dreaming of Nebuchadnezzar may suggest that you are seeking greater leadership roles or the need to take control of a situation in your waking life. It symbolizes your desire to be in charge, make important decisions, and guide others towards a common vision. This dream encourages you to develop your leadership skills, assert yourself confidently, and take responsibility for your actions.

Historical Connection: Nebuchadnezzar is a prominent historical figure associated with Babylonian history. Dreaming of Nebuchadnezzar may symbolize your fascination with history, ancient civilizations, or a connection to your cultural heritage. It reflects your interest in learning from the past, understanding the lessons of history, and appreciating the rich tapestry of human civilization. This dream encourages you to explore your roots, study history, and embrace the wisdom of ancient cultures.

Balancing Power and Responsibility: Nebuchadnezzar's reign highlights the delicate balance between power and responsibility. Dreaming of Nebuchadnezzar may indicate that you are grappling with finding the right balance between asserting your power and shouldering the responsibilities that come with it. It reminds you to consider the ethical implications of your actions, exercise authority responsibly, and lead with integrity.

Remember, dear friend, that the interpretation of dreaming about Nebuchadnezzar is personal and unique to you. Reflect on the specific circumstances, emotions, and events within the dream to uncover the deeper message that Nebuchadnezzar holds for you. Embrace the qualities of leadership, ambition, and the pursuit of greatness, and allow them to inspire you to reach your fullest potential.

May your dreams of Nebuchadnezzar ignite the flame of ambition, instill confidence in your leadership abilities, and guide you towards a path of personal and professional fulfillment.

Nammu (Goddess): Nammu was a primordial goddess in Babylonian mythology associated with creation and the primeval waters. Dreaming of Nammu might symbolize fertility, creativity, or the emergence of new beginnings.

Ah, Nammu, the primordial goddess of creation and the sacred waters! Dreaming of Nammu carries profound symbolism and represents the emergence of new beginnings, creativity, and fertility. Let's explore the possible meanings behind dreaming of Nammu:

Creation and New Beginnings: Nammu, as the primordial goddess, is associated with the creation of the world and the emergence of life. Dreaming of Nammu signifies the awakening of new possibilities, the birth of ideas, and the potential for fresh starts in your life. It suggests that you are in a phase of transformation and renewal, ready to embark on a new chapter filled with growth and opportunities. This dream encourages you to embrace change, tap into your creative potential, and trust in the natural cycles of life.

Fertility and Nurturing: Nammu's connection to the primeval waters symbolizes fertility and nurturing energy. Dreaming of Nammu may indicate a desire for growth and abundance in various areas of your life. It can represent the fertile ground for new projects, relationships, or personal development. This dream encourages you to cultivate a nurturing mindset, be open to receiving blessings, and take proactive steps to nurture your dreams and aspirations.

Creative Expression: Nammu's association with creativity suggests that dreaming of her signifies a need for artistic expression and the exploration of your creative potential. It encourages you to tap into your imagination, express yourself through various artistic mediums, and honor your unique creative impulses. This dream reminds you of the transformative power of creativity and encourages you to embrace your artistic side.

Connection to Primordial Energies: Nammu's status as a primordial goddess signifies a deep connection to ancient, primal energies. Dreaming of Nammu may indicate a longing to reconnect with your roots, tap into ancestral wisdom, or embrace the timeless wisdom of the natural world. It encourages you to explore spiritual practices, connect with the elements, and honor the ancient wisdom within you.

Embracing the Unknown: Nammu's association with the primeval waters represents the mysterious and unknown aspects of life. Dreaming of Nammu may suggest that you are embarking on a journey of self-discovery, ready to dive into the depths of your subconscious mind and explore the hidden realms within you. It encourages you to embrace the unknown, trust in your intuitive guidance, and navigate the uncharted territories of your life with courage and curiosity.

Remember, dear friend, that the interpretation of dreaming about Nammu is personal and unique to you. Reflect on the specific circumstances, emotions, and events within the dream to uncover the deeper message that Nammu holds for you. Embrace the creative and fertile energy that Nammu represents, and allow it to inspire you to bring forth new beginnings, nurture your dreams, and honor the ancient wisdom within you.

May your dreams of Nammu awaken the creative forces within, nurture the seeds of new beginnings, and guide you on a path of growth, abundance, and connection to the primordial energies of creation.

Nippur: Nippur was an important religious center in ancient Babylon, dedicated to the god Enlil. Dreaming of Nippur might symbolize spiritual connection, divine guidance, or the need for inner wisdom.

Ah, Nippur, the sacred religious center dedicated to the mighty god Enlil! Dreaming of Nippur carries profound symbolism and represents a connection to spirituality, divine guidance, and the pursuit of inner wisdom. Let's explore the possible meanings behind dreaming of Nippur:

Spiritual Connection: Nippur served as a significant religious center in ancient Babylon, and dreaming of Nippur signifies a deepening of your spiritual connection. It indicates a desire for a closer relationship with the divine, a yearning for higher meaning and purpose in your life. This dream suggests that you are on a quest for spiritual growth and seeking a profound connection with something greater than yourself. It encourages you to explore spiritual practices, connect with your inner self, and find solace in the sacred.

Divine Guidance: Nippur's association with the god Enlil suggests that dreaming of Nippur represents a need for divine guidance and wisdom. It signifies a longing for direction and support in navigating life's challenges. This dream may indicate that you are seeking answers, clarity, or a sense of purpose. It encourages you to trust in the guidance of the divine, listen to your intuition, and embrace the wisdom that comes from within. Pay attention to signs and synchronicities in your waking life, as they may hold valuable messages from the universe.

Inner Wisdom: Nippur was a place where ancient wisdom was revered, and dreaming of Nippur symbolizes the quest for inner wisdom and self-discovery. It suggests that you are embarking on a journey of self-reflection, seeking deeper understanding and knowledge about yourself and the world around you. This dream encourages you to explore your own inner landscape, delve into your subconscious mind, and tap into the wellspring of wisdom within you. Trust your instincts, embrace your intuition, and honor the innate wisdom that resides in your heart and soul.

Sacred Space and Ritual: Nippur was a center of religious rituals and sacred practices. Dreaming of Nippur may signify a need for sacredness and ritual in your life. It could be a reminder to create sacred space for yourself, to engage in spiritual practices that bring you comfort and peace. This dream encourages you to honor your spiritual needs, establish rituals that nourish your soul, and create a sense of sacredness in your everyday life.

Remember, dear friend, that the interpretation of dreaming about Nippur is personal and unique to you. Reflect on the specific circumstances, emotions, and events within the dream to uncover the deeper message that Nippur holds for you. Embrace the spiritual connection, divine guidance, and inner wisdom that Nippur represents, and allow them to guide you on your path of spiritual growth, self-discovery, and connection to the sacred.

May your dreams of Nippur awaken your spiritual senses, guide you towards inner wisdom, and nurture your connection to the divine, leading you on a journey of spiritual fulfillment and deepening understanding.

Nisaba (Goddess): Nisaba was the goddess of writing, accounting, and wisdom in Babylonian mythology. Dreaming of Nisaba might symbolize intellectual pursuits, knowledge, or the pursuit of wisdom and learning.

Ah, Nisaba, the revered goddess of writing, accounting, and wisdom in Babylonian mythology! Dreaming of Nisaba carries profound symbolism and signifies a connection to intellectual pursuits, knowledge, and the pursuit of wisdom and learning. Let's explore the possible meanings behind dreaming of Nisaba:

Intellectual Pursuits: Nisaba's association with writing and accounting indicates that dreaming of Nisaba symbolizes a deep engagement with intellectual pursuits. It signifies a thirst for knowledge, a passion for learning, and a desire to expand your understanding of the world. This dream suggests that you are on a quest for intellectual growth, seeking to acquire new information, skills, or insights. It encourages you to embrace your curiosity, engage in intellectual activities, and explore areas of study or interests that captivate your mind.

Wisdom and Guidance: Nisaba's role as the goddess of wisdom implies that dreaming of Nisaba represents a quest for wisdom and guidance in your life. It signifies a desire to access deeper insights, gain clarity, and make informed decisions. This dream may indicate that you are seeking wise counsel, mentorship, or spiritual guidance. It encourages you to trust your inner wisdom, seek out sources of knowledge and wisdom, and embrace the teachings that resonate with your soul. Embracing Nisaba's energy in your dream signifies a path of enlightenment and growth through the pursuit of wisdom.

Creative Expression: Nisaba's association with writing suggests that dreaming of Nisaba symbolizes the need for creative expression. It signifies a desire to communicate, share ideas, or express yourself through written or verbal means. This dream encourages you to explore different forms of creative expression, such as writing, storytelling, or artistic endeavors. It invites you to tap into your creativity and harness the power of words to convey your thoughts, emotions, and experiences.

Personal Transformation: Nisaba's presence in your dream may also indicate a transformative journey of self-discovery and personal growth. It suggests that you are ready to delve deep into your own wisdom, challenge your existing beliefs, and expand your understanding of yourself and the world. This dream invites you to embrace lifelong learning, embrace personal development, and cultivate a mindset of continuous growth and self-improvement.

Remember, dear friend, that the interpretation of dreaming about Nisaba is personal and unique to you. Reflect on the specific circumstances, emotions, and events within the dream to uncover the deeper message that Nisaba holds for you. Embrace the intellectual pursuits, wisdom, and creative expression that Nisaba represents, and allow them to guide you on your path of knowledge, self-discovery, and personal transformation.

May your dreams of Nisaba inspire you to embark on a lifelong quest for knowledge, wisdom, and creative expression, leading you to new depths of understanding, self-discovery, and personal growth.

Numerology: Babylonians were skilled mathematicians and used numerical systems extensively. Dreaming of numerology might symbolize hidden meanings, patterns, or the need for logical analysis and understanding.

Ah, numerology, the ancient art of understanding the hidden meanings and patterns behind numbers. Dreaming of numerology in the context of Babylonian culture carries significant symbolism and signifies a deep desire to uncover hidden meanings, explore patterns, and gain a deeper understanding of the world. Let's delve into the possible meanings behind dreaming of numerology:

Hidden Meanings: Numerology is all about uncovering hidden meanings and messages encoded within numbers. Dreaming of numerology suggests that you have a strong intuition that there is more to the surface-level events and experiences in your life. You are seeking deeper insights, looking for the underlying patterns and meanings that can provide you with a profound understanding of yourself and the world around you. This dream encourages you to trust your intuition, pay attention to synchronicities, and explore the hidden layers of existence.

Patterns and Order: Numerology is deeply rooted in the concept of patterns and order. Dreaming of numerology may indicate a desire for structure and logical analysis in your life. You are seeking a sense of order amidst the chaos and complexity of your experiences. This dream suggests that you have a natural inclination towards recognizing patterns and connecting the dots. It encourages you to embrace your analytical abilities and look for the underlying order that governs various aspects of your life.

Self-Reflection and Self-Discovery: Numerology is often used as a tool for self-reflection and self-discovery. Dreaming of numerology may signify a deep desire to gain insights into your own personality, strengths, and challenges. You are on a quest for self-understanding and personal growth. This dream invites you to explore your own numerical vibrations, such as your birth date or name, and reflect on how they influence your life. It encourages you to embark on a journey of self-discovery and embrace the unique qualities that make you who you are.

Seeking Guidance: Numerology is often used as a means to seek guidance and insight into life's challenges and decisions. Dreaming of numerology suggests that you are seeking guidance and wisdom to navigate through important choices and situations. You are open to the idea that numbers hold symbolic meanings and can provide valuable guidance. This dream encourages you to explore various divination methods, such as numerology or astrology, to gain insights into your life's path and make informed decisions.

Remember, dear friend, that the interpretation of dreaming about numerology is personal and unique to you. Reflect on the specific circumstances, emotions, and events within the dream to uncover the deeper message that numerology holds for you. Embrace the curiosity, analytical mindset, and desire for self-discovery that numerology represents, and allow them to guide you on your path of uncovering hidden meanings, patterns, and self-understanding.

May your dreams of numerology inspire you to delve deep into the mysteries of existence, recognize the hidden patterns that shape your life, and embrace the wisdom and guidance that numbers can provide along your journey of self-discovery and personal growth.

Nergal (God): Nergal was a deity associated with war and the underworld in Babylonian mythology. Dreaming of Nergal might symbolize inner conflicts, transformation, or the need for courage and strength in facing challenges.

Ah, Nergal, the formidable deity associated with war and the underworld in Babylonian mythology. Dreaming of Nergal carries significant symbolism and represents various aspects of your inner world and personal journey. Let's explore the possible meanings behind dreaming of Nergal:

Inner Conflicts: Nergal's association with war suggests that dreaming of him may symbolize inner conflicts or battles within yourself. It signifies the presence of opposing forces or conflicting desires within your psyche. This dream indicates the need to confront and address these inner conflicts, finding resolution and harmony amidst the turmoil. It encourages you to delve deep into your own psyche, acknowledge the various aspects of your personality, and seek a balanced integration of these conflicting elements.

Transformation: Nergal's connection to the underworld signifies transformation and the journey into the depths of the subconscious. Dreaming of Nergal suggests a profound transformation taking place within you. It indicates a period of inner growth, shedding old beliefs and patterns, and embracing new aspects of yourself. This dream encourages you to embrace the transformative power of your experiences, even in the face of challenges or difficult emotions. It symbolizes the potential for personal growth and rebirth.

Courage and Strength: Nergal's association with war also signifies courage, strength, and resilience. Dreaming of Nergal may symbolize the need to tap into your inner strength and face challenges head-on. It is a reminder that you possess the inner resources to overcome obstacles and emerge stronger from difficult situations. This dream encourages you to harness your courage, persevere through adversity, and stand firm in your convictions.

Confronting Shadows: Nergal's connection to the underworld points to the realm of shadows and the need to confront your deepest fears and hidden aspects of yourself. Dreaming of Nergal suggests a call to explore your shadow side, the parts of yourself that you may have repressed or denied. It encourages you to embrace and integrate these shadow aspects, as they hold valuable lessons and transformative potential.

Remember, dear friend, that the interpretation of dreaming about Nergal is personal and unique to you. Reflect on the specific circumstances, emotions, and events within the dream to uncover the deeper message that Nergal holds for you. Embrace the symbolism of inner conflicts, transformation, courage, and the exploration of your shadow self that Nergal represents, and allow it to guide you on your path of self-discovery, growth, and embracing the full spectrum of your being.

May your dreams of Nergal empower you to confront your inner conflicts with courage, embrace transformation and growth, and delve fearlessly into the depths of your being, emerging stronger, wiser, and more integrated on your journey of self-discovery.

Netherworld: The ancient Babylonians believed in an underworld known as the netherworld or the realm of the dead. Dreaming of the netherworld might symbolize the exploration of the subconscious, hidden fears, or the desire for spiritual transformation.

Ah, the netherworld, the realm that lies beyond our earthly existence. Dreaming of the netherworld carries profound symbolism and reflects various aspects of your inner self and spiritual journey. Let's delve into the possible meanings behind dreaming of the netherworld:

Exploration of the Subconscious: The netherworld represents the depths of the subconscious mind, a realm where hidden thoughts, emotions, and desires reside. Dreaming of the netherworld suggests a journey into your own subconscious, a call to explore the hidden aspects of your psyche. It signifies a desire for self-discovery, understanding, and healing. This dream invites you to embrace the opportunity to delve deep within, uncovering hidden fears, desires, and unresolved issues that may be influencing your waking life.

Confronting Fears: The netherworld also symbolizes the realm of the unknown and the mysterious. Dreaming of the netherworld may indicate a need to confront your deepest fears and anxieties. It urges you to confront the shadows within yourself and face your fears head-on. This dream invites you to embrace the transformative power of facing your fears, acknowledging their presence, and working towards their resolution. By doing so, you can find liberation and personal growth.

Spiritual Transformation: The netherworld represents a realm of transition and spiritual transformation. Dreaming of the netherworld may symbolize a desire for profound change or spiritual growth. It suggests that you are ready to undergo a significant transformation in your life, shedding old patterns and embracing new ways of being. This dream invites you to explore your spiritual journey, seek guidance, and connect with your inner wisdom for personal and spiritual evolution.

Honoring Ancestors: In Babylonian culture, the netherworld was associated with ancestral spirits and the afterlife. Dreaming of the netherworld may signify a connection to your ancestral roots, a call to honor and seek guidance from your ancestors. It invites you to embrace the wisdom and guidance of those who came before you, tapping into the collective wisdom of your lineage.

Remember, dear friend, that the interpretation of dreaming about the netherworld is personal and unique to you. Reflect on the specific elements, emotions, and events within the dream to uncover the deeper message that the netherworld holds for you. Embrace the symbolism of exploring the subconscious, confronting fears, seeking transformation, and connecting with your ancestral roots that the netherworld represents. Allow it to guide you on your path of self-discovery, healing, and spiritual growth.

May your dreams of the netherworld lead you on a transformative journey of self-exploration, fearlessly facing your

shadows, embracing spiritual growth, and connecting with the
wisdom of your ancestors.

O:

Omens: Babylonians placed great importance on interpreting
omens and signs in dreams. Dreaming of omens might symbolize
the anticipation of future events, the need for guidance, or the
desire for foresight.

Indeed, the Babylonians held a deep reverence for omens and
signs, believing that they held profound meaning and insights into
the future. Dreaming of omens can carry significant symbolism and
offer guidance in various aspects of life. Let's explore the possible
meanings behind dreaming of omens:

Anticipation of Future Events: Dreaming of omens signifies an
awareness and anticipation of future events. It suggests that you are
attuned to the subtle signs and signals in your waking life, seeking
clues and indications of what lies ahead. This dream encourages
you to pay attention to synchronicities and subtle messages in your
surroundings, as they may hold valuable insights and guidance for
your path.

Need for Guidance: Dreaming of omens reflects a deep desire
for guidance and clarity in your life. It indicates that you may be
seeking answers to important questions or uncertainties. This
dream invites you to trust your intuition and inner wisdom, as well
as to remain open to signs and messages from the universe. It
encourages you to be receptive to the guidance that presents itself
to you in various forms.

Desire for Foresight: Dreaming of omens may also symbolize
a longing for foresight and the ability to navigate future challenges
with wisdom and insight. It suggests a desire to gain a deeper
understanding of the events and circumstances that lie ahead. This

dream invites you to cultivate your intuition, expand your awareness, and develop your ability to read the signs and symbols that life presents to you.

Connection to the Divine: Dreaming of omens signifies a connection to the divine and the belief in the interconnectedness of all things. It reflects a deep spirituality and an understanding that the universe communicates with us through signs and symbols. This dream invites you to cultivate a sense of awe and reverence for the mysteries of life, and to embrace a mindset of trust and surrender to the divine guidance that is available to you.

Remember, dear dreamer, that the interpretation of dreaming of omens is personal and unique to you. Pay attention to the specific symbols, feelings, and events within the dream, as they hold the key to understanding the message and guidance it offers. Embrace your intuition, remain open to signs in your waking life, and trust in the wisdom of the universe as you navigate your journey.

May your dreams of omens bring you clarity, guidance, and a deeper connection to the divine. May you trust in the signs and symbols that present themselves to you, and may they illuminate your path with insight and foresight.

Oracles: Oracles were individuals believed to have the ability to communicate with the divine and provide guidance and prophecy. Dreaming of oracles might symbolize seeking divine wisdom, the need for clarity, or the desire for spiritual guidance.

Indeed, oracles held great significance in ancient Babylonian culture as conduits of divine communication and sources of wisdom and guidance. Dreaming of oracles can carry profound symbolism and reflect a deep yearning for spiritual connection and guidance. Let's explore the possible meanings behind dreaming of oracles:

Seeking Divine Wisdom: Dreaming of oracles signifies a strong desire to tap into divine wisdom and receive guidance from a higher source. It suggests that you are seeking answers to important questions or seeking clarity in a particular aspect of your life. This dream invites you to open yourself up to receiving spiritual insights and to trust in the wisdom that comes from a higher realm.

Need for Clarity: Dreaming of oracles reflects a need for clarity and understanding in your life. It suggests that you may be facing a situation or decision where you seek guidance and a deeper understanding of the underlying truth. This dream encourages you to trust in your intuition and inner guidance, and to seek out sources of wisdom and knowledge that can provide clarity in your current circumstances.

Desire for Spiritual Guidance: Dreaming of oracles symbolizes a longing for spiritual guidance and support. It reflects a recognition that there are higher forces at play and a desire to connect with them for guidance and direction. This dream invites you to deepen your spiritual practices, such as meditation, prayer, or contemplation, in order to cultivate a stronger connection with the divine and receive the guidance you seek.

Recognition of Divine Presence: Dreaming of oracles signifies a recognition of the presence of the divine in your life. It reflects an awareness of the interconnectedness of all things and the belief that there is a greater purpose and meaning behind your experiences. This dream invites you to cultivate a sense of reverence and openness to the divine presence, and to embrace the guidance and support that is available to you.

Remember, dear dreamer, that the interpretation of dreaming of oracles is unique to you and your personal experiences. Pay attention to the specific symbols, feelings, and messages within the dream, as they hold the key to understanding the guidance and wisdom it offers. Embrace your spiritual journey, seek out sources of wisdom and insight, and trust in the divine guidance that is available to you.

May your dreams of oracles bring you clarity, guidance, and a deeper connection to the divine. May you trust in the wisdom and support that flows from the higher realms, and may it illuminate your path with truth and understanding.

Offering: Offerings were commonly made in Babylonian religious rituals to appease deities or seek their favor. Dreaming of an offering might symbolize a desire for divine intervention, the need for sacrifice, or the expression of gratitude.

Dreaming of an offering holds profound symbolism in ancient Babylonian culture and can carry various meanings and interpretations. Let's explore the possible meanings behind dreaming of an offering:

Divine Intervention: Dreaming of making an offering suggests a desire for divine intervention or assistance in your life. It signifies a recognition that there are higher powers at play and a willingness to seek their guidance, support, or favor. This dream invites you to surrender your concerns or challenges to the divine and trust in their wisdom and assistance.

Sacrifice and Dedication: Dreaming of making an offering symbolizes a willingness to make sacrifices or dedicate yourself to a higher purpose. It reflects your commitment to something greater than yourself and your readiness to invest time, energy, or resources into that pursuit. This dream encourages you to consider what you are willing to give up or devote yourself to in order to align with your values and spiritual path.

Expression of Gratitude: Dreaming of making an offering can also represent a deep sense of gratitude and appreciation. It signifies a recognition of the blessings and abundance in your life and a desire to express gratitude to the divine or others who have supported you. This dream invites you to cultivate an attitude of gratitude and to express appreciation for the gifts and blessings you receive.

Seeking Divine Favor: Dreaming of making an offering suggests a desire to seek divine favor or blessings. It reflects a belief that by making an offering or demonstrating devotion, you can attract positive energies and opportunities into your life. This dream encourages you to explore ways to connect with the divine and to deepen your spiritual practices in order to enhance your connection and receive the blessings you seek.

Remember, dear dreamer, that the interpretation of dreaming of an offering is unique to you and your personal experiences. Pay attention to the specific symbols, emotions, and messages within the dream, as they hold the key to understanding the deeper significance and guidance it offers. Embrace the spirit of giving, gratitude, and devotion in your waking life, and may your offerings, whether material or spiritual, be met with divine blessings and favor.

May your dreams of making offerings bring you closer to the divine, deepen your connection to the sacred, and foster a spirit of gratitude and devotion in your heart. May you receive the blessings and guidance you seek as you navigate your spiritual journey.

Obelisk: Obelisks were tall, slender monuments used to commemorate significant events or deities. Dreaming of an obelisk might symbolize monumentality, legacy, or the desire for recognition and remembrance.

Dreaming of an obelisk carries profound symbolism and can have various interpretations. Here are some possible meanings behind dreaming of an obelisk:

Monumentality and Significance: An obelisk is a towering monument that symbolizes grandeur, significance, and permanence. Dreaming of an obelisk may reflect your aspirations for greatness, the desire to leave a lasting impact, or the need to be recognized for your achievements. It signifies a longing for a sense of monumentality in your life, whether it be through your accomplishments, contributions, or the mark you make on the world.

Legacy and Remembrance: Obelisks were often erected to commemorate important events, individuals, or deities. Dreaming of an obelisk may indicate a desire to create a lasting legacy, to be remembered by future generations, or to leave behind a meaningful imprint. It may also represent a longing to connect with your ancestral or cultural heritage, seeking to honor and preserve the wisdom and traditions of the past.

Ambition and Recognition: The towering presence of an obelisk can symbolize ambition and the desire for recognition. Dreaming of an obelisk may reflect your aspirations for success, fame, or influence. It suggests a drive to achieve greatness, to stand out from the crowd, or to make a significant impact in your chosen field or area of interest. This dream invites you to embrace your ambitions and pursue your goals with determination and perseverance.

Symbol of Spirituality and Divinity: In ancient civilizations, obelisks were often associated with spiritual or religious significance. Dreaming of an obelisk may represent a deepening connection with the divine, a spiritual awakening, or a longing for higher truths and wisdom. It can symbolize the quest for spiritual growth, enlightenment, and alignment with higher principles and values.

When interpreting your dream of an obelisk, consider the specific context, emotions, and personal associations you have with the symbol. Reflect on how it relates to your current life circumstances, goals, and aspirations. The dream may be urging you to embrace your ambitions, leave a meaningful legacy, or seek spiritual growth and alignment.

Embrace the symbolism of the obelisk in your waking life, and strive to live a life of significance and purpose. May your aspirations be realized, your legacy be meaningful, and your connection with the divine deepen as you embark on your journey of self-discovery and growth.

Oasis: In the arid Babylonian landscape, oases were considered places of refuge and abundance. Dreaming of an oasis might symbolize finding solace, renewal, or the need for emotional nourishment.

Dreaming of an oasis holds significant symbolism and can carry various interpretations. Here are some possible meanings behind dreaming of an oasis:

Emotional Nourishment and Renewal: An oasis is a symbol of abundance, refreshment, and vitality amidst a barren and arid landscape. Dreaming of an oasis may indicate a need for emotional nourishment, rejuvenation, and renewal in your life. It suggests that you are seeking a source of comfort, healing, and replenishment to restore your energy and well-being.

Finding Inner Peace and Tranquility: Oases are often associated with serenity, calmness, and a sense of harmony. Dreaming of an oasis may signify a longing for inner peace, balance, and tranquility in the midst of life's challenges. It suggests a desire to find a sanctuary within yourself or to seek out peaceful environments that can provide solace and relaxation.

Symbol of Hope and Resilience: In the arid Babylonian landscape, oases were seen as symbols of hope and resilience, as they offered life-giving water and sustenance. Dreaming of an oasis may reflect your inner strength, resilience, and the ability to find hope and inspiration even in difficult times. It signifies your capacity to navigate through challenges and find sources of nourishment and support.

Seeking Refuge and Escape: Oases served as refuge and shelter from the harsh conditions of the surrounding environment. Dreaming of an oasis may indicate a desire to escape from the pressures, stresses, or demands of your daily life. It suggests a need for respite, a temporary break from responsibilities, or a longing for a peaceful and nurturing environment where you can recharge and find sanctuary.

When interpreting your dream of an oasis, consider the specific details, emotions, and personal associations you have with the symbol. Reflect on how it relates to your current circumstances, emotional state, and overall well-being. The dream may be inviting you to prioritize self-care, seek moments of tranquility, or find sources of nourishment and renewal in your life.

Embrace the symbolism of the oasis in your waking life, and strive to create spaces of serenity, balance, and emotional well-being. Allow yourself moments of retreat and self-care, and cultivate resilience and hope as you navigate through life's challenges. May you find solace and renewal along your journey.

Oil: Oil held great importance in Babylonian culture for various purposes, including religious rituals and illumination. Dreaming of oil might symbolize anointing, purification, or the need for spiritual enlightenment.

Dreaming of oil carries significant symbolism and can have various meanings. Here are some possible interpretations of dreaming about oil:

Anointing and Blessing: Oil was commonly used in ancient Babylonian culture for anointing rituals, symbolizing consecration and divine favor. Dreaming of oil may suggest a need for spiritual guidance, protection, or a sense of being chosen or blessed. It can symbolize a recognition of your own unique qualities and the potential for growth and transformation.

Purification and Cleansing: Oil was also used for purification purposes in Babylonian rituals. Dreaming of oil may indicate a need for inner cleansing, releasing negativity, or letting go of emotional burdens. It can symbolize a desire to purify your thoughts, emotions, and actions, and seek a sense of renewal and clarity.

Illumination and Enlightenment: Oil was used to light lamps and provide illumination in Babylonian culture. Dreaming of oil may symbolize a quest for knowledge, wisdom, or spiritual enlightenment. It can signify a desire to gain deeper insights, expand your awareness, or find clarity and guidance in your life's journey.

Abundance and Prosperity: Oil was also associated with prosperity and abundance in Babylonian culture, as it was used for trading and commerce. Dreaming of oil may indicate the potential for financial or material prosperity. It can symbolize the manifestation of resources, opportunities, and abundance in your life.

Lubrication and Flexibility: Oil's lubricating properties represent smoothness and flexibility. Dreaming of oil may suggest the need to navigate challenges or relationships with greater ease and adaptability. It can symbolize the importance of finding balance, flexibility, and harmonious interactions in your personal and professional life.

When interpreting your dream of oil, consider the specific context, emotions, and personal associations you have with the symbol. Reflect on how it relates to your current circumstances, spiritual journey, or aspirations. The dream may be inviting you to seek inner illumination, embrace spiritual practices, or find balance and prosperity in various aspects of your life.

Embrace the symbolism of oil in your waking life, and explore ways to nurture your spiritual well-being, pursue knowledge and wisdom, and cultivate a sense of abundance and flexibility. May you find anointing and enlightenment along your path.

Onyx: Onyx was a precious gemstone valued in ancient Babylon. Dreaming of onyx might symbolize strength, protection, or the need for grounding and stability.

Dreaming of onyx can carry various symbolic meanings. Here are some possible interpretations of dreaming about onyx:

Strength and Resilience: Onyx is known for its strength and durability. Dreaming of onyx may symbolize inner strength, resilience, and the ability to overcome challenges. It can serve as a reminder of your own inner power and the ability to navigate difficult situations with grace and stability.

Protection and Grounding: Onyx is often associated with protective qualities. Dreaming of onyx may indicate a need for protection, whether it be physical, emotional, or spiritual. It can symbolize the importance of establishing boundaries and creating a sense of security in your life. Additionally, onyx is grounding in nature, and dreaming of onyx may suggest a need for stability, balance, and a connection with the earth.

Self-Control and Emotional Stability: Onyx is believed to have a calming effect on emotions and is associated with promoting self-control. Dreaming of onyx may symbolize the need for emotional stability and self-discipline. It can be a reminder to maintain composure, stay centered, and approach challenges with a level-headed perspective.

Inner Transformation: Onyx is a stone that encourages self-reflection and inner growth. Dreaming of onyx may signify a period of personal transformation and self-discovery. It can symbolize the need to delve deep within yourself, confront your shadow aspects, and embrace personal growth and self-improvement.

Beauty and Elegance: Onyx is a visually striking gemstone with its contrasting bands of color. Dreaming of onyx may represent a desire for beauty, elegance, and refinement in your life. It can symbolize the importance of aesthetics, artistry, and creating a sense of harmony and balance in your surroundings.

When interpreting your dream of onyx, consider the specific context and emotions associated with it. Reflect on how it relates to your current circumstances, challenges, or aspirations. The dream may be inviting you to embrace your inner strength, establish boundaries, seek emotional stability, or embark on a journey of personal transformation and self-improvement.

Embrace the symbolism of onyx in your waking life, and consider incorporating its qualities into your daily practices. Whether it is through grounding exercises, setting clear boundaries, or cultivating emotional stability, may the symbolism of onyx guide you towards strength, protection, and inner transformation.

P:

Palace: Palaces were grand structures that symbolized power and opulence in ancient Babylon. Dreaming of a palace might symbolize luxury, authority, or the desire for status and recognition. Dreaming of a palace can carry various symbolic meanings. Here are some possible interpretations of dreaming about a palace:

Power and Authority: Palaces were associated with kings and rulers, representing their authority and influence. Dreaming of a palace may symbolize your own sense of power and authority. It can indicate a desire for recognition, leadership, or a need to assert control in your life. Alternatively, it may suggest that you are feeling empowered and confident in your abilities.

Opulence and Luxury: Palaces were known for their grandeur and lavishness. Dreaming of a palace may reflect a desire for a luxurious and abundant lifestyle. It can symbolize a longing for material wealth, comfort, or the enjoyment of the finer things in life. It may also suggest a need to indulge in self-care and treat yourself with kindness and indulgence.

Status and Recognition: Palaces were symbols of prestige and status in ancient Babylon. Dreaming of a palace may represent your aspirations for recognition and success. It can symbolize your desire to be acknowledged and respected for your achievements. Alternatively, it may reflect a need to feel validated and appreciated in your personal or professional life.

Inner Sanctum and Personal Space: Palaces often had private chambers and inner sanctums for the rulers. Dreaming of a palace may indicate a need for personal space, solitude, or privacy. It can symbolize a desire to retreat from the external world and reconnect with your inner self. It may suggest the importance of creating a sanctuary or sacred space for self-reflection and rejuvenation.

Legacy and Longevity: Palaces were built to last and often became symbols of a ruler's legacy. Dreaming of a palace may represent a desire to leave a lasting impact or build a strong foundation for the future. It can symbolize your aspirations for long-term success, stability, and the creation of a lasting legacy.

When interpreting your dream of a palace, consider the specific details, emotions, and interactions within the dream. Reflect on how it relates to your personal circumstances, goals, and desires. The dream may be inviting you to tap into your own power and authority, seek luxury and abundance, or cultivate a sense of inner sanctum and personal space.

Embrace the symbolism of the palace in your waking life and explore ways to incorporate its qualities. This may involve setting goals for personal and professional success, creating a space that reflects your style and comfort, or seeking opportunities to assert your authority and influence.

Priest: Priests played a significant role in Babylonian religious rituals and were intermediaries between the people and the gods. Dreaming of a priest might symbolize spirituality, guidance, or the need for divine connection.

Dreaming of a priest can carry various symbolic meanings. Here are some possible interpretations of dreaming about a priest:

Spirituality and Connection: Priests were regarded as spiritual leaders and mediators between the earthly realm and the divine. Dreaming of a priest may symbolize a deepening of your spiritual connection or a desire to explore your spiritual beliefs. It can represent a need for guidance, wisdom, or the search for a higher purpose in life. The presence of a priest in your dream may suggest that you are seeking spiritual support and insight.

Rituals and Ceremonies: Priests played a central role in religious rituals and ceremonies in ancient Babylon. Dreaming of a priest may indicate the importance of rituals, traditions, or symbolic actions in your life. It can symbolize the need for structure, discipline, or a sense of sacredness in your daily routines. The dream may be urging you to pay attention to the spiritual or ceremonial aspects of your life and find meaning in them.

Wisdom and Guidance: Priests were often seen as wise individuals with deep knowledge of spiritual matters. Dreaming of a priest may symbolize the need for wise counsel or guidance in your waking life. It can represent a quest for knowledge, understanding, or seeking answers to profound questions. The presence of a priest in your dream may suggest that you are looking for someone to offer guidance and support in important decisions or challenges.

Healing and Blessings: Priests were also associated with healing and offering blessings in Babylonian culture. Dreaming of a priest may signify the need for healing, both physically and emotionally. It can symbolize a desire for spiritual or energetic cleansing, as well as the hope for divine intervention or blessings in your life. The dream may be a reminder to seek inner peace, restoration, and the support of higher forces.

Ritualistic Behavior and Tradition: Priests often followed specific rituals and adhered to traditional practices. Dreaming of a priest may represent a need for structure, order, or adherence to rituals and routines in your waking life. It can symbolize the importance of tradition, ceremony, or maintaining a sense of stability and continuity. The presence of a priest in your dream may suggest that you are seeking a sense of grounding and stability amidst uncertainty.

Consider the specific details, interactions, and emotions within the dream to gain further insight into its meaning. Reflect on how the symbolism of the priest relates to your current life circumstances, spiritual journey, and quest for guidance. Embrace the qualities represented by the priest, such as wisdom, spirituality, and connection, and seek ways to incorporate them into your waking life.

Prophecy: Prophecy and divination were important practices in ancient Babylon, where individuals sought to interpret signs and predict the future. Dreaming of a prophecy might symbolize a message from the divine, foresight, or the need for insight into future events.

Dreaming of a prophecy can hold significant meaning and symbolism. Here are some possible interpretations of dreaming about a prophecy:

Intuition and Inner Guidance: Prophecies are often associated with receiving messages from a higher source or tapping into one's intuition. Dreaming of a prophecy may symbolize the importance of trusting your inner wisdom and guidance. It can indicate that you have access to deep intuitive insights or that your subconscious mind is trying to convey important information to you. The dream may be urging you to pay attention to your instincts and trust your inner voice.

Future Events and Premonitions: Prophecies are often linked to the ability to foresee future events. Dreaming of a prophecy may suggest that you have an awareness or premonition about something that is yet to occur. It can symbolize your subconscious mind processing information and providing you with glimpses of what may lie ahead. The dream may be inviting you to reflect on the significance of these insights and take appropriate action or make informed decisions.

Divine Guidance and Higher Purpose: Prophecies are often associated with messages from the divine or a higher power. Dreaming of a prophecy may indicate a deep connection to the spiritual realm or a sense of divine guidance in your life. It can symbolize that you are on a path aligned with your higher purpose or that there are spiritual forces working in your favor. The dream may be a reminder to trust in the greater plan and have faith in the guidance and support available to you.

Self-Reflection and Personal Transformation: Prophecies can also represent personal growth and transformation. Dreaming of a prophecy may symbolize a period of change and evolution in your life. It can indicate that you are being called to embrace new opportunities, release old patterns, or step into a higher version of yourself. The dream may be inviting you to explore your inner potential and embrace the transformative journey that lies ahead.

Seeking Answers and Clarity: Prophecies often offer insights and answers to pressing questions or uncertainties. Dreaming of a prophecy may symbolize a desire for clarity, understanding, or resolution in your waking life. It can represent a need for guidance or a search for meaning and purpose. The dream may be encouraging you to reflect on your current circumstances, seek answers within yourself, or seek wise counsel to gain the clarity you are seeking.

Consider the specific details, symbols, and emotions within the dream to gain further insight into its meaning. Reflect on how the prophecy relates to your current life situation, aspirations, and inner quest for understanding. Embrace the messages and guidance received in the dream, and consider how you can apply them to your waking life to navigate challenges, make decisions, and align with your higher purpose.

Planet: Babylonians were skilled astronomers and observed celestial bodies, including planets. Dreaming of a planet might symbolize cosmic forces, influence, or the need to align oneself with the greater universe.

Dreaming of a planet can carry various meanings and symbolism. Here are some possible interpretations:

Expansion and Growth: Planets are often associated with expansion and growth, both on a personal and universal level. Dreaming of a planet may symbolize your desire for personal growth, development, and the pursuit of new experiences. It can represent a call to explore new horizons, expand your knowledge, or embrace opportunities for personal transformation.

Cosmic Energy and Influence: Planets are celestial bodies with their own energetic qualities and influences. Dreaming of a planet may symbolize the presence of cosmic energy in your life. It can suggest that you are being influenced by certain energetic forces or that you have the potential to tap into higher realms of consciousness. The dream may be an invitation to connect with your spirituality, align your actions with your values, or explore mystical or metaphysical aspects of life.

Archetypal Energies: Planets are often associated with specific archetypal energies and qualities. Dreaming of a planet may reflect the activation or integration of these archetypal energies within you. For example, dreaming of Mars might symbolize assertiveness, passion, and the need for action, while dreaming of Venus might symbolize love, harmony, and the pursuit of beauty. Consider the specific planet in your dream and its associated qualities to gain further insight into its meaning.

Balance and Harmony: Planets are part of a larger cosmic system and are held in balance by gravitational forces. Dreaming of a planet may symbolize the need for balance and harmony in your life. It can represent the importance of finding equilibrium between different aspects of yourself or different areas of your life. The dream may be encouraging you to pay attention to your inner and outer balance and make necessary adjustments to restore harmony.

Cosmic Connection and Unity: Planets exist within a vast cosmic network, interconnected and part of a larger whole. Dreaming of a planet may symbolize your desire for connection, unity, and a sense of belonging to something greater than yourself. It can represent your longing for a deeper understanding of the universe and your place within it. The dream may be an invitation to explore your interconnectedness with others, nature, or the divine.

Consider the specific planet in your dream, its characteristics, and any other details or emotions associated with it to gain a deeper understanding of its meaning. Reflect on how the symbolism of the planet resonates with your current life circumstances, aspirations, or spiritual journey. Embrace the messages and energies of the planet and seek to align yourself with the cosmic forces at play in your life.

Palm: Palms were significant in Babylonian symbolism, often associated with fertility, abundance, and protection. Dreaming of a palm might symbolize vitality, growth, or the need for nurturing and care. Dreaming of a palm tree or palm in Babylonian symbolism can carry several meanings and interpretations:

Fertility and Abundance: Palms were often associated with fertility and abundance in Babylonian culture. Dreaming of a palm tree might symbolize a period of growth, prosperity, and abundance in your life. It can signify the fruition of your efforts, the successful completion of a project, or the beginning of a period of abundance and prosperity.

Nurturing and Protection: Palms were also seen as protective symbols in Babylonian culture. Dreaming of a palm tree might represent a need for nurturing and protection. It can suggest that you seek a safe and secure environment in which you can grow and flourish. The dream may be a reminder to create a supportive and nurturing space for yourself or to seek the guidance and protection of others.

Vitality and Renewal: Palms are known for their resilience and ability to thrive in challenging conditions. Dreaming of a palm tree might symbolize vitality, resilience, and the ability to adapt to difficult circumstances. It can represent your inner strength, endurance, and capacity to overcome obstacles. The dream may be urging you to tap into your inner resources and find the resilience to navigate through challenges.

Spiritual Significance: Palms have also held spiritual significance in various cultures, including Babylonian mythology.

Dreaming of a palm tree might symbolize a spiritual journey, awakening, or connection to higher realms. It can represent a quest for spiritual growth, enlightenment, or a desire to deepen your connection with the divine.

Tropical Paradise and Relaxation: Palms are often associated with tropical landscapes and a sense of relaxation and tranquility. Dreaming of a palm tree might symbolize a longing for a peaceful and harmonious environment. It can represent your desire for rest, relaxation, and a break from the stresses of daily life. The dream may be encouraging you to create moments of calm and serenity amidst the busyness of your life.

Consider the specific context, emotions, and details in your dream to further interpret the meaning of the palm symbol. Reflect on how it relates to your current life situation, aspirations, or desires. Embrace the symbolism of the palm tree and seek to cultivate abundance, protection, resilience, and inner growth in your life.

Prayers: Prayers were an integral part of religious practices in ancient Babylon. Dreaming of prayers might symbolize spiritual devotion, seeking guidance, or the need for divine intervention.

Dreaming of a palm tree or palm in Babylonian symbolism can carry several meanings and interpretations:

Fertility and Abundance: Palms were often associated with fertility and abundance in Babylonian culture. Dreaming of a palm tree might symbolize a period of growth, prosperity, and abundance in your life. It can signify the fruition of your efforts, the successful completion of a project, or the beginning of a period of abundance and prosperity.

Nurturing and Protection: Palms were also seen as protective symbols in Babylonian culture. Dreaming of a palm tree might represent a need for nurturing and protection. It can suggest that you seek a safe and secure environment in which you can grow and flourish. The dream may be a reminder to create a supportive and nurturing space for yourself or to seek the guidance and protection of others.

Vitality and Renewal: Palms are known for their resilience and ability to thrive in challenging conditions. Dreaming of a palm tree might symbolize vitality, resilience, and the ability to adapt to difficult circumstances. It can represent your inner strength, endurance, and capacity to overcome obstacles. The dream may be urging you to tap into your inner resources and find the resilience to navigate through challenges.

Spiritual Significance: Palms have also held spiritual significance in various cultures, including Babylonian mythology. Dreaming of a palm tree might symbolize a spiritual journey, awakening, or connection to higher realms. It can represent a quest for spiritual growth, enlightenment, or a desire to deepen your connection with the divine.

Tropical Paradise and Relaxation: Palms are often associated with tropical landscapes and a sense of relaxation and tranquility. Dreaming of a palm tree might symbolize a longing for a peaceful and harmonious environment. It can represent your desire for rest, relaxation, and a break from the stresses of daily life. The dream may be encouraging you to create moments of calm and serenity amidst the busyness of your life.

Consider the specific context, emotions, and details in your dream to further interpret the meaning of the palm symbol. Reflect on how it relates to your current life situation, aspirations, or desires. Embrace the symbolism of the palm tree and seek to cultivate abundance, protection, resilience, and inner growth in your life.

Papyrus: Papyrus was a writing material used in ancient Babylon, particularly for recording important texts. Dreaming of papyrus might symbolize communication, knowledge, or the need to express oneself through writing or other forms of creative expression.

Dreaming of papyrus in the context of ancient Babylonian symbolism can carry several meanings:

Communication and Expression: Papyrus was a medium for recording and preserving information in ancient Babylon. Dreaming of papyrus might symbolize a desire for effective communication or the need to express yourself more clearly. It could suggest that you have important ideas, thoughts, or emotions that need to be conveyed or shared with others.

Knowledge and Learning: Papyrus was used for writing and documenting knowledge in ancient Babylon. Dreaming of papyrus might symbolize a thirst for knowledge, learning, or intellectual pursuits. It could represent a desire to acquire new information, explore new ideas, or delve into areas of interest that can expand your understanding of the world.

Preservation and Legacy: Papyrus was used to preserve important texts and records in ancient Babylon. Dreaming of papyrus might symbolize the importance of preserving your own experiences, wisdom, or legacy. It could signify a need to document or remember significant events, lessons learned, or personal achievements. The dream may be urging you to create a lasting impact or leave a meaningful legacy.

Creativity and Artistry: Papyrus was also used for artistic purposes, such as creating intricate designs and illustrations. Dreaming of papyrus might symbolize your creative potential and the need to express yourself artistically. It could signify a call to explore your artistic abilities, engage in creative projects, or find new ways to express your unique perspective and talents.

Historical or Cultural Connection: Papyrus is closely associated with ancient civilizations, including Babylon. Dreaming of papyrus might symbolize a connection to history, ancestry, or cultural heritage. It could suggest that you are exploring your roots, seeking to understand your origins, or feeling a deep connection to the traditions and wisdom of the past.

Consider the specific details, emotions, and context of your dream to further interpret the meaning of papyrus. Reflect on how it resonates with your current life circumstances, aspirations, or desires. Embrace the symbolism of papyrus as a symbol of communication, knowledge, creativity, and the preservation of important ideas or experiences.

Pigeon: Pigeons were often associated with messages and communication in ancient Babylonian culture. Dreaming of a pigeon might symbolize the need for communication, news, or the arrival of important information.

In the context of ancient Babylonian symbolism, dreaming of a pigeon can carry several meanings:

Communication: Pigeons were often used as messengers in ancient Babylonian culture. Dreaming of a pigeon might symbolize the need for clear and effective communication. It could suggest a desire to express yourself or convey an important message to others. The dream may be highlighting the importance of open and honest communication in your personal or professional relationships.

News and Information: Pigeons were carriers of news and information in ancient times. Dreaming of a pigeon might symbolize the arrival of significant news or the need to pay attention to important information that is coming your way. It could signify that there are messages or insights that you need to be aware of or that important news is about to reach you.

Connection to the Divine: Pigeons were also associated with divine messages and spiritual communication in Babylonian culture. Dreaming of a pigeon might symbolize a connection to the spiritual realm or a message from the divine. It could suggest that you are receiving guidance or support from higher forces and that you should pay attention to your intuition or inner wisdom.

Peace and Harmony: Pigeons are often seen as symbols of peace and tranquility. Dreaming of a pigeon might symbolize a need for peace, reconciliation, or finding harmony in your life. It could suggest a desire to resolve conflicts, restore balance, or create a peaceful environment in your relationships or surroundings.

Freedom and Liberation: Pigeons are known for their ability to fly and navigate freely in the sky. Dreaming of a pigeon might symbolize a longing for freedom, independence, or liberation. It could signify a desire to break free from constraints, limitations, or emotional burdens that are holding you back.

Consider the specific details and emotions in your dream to further interpret the meaning of the pigeon symbol. Reflect on how it resonates with your current life circumstances, relationships, or aspirations. Embrace the symbolism of the pigeon as a messenger, a symbol of peace, connection, freedom, and the arrival of important information or insights.

Q:

Queenship: In ancient Babylon, queenship represented power and authority. Dreaming of queenship might symbolize leadership, influence, or the desire for control and sovereignty.

Dreaming of queenship in the context of ancient Babylonian symbolism can indeed carry several meanings:

Leadership and Authority: Queenship symbolizes a position of leadership and authority. Dreaming of queenship might indicate your own desire for power, influence, and control in your personal or professional life. It suggests a yearning to take charge and be in a position of command and decision-making.

Empowerment and Self-Confidence: Dreaming of queenship can also symbolize a sense of empowerment and self-confidence. It signifies recognizing your own worth, strength, and capabilities. The dream may be urging you to step into your own power, embrace your leadership qualities, and assert yourself in various aspects of your life.

Feminine Power and Wisdom: Queenship is often associated with feminine power and wisdom. Dreaming of queenship might represent your connection to feminine energy, intuition, and emotional intelligence. It may suggest the need to embrace and nurture these aspects of yourself, tapping into your innate wisdom and intuition to navigate through challenges.

Control and Independence: Queenship represents a sense of control and independence. Dreaming of queenship might indicate a desire for autonomy and the ability to make decisions for yourself. It suggests a longing for freedom and the ability to shape your own destiny without being constrained by external influences.

Responsibility and Accountability: Queenship comes with responsibilities and accountability. Dreaming of queenship might symbolize your recognition of the need to take charge of your life, make responsible choices, and be accountable for the outcomes. It implies a readiness to accept the challenges and obligations that come with leadership roles.

Reflect on the emotions, situations, and circumstances within the dream to gain further insight into its meaning. Consider how the symbolism of queenship resonates with your own desires, aspirations, and personal growth. Embrace the symbolism of queenship as a representation of power, leadership, empowerment, and the ability to shape your own destiny.

R:

Ruler: In ancient Babylon, rulers held significant power and were seen as embodiments of divine authority. Dreaming of a ruler might symbolize leadership, guidance, or the need for direction in one's life.

Dreaming of a ruler in the context of ancient Babylonian symbolism can carry several meanings:

Leadership and Authority: Dreaming of a ruler signifies a desire for leadership and authority in your own life. It may indicate your longing to take control, make important decisions, and guide others. This dream symbolizes your aspirations for power and influence.

Guidance and Direction: A ruler represents someone who provides guidance and direction. Dreaming of a ruler may indicate that you are seeking guidance in your life, whether it's from a mentor, a higher power, or your own inner wisdom. It suggests a need for clarity and a sense of purpose.

Divine Connection: In ancient Babylon, rulers were seen as embodiments of divine authority. Dreaming of a ruler may symbolize a connection to higher realms or a desire for spiritual guidance. It signifies your yearning for a deeper connection with the divine and a sense of purpose beyond the material world.

Responsibility and Accountability: Rulers bear the weight of responsibility and are accountable for their decisions. Dreaming of a ruler may indicate that you are recognizing the need to take responsibility for your own life and actions. It implies a willingness to embrace the challenges and obligations that come with leadership roles.

Order and Structure: Rulers bring order and structure to their domains. Dreaming of a ruler may symbolize a desire for order and stability in your life. It suggests that you seek a sense of control and organization in your personal or professional affairs.

Reflect on the emotions and circumstances within the dream to gain further insight into its meaning. Consider how the symbolism of a ruler resonates with your own aspirations, desires, and responsibilities. Embrace the symbolism of a ruler as a representation of leadership, guidance, and the ability to shape your own path.

River: The Tigris and Euphrates rivers played a crucial role in Babylonian civilization. Dreaming of a river might symbolize the flow of life, emotions, or the need to navigate through different stages or challenges.

Dreaming of a river in the context of ancient Babylonian symbolism carries several significant meanings:

Life and Vitality: The river represents the flow of life and vitality. Dreaming of a river symbolizes the dynamic nature of existence, the continuous movement and energy that propels you forward. It signifies the ebb and flow of emotions, experiences, and the passage of time.

Emotional Journey: A river often represents emotions and the depths of the subconscious. Dreaming of a river can indicate the need to navigate and understand your own emotions. It suggests the importance of acknowledging and exploring your feelings to gain insight and personal growth.

Transition and Change: Rivers are natural forces of change and transformation. Dreaming of a river may symbolize a period of transition or significant changes in your life. It suggests that you are entering a new phase, adapting to circumstances, and embracing the opportunities for growth and renewal.

Navigation and Direction: Rivers are pathways that guide you along your journey. Dreaming of a river can represent the need to navigate through challenges and make choices. It signifies the importance of finding the right direction and staying on course to achieve your goals.

Abundance and Prosperity: In the context of Babylonian civilization, rivers were essential for agriculture and prosperity. Dreaming of a river may symbolize abundance, fertility, and the potential for growth and prosperity in various aspects of your life.

Reflect on the characteristics of the river in your dream, such as its size, speed, clarity, or obstacles, to gain further insight into its meaning. Consider the emotions and sensations you experienced during the dream to understand its significance in relation to your waking life. Embrace the symbolism of the river as a reminder to flow with the currents of life, adapt to changes, and navigate through your experiences with resilience and grace.

Ritual: Rituals held great importance in Babylonian religious practices. Dreaming of a ritual might symbolize the need for structure, order, or the desire for a sense of sacredness and meaning in life.

Dreaming of a ritual in the context of ancient Babylonian symbolism carries several significant meanings:

Connection to the Divine: Rituals were a means of connecting with the divine in Babylonian culture. Dreaming of a ritual may symbolize your desire for a deeper connection with the spiritual or higher realms. It suggests a need for sacredness and meaning in your life, and the desire to engage in practices that bring you closer to your spiritual or higher self.

Structure and Order: Rituals in Babylonian culture followed a specific structure and order. Dreaming of a ritual can symbolize your need for structure, routine, and organization in your waking life. It may suggest that you seek a sense of stability and clarity, and you desire to establish rituals or routines that bring a sense of order and purpose to your daily activities.

Transformation and Renewal: Rituals often involved transformative elements and symbolized renewal. Dreaming of a ritual may indicate a desire for personal growth, healing, or a fresh start. It suggests that you are ready to release old patterns, beliefs, or energies that no longer serve you, and you are open to embracing new beginnings and transformation in your life.

Connection with Community: Rituals were often communal activities, bringing people together in shared experiences. Dreaming of a ritual may symbolize your need for connection, belonging, and a sense of community. It suggests a desire to engage with others in meaningful ways, to participate in shared traditions or practices, and to find a sense of unity and support.

Symbolism and Meaning: Rituals were rich in symbolism and meaning in Babylonian culture. Dreaming of a ritual may signify your desire for deeper understanding, symbolism, and significance in your waking life. It suggests a need to explore the deeper layers of your experiences, emotions, and actions, and to find meaning in the rituals or practices you engage in.

Consider the specific elements and actions within the ritual in your dream, as well as the emotions and sensations you experienced. Reflect on how these elements relate to your current life circumstances, your spiritual or personal journey, and your overall sense of well-being. Embrace the symbolism of the ritual as a reminder to infuse your life with sacredness, meaning, and purpose.

Roaring: The sound of roaring, particularly associated with lions, held symbolic significance in ancient Babylon. Dreaming of roaring might symbolize power, strength, or the need to assert oneself and make a bold statement.

Dreaming of roaring, especially in the context of ancient Babylonian symbolism, carries significant meanings:

Power and Strength: Roaring is often associated with powerful and mighty creatures like lions. Dreaming of roaring may symbolize your inner strength, courage, and assertiveness. It suggests that you have a strong presence and the ability to command attention and authority. It could be a sign that you are embracing your personal power and standing up for yourself in various aspects of your life.

Expression and Communication: Roaring is a form of vocal expression. Dreaming of roaring may symbolize the need to communicate your thoughts, emotions, or desires in a bold and assertive manner. It suggests a desire to be heard, to make your presence known, and to express yourself authentically without holding back.

Assertion and Boundaries: Roaring is often associated with establishing territory and asserting dominance. Dreaming of roaring may symbolize the need to set boundaries and assert yourself in challenging situations. It can represent your willingness to defend your personal space, beliefs, or values, and to stand up for what you believe in.

Release of Emotions: Roaring can be an expression of intense emotions. Dreaming of roaring may indicate a need to release pent-up emotions or frustrations. It suggests that you have strong emotions that are seeking an outlet, and you may need to find healthy ways to express and process them.

Confidence and Assertiveness: Roaring is a bold and confident action. Dreaming of roaring may symbolize a growing sense of self-assurance, assertiveness, and confidence. It indicates that you are embracing your personal power and are ready to take charge of your life and pursue your goals with determination.

Reflect on the context and emotions surrounding the roaring in your dream to gain further insights. Consider how these interpretations align with your current life circumstances, challenges, or aspirations. Embrace the symbolism of roaring as a reminder to embrace your inner strength, express yourself boldly, and assertively navigate the situations and relationships in your waking life.

Royal Court: The royal court was the center of political and social life in Babylon. Dreaming of a royal court might symbolize social status, influence, or the desire for recognition and respect from others.

Dreaming of a royal court, with its significance in ancient Babylonian culture, carries several symbolic meanings:

Status and Recognition: The royal court was associated with high social status and influence. Dreaming of a royal court may symbolize your desire for recognition, respect, and acknowledgement from others. It suggests a longing to be seen as important and valued in your social or professional circles.

Power and Authority: The royal court represented a place of power and decision-making. Dreaming of a royal court may symbolize your own aspirations for power, authority, or leadership in your personal or professional life. It suggests a desire to have control over your circumstances and make significant decisions that affect your own life and the lives of others.

Social Interactions: The royal court was a hub of social interactions, where individuals from different backgrounds came together. Dreaming of a royal court may symbolize your social life, relationships, and the dynamics within your social circle. It could signify a desire for meaningful connections, social recognition, or involvement in important social events.

Validation and Acceptance: In the royal court, individuals sought validation and acceptance from the ruler and others in positions of influence. Dreaming of a royal court may symbolize your need for validation, acceptance, and approval from others. It suggests a desire to be accepted and appreciated for your skills, talents, and contributions.

Ambition and Success: The royal court was a place where ambitious individuals sought opportunities for advancement and success. Dreaming of a royal court may symbolize your own ambitions, career aspirations, or desire for personal achievement. It suggests that you are seeking recognition and success in your chosen endeavors and are willing to put in the effort to reach your goals.

Consider the specific dynamics and emotions within the royal court in your dream to gain a deeper understanding of its symbolic meaning. Reflect on how these interpretations align with your current life circumstances, goals, and desires. The dream may serve as a reminder to assert yourself, seek recognition, or pursue your ambitions with confidence and determination.

Riches: Babylon was known for its wealth and prosperity. Dreaming of riches might symbolize abundance, success, or the desire for material and financial well-being.

Dreaming of riches, associated with the wealth and prosperity of Babylon, carries several symbolic meanings:

Abundance and Prosperity: Babylon was renowned for its riches, trade, and economic prosperity. Dreaming of riches may symbolize your desire for abundance and financial well-being. It reflects a longing for material comfort, security, and the fulfillment of your material needs and desires.

Success and Achievement: The wealth of Babylon represented success and achievement. Dreaming of riches may symbolize your aspirations for success, recognition, and accomplishment in your personal or professional life. It suggests a desire to achieve financial goals, gain a higher social status, or be recognized for your achievements and contributions.

Value and Worth: The concept of riches is often associated with value and worth. Dreaming of riches may symbolize your recognition of your own value and worth as an individual. It signifies a desire to be acknowledged and appreciated for your unique qualities, skills, and talents.

Materialism and Attachment: The desire for riches can also reflect a preoccupation with material possessions and a tendency to attach your self-worth to material wealth. Dreaming of riches may serve as a reminder to evaluate your relationship with materialism and the extent to which you derive happiness and fulfillment from external possessions.

Inner Resources: While riches are often associated with external wealth, they can also symbolize inner resources and qualities. Dreaming of riches may indicate a need to recognize and develop your inner resources, such as your talents, knowledge, or emotional well-being. It suggests a desire to cultivate and harness your inner wealth to create a fulfilling and prosperous life.

Consider the emotions and context within your dream to gain a deeper understanding of its symbolic meaning. Reflect on how these interpretations resonate with your current life circumstances, values, and goals. The dream may serve as a reminder to pursue a balanced approach to wealth and success, emphasizing the importance of inner richness and fulfillment alongside material abundance.

Ruins: Ancient Babylon was a city of great architectural marvels, and its ruins hold historical significance. Dreaming of ruins might symbolize the passage of time, the transient nature of life, or the need for reflection and introspection.

Dreaming of ruins, associated with the ancient city of Babylon, carries several symbolic meanings:

Passage of Time: Ruins are remnants of the past, representing the passage of time and the impermanence of human existence. Dreaming of ruins may symbolize your awareness of the transient nature of life. It serves as a reminder to appreciate the present moment and to reflect on the lessons and experiences of the past.

Transformation and Rebirth: Ruins can also symbolize the process of transformation and rebirth. They represent the transition from one phase of life to another. Dreaming of ruins may indicate that you are going through a period of change or facing the need for personal growth. It suggests the importance of letting go of the past and embracing new beginnings.

Reflection and Introspection: Ruins evoke a sense of contemplation and reflection. Dreaming of ruins may symbolize the need for introspection and self-examination. It suggests a time for self-reflection, evaluating past choices, and considering how they have shaped your present circumstances. It encourages you to learn from your past and make wiser decisions moving forward.

Historical and Cultural Significance: Ruins often hold historical and cultural significance. Dreaming of ruins may symbolize your connection to history, heritage, or the collective consciousness of humanity. It signifies a sense of awe and appreciation for the wisdom and experiences of those who came before you.

Resilience and Strength: Despite their dilapidated state, ruins can also symbolize resilience and strength. They stand as a testament to the endurance of human creations and the capacity to rebuild and adapt. Dreaming of ruins may symbolize your inner resilience and ability to overcome challenges. It reminds you of your strength and resourcefulness in the face of adversity.

Consider the emotions, surroundings, and context within your dream to gain a deeper understanding of its symbolic meaning. Reflect on how these interpretations resonate with your current life circumstances, emotions, and personal journey. The dream may provide insights into your mindset, the need for self-reflection, or the embracing of change and growth in your life.

Revelation: Babylonians believed in divine messages and revelations. Dreaming of a revelation might symbolize the unveiling of hidden truths, insights, or the need for a deeper understanding of oneself and the world.

Dreaming of a revelation carries significant symbolic meaning:

Unveiling of Hidden Truths: A revelation in a dream represents the unveiling of hidden truths or knowledge. It signifies a moment of clarity and understanding, where previously obscured aspects of your life or the world are revealed to you. It suggests that you are ready to receive deeper insights and gain a new perspective on matters that were once unclear or confusing.

Spiritual Awakening: Dreaming of a revelation can symbolize a spiritual awakening or a deeper connection to the divine. It signifies that you are open to receiving spiritual guidance and are seeking higher truths and wisdom. It may indicate a shift in your consciousness or an increased awareness of spiritual dimensions and energies.

Self-Discovery and Personal Growth: A revelation in a dream may represent a journey of self-discovery and personal growth. It suggests that you are on a path of uncovering your true self, understanding your desires, and discovering your purpose in life. The revelation may provide valuable insights into your strengths, weaknesses, and hidden potentials.

Transformation and Change: A revelation often leads to transformation and change. Dreaming of a revelation may symbolize a significant turning point in your life, where you are called to let go of old patterns, beliefs, or behaviors that no longer serve you. It encourages you to embrace growth, make positive changes, and align with your authentic self.

Guidance and Direction: A revelation in a dream can serve as guidance and direction in your waking life. It may be a message from your subconscious or the divine, offering guidance on important decisions or providing solutions to challenges you are facing. Pay attention to the details and symbolism within the revelation, as they may hold valuable insights for your path ahead.

Dreaming of a revelation signifies a profound shift in your understanding and perception. It invites you to embrace new knowledge, spiritual insights, and personal growth opportunities. Reflect on the emotions, symbols, and messages within the dream to gain a deeper understanding of the specific revelations being presented to you.

S:

Sun: The sun was a powerful symbol in Babylonian culture, representing divinity, light, and vitality. Dreaming of the sun might symbolize enlightenment, energy, or the pursuit of knowledge and truth.

Dreaming of the sun carries significant symbolic meanings:

Enlightenment and Illumination: The sun is often associated with enlightenment and the illumination of knowledge. Dreaming of the sun may symbolize a desire for wisdom, understanding, and spiritual growth. It represents the pursuit of knowledge, truth, and a deeper understanding of oneself and the world.

Vitality and Energy: The sun is a source of energy and life. Dreaming of the sun may symbolize vitality, strength, and the need for renewal and rejuvenation. It can represent a surge of energy and motivation in your life, inspiring you to take action, pursue your goals, and embrace a positive outlook.

Divine Presence and Guidance: In Babylonian culture, the sun was often associated with divinity and represented the presence of the gods. Dreaming of the sun may symbolize a connection to the divine, spiritual guidance, or a higher power watching over you. It signifies a sense of protection, support, and divine intervention in your life's journey.

Enlightenment and Awareness: The sun's brightness and radiance can represent clarity of thought and heightened awareness. Dreaming of the sun may indicate a need for clarity in your life, where you are seeking a deeper understanding of yourself and your circumstances. It encourages you to shine a light on any areas of confusion or uncertainty and to gain a clearer perspective.

Growth and Transformation: The sun's energy is associated with growth, both physically and metaphorically. Dreaming of the sun may symbolize personal growth, transformation, and the blossoming of potential. It represents a period of positive change, expansion, and the realization of your full potential.

Dreaming of the sun is a powerful symbol of enlightenment, energy, and vitality. It signifies a desire for knowledge, a connection to the divine, and the potential for growth and transformation. Pay attention to the emotions, sensations, and messages within the dream to gain deeper insights into the specific meaning and significance of the sun in your dream.

Snake: Snakes held symbolic significance in Babylonian mythology and were associated with both positive and negative aspects. Dreaming of a snake might symbolize transformation, healing, wisdom, or the need to confront hidden fears or desires.

Dreaming of a snake carries various symbolic meanings:

Transformation and Rebirth: In Babylonian mythology, snakes were often associated with transformation and rebirth due to their ability to shed their skin. Dreaming of a snake may symbolize personal transformation, growth, and the shedding of old habits or beliefs. It can indicate a period of change and renewal in your life.

Wisdom and Knowledge: Snakes were also regarded as symbols of wisdom and knowledge in Babylonian culture. Dreaming of a snake may suggest a need for deeper understanding, intuition, or the pursuit of wisdom. It can signify the importance of tapping into your inner wisdom and trusting your instincts.

Healing and Renewal: Snakes have long been associated with healing and renewal, as their venom can also be used in medicinal practices. Dreaming of a snake may symbolize the need for healing, either physically, emotionally, or spiritually. It can represent a period of rejuvenation and the potential for overcoming challenges or obstacles.

Hidden Fears or Desires: Snakes are often associated with primal instincts and symbolize our deepest fears and desires. Dreaming of a snake may indicate the need to confront and address hidden fears, repressed emotions, or unfulfilled desires. It can serve as a reminder to explore and integrate aspects of yourself that you may have been avoiding.

Dual Nature and Ambiguity: Snakes in Babylonian mythology had both positive and negative connotations, representing the duality of their nature. Dreaming of a snake may reflect ambiguity or mixed feelings about a situation or person in your life. It suggests the need to navigate between opposing forces or find balance in conflicting aspects of yourself or your circumstances.

It's essential to consider the context and your personal associations with snakes when interpreting a dream. Pay attention to the emotions, actions, and interactions within the dream to gain a deeper understanding of its specific meaning for you.

Sky: The vastness of the sky was revered by ancient Babylonians, who observed celestial bodies and interpreted celestial events. Dreaming of the sky might symbolize expansiveness, spirituality, or the need for a broader perspective on life.

Dreaming of the sky can carry various symbolic meanings:

Freedom and Expansion: The sky represents vastness and freedom. Dreaming of the sky may symbolize a desire for liberation, breaking free from limitations, or expanding your horizons. It can indicate a longing for greater possibilities and the need to explore new avenues in life.

Spirituality and Transcendence: The sky has long been associated with the realm of the divine and spiritual experiences. Dreaming of the sky may symbolize a connection to the spiritual or higher realms. It can suggest a need for spiritual growth, seeking guidance, or finding meaning beyond the material world.

Perspective and Clarity: The sky offers a broader perspective and a sense of clarity. Dreaming of the sky may represent the need to gain a higher perspective on a situation or to see things from a different angle. It can indicate a desire for clarity, insight, or a shift in your understanding of a particular issue.

Hope and Possibility: The sky is often associated with hope, as it holds the promise of a new day and the infinite possibilities that lie ahead. Dreaming of the sky may symbolize optimism, aspirations, or the belief in the potential for positive change. It can signify a hopeful outlook or the need to maintain faith in challenging times.

Emotions and Mood: The sky can reflect the emotional landscape within us. Dreaming of the sky may mirror your emotional state, with clear skies representing peace and serenity, stormy skies reflecting inner turmoil, or a vibrant sunset symbolizing emotional transformation and release.

As with any dream symbol, it's important to consider the context and personal associations to gain a more specific interpretation. Reflect on your emotions, the overall atmosphere of the dream, and any significant details that stood out to you to uncover the deeper meaning behind dreaming of the sky.

Statues: Babylonians crafted intricate statues representing deities, kings, and other figures. Dreaming of statues might symbolize reverence, idolatry, or the need to embody certain qualities or ideals.

Dreaming of statues can hold various symbolic meanings:

Representation and Presence: Statues are physical representations of beings or concepts. Dreaming of statues may symbolize the presence or influence of someone or something in your life. It can indicate the need to recognize and acknowledge the qualities or aspects represented by the statue.

Symbolism and Meaning: Statues often carry symbolic significance. Dreaming of statues may suggest the need to explore and understand the deeper meaning behind certain symbols or archetypes. It can signify a search for wisdom, knowledge, or guidance in your waking life.

Immortality and Legacy: Statues can represent immortality and the desire for a lasting legacy. Dreaming of statues may symbolize the longing for permanence, recognition, or leaving a mark on the world. It can reflect aspirations for achieving greatness or making a significant impact in your personal or professional endeavors.

Reverence and Idolatry: Statues are often associated with reverence and worship. Dreaming of statues may reflect a deep respect or admiration for someone or something in your life. It can also indicate the danger of idolizing or placing too much emphasis on external figures or ideals, reminding you to maintain a balanced perspective.

Frozen or Stagnant Energy: Statues are fixed in their form and often lack movement. Dreaming of statues may symbolize a sense of stagnation, rigidity, or being stuck in a particular mindset or situation. It can signify the need to break free from limiting beliefs, embrace change, or invite more fluidity and dynamism into your life.

Consider the specific details of the statues in your dream, their condition, and the emotions they evoke to gain a more nuanced understanding of their symbolism. Reflect on your own attitudes towards reverence, the quest for immortality, and the balance between honoring tradition and embracing growth and change.

Star: Babylonians were skilled astronomers and held stars in high regard. Dreaming of a star might symbolize guidance, inspiration, or the pursuit of dreams and aspirations.

Dreaming of a star can hold various symbolic meanings:

Guidance and Direction: Stars have been used throughout history as navigational tools. Dreaming of a star may symbolize the need for guidance or direction in your life. It can represent a source of inspiration or a guiding light that helps you find your path or make important decisions.

Inspiration and Aspirations: Stars are often associated with dreams, goals, and aspirations. Dreaming of a star may signify a desire for personal growth, success, or the pursuit of your passions. It can represent the spark of inspiration that motivates you to reach for the stars and manifest your true potential.

Divine or Spiritual Connection: Stars have been associated with divinity and the spiritual realm in many cultures. Dreaming of a star may symbolize a connection to higher consciousness, spiritual enlightenment, or the presence of divine guidance in your life. It can represent a reminder to stay connected to your inner wisdom and trust in the cosmic order.

Hope and Optimism: Stars often evoke a sense of wonder and beauty. Dreaming of a star may symbolize hope, optimism, and a positive outlook on life. It can be a sign of encouragement during challenging times, reminding you to keep your faith and believe in brighter days ahead.

Individuality and Uniqueness: Stars are distinct and unique in their appearance. Dreaming of a star may symbolize embracing your individuality, celebrating your unique qualities, and recognizing your own inner light. It can be a reminder to shine brightly and let your true self be seen.

Consider the context of the dream, the specific characteristics of the star, and the emotions it evokes to gain a deeper understanding of its symbolism. Reflect on how the qualities associated with stars resonate with your own life circumstances and aspirations.

Sanctuary: Sanctuaries were sacred spaces where people sought solace and divine connection. Dreaming of a sanctuary might symbolize inner peace, spiritual refuge, or the need for introspection and self-care.

Dreaming of a sanctuary can hold several symbolic meanings:

Inner Peace and Serenity: A sanctuary is a place of tranquility and calmness. Dreaming of a sanctuary may symbolize a longing for inner peace, emotional stability, and a break from the chaos of daily life. It can represent the need to create a sacred space within yourself where you can find solace and recharge.

Spiritual Connection and Guidance: Sanctuaries are often associated with spirituality and the divine. Dreaming of a sanctuary may symbolize a desire for a deeper connection with the spiritual realm or a need for guidance and support from higher powers. It can be a reminder to seek moments of introspection and reflection to nourish your spiritual well-being.

Healing and Rejuvenation: Sanctuaries are places where people go to heal and rejuvenate their mind, body, and soul. Dreaming of a sanctuary may symbolize the need for self-care, emotional healing, or a period of rest and rejuvenation. It can be a signal to prioritize your well-being and find ways to replenish your energy.

Safety and Protection: Sanctuaries are often seen as safe havens, providing protection from external pressures and challenges. Dreaming of a sanctuary may symbolize the need for a sanctuary in your waking life, a place where you feel safe, secure, and free from judgment. It can also represent a desire to establish boundaries and create a nurturing environment for yourself.

Sacredness and Ritual: Sanctuaries are associated with sacredness and rituals. Dreaming of a sanctuary may symbolize the importance of incorporating rituals or meaningful practices into your life. It can be a reminder to honor your spiritual or personal beliefs and create sacred moments that bring meaning and purpose to your daily existence.

Consider the emotions and sensations you experienced in the dream and how they relate to the idea of a sanctuary. Reflect on the areas of your life where you may be seeking solace, guidance, or rejuvenation. Use the symbolism of the sanctuary to inspire you to create moments of peace and sacredness in your waking life.

Scribe: Scribes played a vital role in Babylonian society, recording information and preserving knowledge. Dreaming of a scribe might symbolize communication, learning, or the need to express oneself through writing or other forms of expression.

Dreaming of a scribe can hold several symbolic meanings:

Communication and Expression: Scribes were skilled in the art of written communication. Dreaming of a scribe may symbolize the need for effective and clear communication in your waking life. It can signify a desire to express yourself more eloquently or to find a creative outlet for self-expression.

Learning and Knowledge: Scribes were responsible for recording and preserving knowledge. Dreaming of a scribe may symbolize a thirst for learning, a desire for intellectual growth, or the need to acquire new information or skills. It can indicate a period of seeking wisdom or a call to engage in educational pursuits.

Organization and Order: Scribes were known for their meticulousness and attention to detail. Dreaming of a scribe may symbolize the need for organization and order in your life. It can represent a desire to bring structure to chaotic areas or to prioritize tasks and responsibilities.

Preserving History and Legacy: Scribes were custodians of historical records and contributed to the preservation of cultural heritage. Dreaming of a scribe may symbolize the importance of remembering and honoring your personal history, heritage, and legacy. It can signify a need to reflect on the past, learn from it, and carry forward valuable lessons.

Honing Skills and Craftsmanship: Scribes honed their craft through practice and dedication. Dreaming of a scribe may symbolize the importance of honing your skills and striving for excellence in your chosen field. It can be a reminder to invest time and effort in developing your talents and to take pride in the craftsmanship of your work.

Consider the role of the scribe in your dream and the emotions and actions associated with it. Reflect on how these symbols relate to your waking life and the areas where you may need to enhance communication, pursue learning, establish order, honor your history, or refine your skills. Use the symbolism of the scribe as inspiration to embrace self-expression, seek knowledge, and strive for excellence.

Serpent: Serpents were powerful symbols associated with deities and the forces of nature in ancient Babylon. Dreaming of a serpent might symbolize regeneration, wisdom, or the need to tap into primal instincts or energy.

Dreaming of a serpent can hold various symbolic meanings:

Transformation and Rebirth: Serpents are often associated with shedding their skin, symbolizing transformation and rebirth. Dreaming of a serpent may indicate a period of personal growth and renewal in your life. It can represent the shedding of old patterns, beliefs, or behaviors, and the emergence of a new and transformed self.

Wisdom and Knowledge: Serpents have been regarded as symbols of wisdom and secret knowledge in many cultures. Dreaming of a serpent may symbolize the need to tap into your inner wisdom or the pursuit of deeper understanding and insight. It can signify a call to explore your subconscious mind and to uncover hidden truths or knowledge within yourself.

Primal Instincts and Energy: Serpents are often associated with primal instincts and life force energy. Dreaming of a serpent may symbolize the need to reconnect with your instincts, intuition, and vital energy. It can represent a call to embrace your primal nature, trust your instincts, and tap into your innate power.

Healing and Regeneration: Serpents have been associated with healing and regenerative powers in many cultures. Dreaming of a serpent may symbolize the need for healing, both physically and emotionally. It can signify a process of rejuvenation and restoration, allowing you to let go of what no longer serves you and embrace new beginnings.

Dual Nature and Balance: Serpents often embody both positive and negative qualities, representing the balance of opposing forces. Dreaming of a serpent may symbolize the need to find balance in your life, to integrate opposing aspects of yourself, or to reconcile conflicting emotions or desires. It can be a reminder to embrace the wholeness of your being and find harmony within yourself.

Consider the specific context, actions, and emotions associated with the serpent in your dream to gain deeper insight into its symbolic meaning for you. Reflect on how these symbols relate to your waking life and the areas where you may need transformation, wisdom, vitality, healing, or balance. Use the symbolism of the serpent as a guide to navigate your personal journey of growth and self-discovery.

T:

Temple: Temples were central to religious and spiritual life in ancient Babylon. Dreaming of a temple might symbolize divine connection, spirituality, or the need for inner reflection and sacredness.

Dreaming of a temple can hold various symbolic meanings:

Spiritual Connection: Temples were sacred spaces dedicated to worship and spiritual practices. Dreaming of a temple may symbolize a deep desire for spiritual connection, a longing for divine guidance, or a need to explore your own spirituality. It can represent a call to reconnect with your inner self and seek higher wisdom or enlightenment.

Inner Reflection and Sacredness: Temples were places of inner reflection and contemplation. Dreaming of a temple may symbolize the need for introspection, self-discovery, and inner growth. It can signify a call to create sacred space within yourself, to explore your inner world, and to find solace and peace in your own divine essence.

Rituals and Traditions: Temples were often associated with rituals and traditions. Dreaming of a temple may symbolize the need for structure, order, or a connection to established practices in your life. It can represent a call to honor and integrate rituals or traditions that hold significance for you, whether they are spiritual, cultural, or personal.

Community and Connection: Temples were gathering places for communities to come together in worship and celebration. Dreaming of a temple may symbolize the need for community, support, or a sense of belonging. It can signify a desire for connection with like-minded individuals who share similar beliefs or values, or a call to foster deeper connections with the people around you.

Sacredness and Transcendence: Temples were regarded as sacred spaces where individuals could experience a sense of transcendence. Dreaming of a temple may symbolize the longing for something greater than oneself, a desire for a higher purpose or meaning in life. It can signify a call to transcend mundane concerns and tap into a deeper sense of purpose and spirituality.

Consider the specific details of the temple in your dream, such as its condition, atmosphere, activities, or the emotions you felt while being in the temple. Reflect on how these symbols relate to your waking life and the areas where you may need spiritual connection, inner reflection, community, or a sense of the sacred. Use the symbolism of the temple as a guide to explore and nurture your spiritual journey and to create a deeper connection with yourself and the divine.

Tablet: Babylonians used clay tablets for writing, recording information, and preserving knowledge. Dreaming of a tablet might symbolize the need for communication, learning, or the exploration of hidden wisdom and knowledge.

Dreaming of a tablet, particularly a clay tablet like those used by the Babylonians, can hold various symbolic meanings:

Communication and Expression: Tablets were used as a medium for writing and recording information. Dreaming of a tablet may symbolize the need for effective communication, self-expression, or the desire to convey your thoughts and ideas more clearly. It can suggest the importance of finding the right words to express yourself or the need to share information with others.

Learning and Knowledge: Tablets were instrumental in preserving knowledge and wisdom in ancient Babylon. Dreaming of a tablet may symbolize the thirst for knowledge, intellectual pursuits, or the desire for learning and growth. It can represent a call to delve deeper into a subject of interest, to explore new ideas, or to seek hidden wisdom and understanding.

Preservation and Legacy: Tablets were used to preserve important texts and historical records. Dreaming of a tablet may symbolize the need to honor and preserve your own personal history, traditions, or values. It can signify a desire to leave a lasting legacy, to make an impact, or to pass down knowledge and wisdom to future generations.

Hidden Messages and Secrets: Tablets were often inscribed with cuneiform script, which could contain hidden messages or encoded information. Dreaming of a tablet may symbolize the exploration of hidden truths, uncovering secrets, or the need for deeper understanding in a particular area of your life. It can suggest the presence of hidden knowledge or messages that are waiting to be discovered.

Organization and Structure: Tablets were used to organize and structure information. Dreaming of a tablet may symbolize the need for order, clarity, or the establishment of a systematic approach in your life. It can represent a call to organize your thoughts, plans, or goals in a structured manner, or to create a solid foundation for your endeavors.

Consider the specific details of the tablet in your dream, such as its content, condition, or the emotions associated with it. Reflect on how these symbols relate to your waking life and the areas where you may need effective communication, learning, organization, or the exploration of hidden knowledge. Use the symbolism of the tablet as a guide to embrace the pursuit of knowledge, express yourself more effectively, and preserve valuable insights and wisdom in your life.

Tigris: The Tigris River was a significant geographical feature in ancient Babylon. Dreaming of the Tigris might symbolize the flow of emotions, adaptability, or the need to navigate through life's challenges.

Dreaming of the Tigris River, a prominent geographical feature in ancient Babylon, can hold various symbolic meanings:

Flow and Movement: The Tigris River represents the flow of water, which in turn symbolizes the flow of life. Dreaming of the Tigris might symbolize the fluidity of emotions, experiences, and circumstances in your life. It can suggest the need to go with the flow, adapt to changes, and navigate through life's challenges with ease and flexibility.

Emotions and Inner World: Water is often associated with emotions and the subconscious mind. Dreaming of the Tigris River can symbolize the need to explore and understand your emotions on a deeper level. It may indicate a desire to connect with your inner world, acknowledge and navigate your feelings, or find emotional balance and harmony.

Adaptability and Resilience: Rivers are known for their ability to adapt and change course when faced with obstacles. Dreaming of the Tigris can symbolize your own adaptability and resilience in the face of challenges. It may suggest that you have the capacity to flow with the changes and find alternative routes to achieve your goals.

Navigation and Direction: Rivers serve as natural guides for navigation. Dreaming of the Tigris can symbolize the need for guidance and direction in your life. It may suggest that you seek clarity about your path, goals, or decisions, and are in search of a reliable and steady course to follow.

Historical and Cultural Significance: The Tigris River holds historical and cultural significance in the context of ancient Babylon. Dreaming of the Tigris may evoke a sense of connection to history, heritage, or the wisdom of past civilizations. It can symbolize the importance of honoring and embracing your roots and drawing inspiration from the collective wisdom of your cultural background.

Consider the specific details and emotions associated with your dream of the Tigris River. Reflect on how these symbols relate to your waking life experiences, emotions, and aspirations. The Tigris River can serve as a powerful metaphor for navigating life's challenges, embracing emotional flow, seeking guidance, and honoring your cultural heritage.

Tower: Ziggurats, towering structures with religious significance, were present in ancient Babylon. Dreaming of a tower might symbolize ambition, aspirations, or the desire to reach higher levels of consciousness and achievement.

Dreaming of a tower, particularly in the context of ancient Babylonian ziggurats, can carry various symbolic meanings:

Ambition and Aspiration: The tower represents ambition and the desire to achieve great heights. Dreaming of a tower may symbolize your own ambitions, goals, and aspirations in life. It suggests that you have a strong drive for success and are striving to reach new levels of achievement.

Spiritual and Personal Growth: Ziggurats were religious structures associated with the worship of deities in ancient Babylon. Dreaming of a tower can symbolize your spiritual journey and the pursuit of higher levels of consciousness. It may indicate a longing for spiritual growth, self-discovery, and a deeper connection with the divine.

Strength and Stability: Towers are known for their strength and stability. Dreaming of a tower can symbolize your own inner strength and resilience. It suggests that you have a solid foundation and the ability to withstand challenges and adversities in your life.

Perspective and Insight: Towers provide a vantage point from which one can gain a broader perspective. Dreaming of a tower may symbolize the need to gain a new perspective or see things from a higher vantage point. It suggests the importance of stepping back, gaining clarity, and gaining insight into your current situation or challenges.

Isolation and Separation: Towers can also represent isolation or a sense of being separated from others. Dreaming of a tower may indicate feelings of isolation or a desire for solitude and introspection. It can suggest the need for self-reflection and taking time for yourself.

Consider the specific details and emotions associated with your dream of a tower. Reflect on how these symbols relate to your waking life experiences, goals, and aspirations. The tower can serve as a powerful metaphor for ambition, spiritual growth, strength, perspective, and isolation.

Trade: Babylon was a hub of trade and commerce in ancient times. Dreaming of trade might symbolize exchange, negotiation, or the need to find a balance between different aspects of life.

Dreaming of trade, particularly in the context of Babylon's historical significance in commerce, can carry several symbolic meanings:

Exchange and Interaction: Trade involves the exchange of goods, ideas, and services between individuals or communities. Dreaming of trade may symbolize the need for social interaction, collaboration, and the exchange of information or resources. It suggests the importance of building connections and fostering mutually beneficial relationships.

Negotiation and Compromise: Trade often involves negotiation and finding mutually acceptable terms. Dreaming of trade may symbolize the need for negotiation and compromise in your waking life. It suggests the importance of finding a balance and seeking win-win solutions in your personal or professional relationships.

Abundance and Prosperity: Trade can bring about abundance and prosperity. Dreaming of trade may symbolize your desire for material wealth, success, and financial stability. It signifies your ambition and willingness to explore opportunities for growth and prosperity.

Balancing Priorities: Trade requires balancing various factors, such as supply and demand, cost and benefit, and risk and reward. Dreaming of trade may symbolize the need to find a balance in different aspects of your life, such as work and personal life, responsibilities and leisure, or short-term and long-term goals. It suggests the importance of making informed decisions and considering the consequences of your choices.

Adaptability and Flexibility: Trade often involves adapting to changing circumstances and market conditions. Dreaming of trade may symbolize the need for adaptability and flexibility in your approach to life. It suggests the importance of being open to new opportunities, embracing change, and adjusting your strategies as needed.

Consider the specific details and emotions associated with your dream of trade. Reflect on how these symbols relate to your waking life experiences, relationships, and aspirations. The concept of trade encompasses a range of meanings, including exchange, negotiation, abundance, balance, and adaptability.

Treasures: Babylonians valued wealth and possessions. Dreaming of treasures might symbolize abundance, prosperity, or the desire for material and emotional fulfillment.

Dreaming of treasures, particularly in the context of Babylonian culture's value for wealth and possessions, can carry several symbolic meanings:

Abundance and Prosperity: Treasures are often associated with abundance and prosperity. Dreaming of treasures may symbolize your desire for material wealth and financial success. It signifies the potential for experiencing abundance and enjoying the fruits of your labor.

Inner Riches: Beyond material possessions, treasures can also symbolize inner wealth, such as wisdom, knowledge, and personal growth. Dreaming of treasures may signify the importance of nurturing and valuing your inner resources, such as talents, skills, and experiences.

Emotional Fulfillment: Treasures can represent emotional fulfillment and satisfaction. Dreaming of treasures may symbolize your longing for emotional richness, meaningful connections, and experiences that bring joy and fulfillment to your life.

Self-Worth and Value: Treasures are often seen as valuable and precious. Dreaming of treasures may reflect your need to recognize and appreciate your own worth and value. It suggests the importance of honoring and valuing yourself, your talents, and your contributions.

Hidden Potential: Treasures are often hidden or buried, waiting to be discovered. Dreaming of treasures may symbolize untapped potential, hidden talents, or unexplored opportunities in your life. It signifies the importance of exploring and uncovering your true abilities and resources.

Consider the specific details and emotions associated with your dream of treasures. Reflect on how these symbols relate to your waking life experiences, aspirations, and desires for abundance and fulfillment. Treasures can represent both material and inner wealth, highlighting the significance of recognizing and cultivating various forms of richness in your life.

Triumph: Ancient Babylon celebrated military triumphs and victories. Dreaming of triumph might symbolize overcoming obstacles, achieving success, or the need for recognition and accomplishment.

Dreaming of triumph, particularly in the context of Babylonian culture's celebration of military victories, can carry several symbolic meanings:

Overcoming Obstacles: Triumph symbolizes the ability to overcome challenges and obstacles in your life. Dreaming of triumph may signify your determination, resilience, and perseverance in the face of adversity. It represents your inner strength and the belief that you can conquer any challenges that come your way.

Achievement and Success: Triumph is often associated with achieving goals and experiencing success. Dreaming of triumph may symbolize your desire for accomplishment, recognition, and the fulfillment of your ambitions. It reflects your confidence in your abilities and the belief that you can attain greatness.

Self-Confidence and Empowerment: Triumph represents a sense of self-confidence and empowerment. Dreaming of triumph may indicate a growing belief in yourself, your skills, and your capabilities. It suggests that you have the inner strength and determination to overcome any obstacles and achieve your goals.

Recognition and Validation: Triumph often involves recognition and validation from others. Dreaming of triumph may signify your need for acknowledgment and appreciation for your efforts and achievements. It reflects your desire to be seen, respected, and celebrated for your accomplishments.

Celebration and Joy: Triumph is associated with celebration and joyous moments. Dreaming of triumph may symbolize the need for celebration and enjoyment in your life. It signifies the importance of embracing and savoring your victories, both big and small, and finding joy in your achievements.

Consider the specific details and emotions associated with your dream of triumph. Reflect on how these symbols relate to your waking life experiences, goals, and aspirations for success and recognition. Triumph represents the overcoming of challenges and the attainment of goals, highlighting the importance of perseverance, self-confidence, and celebration in your journey towards fulfillment and accomplishment.

Time: Babylonians had an interest in astrology and the measurement of time. Dreaming of time might symbolize the passage of life, the importance of timing, or the need to make the most of the present moment.

Dreaming of time can carry various symbolic meanings:

Passage of Life: Time represents the continuous flow of life and the inevitability of change. Dreaming of time may symbolize your awareness of the passing of time and the transient nature of existence. It can serve as a reminder to cherish each moment, appreciate the present, and make the most of the opportunities that come your way.

Importance of Timing: Time is closely associated with timing and the concept of opportune moments. Dreaming of time may signify your recognition of the significance of timing in various aspects of your life, such as making decisions, taking action, or seizing opportunities. It can reflect your desire to be in sync with the rhythms of life and to make choices at the right time.

Reflection and Evaluation: Time allows for reflection and evaluation of past experiences and future aspirations. Dreaming of time may indicate a need for introspection, self-reflection, and assessment of your life journey. It can serve as a reminder to review your past choices, learn from them, and consider how they have shaped your present circumstances.

Urgency or Impatience: Dreaming of time may suggest a sense of urgency or impatience regarding a particular situation or goal in your life. It can indicate a desire to move forward, achieve results, or meet deadlines. It may also signal the need to manage your time effectively and prioritize your tasks and responsibilities.

Transformation and Growth: Time is often associated with personal growth and transformation. Dreaming of time may symbolize your awareness of the potential for change and development in your life. It can reflect a desire for self-improvement, learning, and evolving into the best version of yourself.

Pay attention to the specific details and emotions associated with your dream of time. Reflect on how these symbols relate to your waking life experiences, your relationship with time, and your attitude towards the past, present, and future. Understanding the symbolic meaning of time in your dream can provide insights into your perception of time, your priorities, and your approach to seizing opportunities and embracing change in your life.

U:

Uruk: Uruk was an ancient city in Mesopotamia, located in present-day Iraq. It was one of the major cities in ancient Babylon. Dreaming of Uruk might symbolize connection to ancient history, exploration, or the search for roots and cultural heritage.

Dreaming of Uruk, the ancient city in Mesopotamia, can carry various symbolic meanings:

Connection to Ancient History: Uruk represents a significant historical and cultural heritage. Dreaming of Uruk may symbolize your connection to the past, an interest in ancient civilizations, or a fascination with history. It can reflect a desire to explore and learn from the wisdom and experiences of previous generations.

Exploration and Adventure: Uruk was a bustling city of trade and innovation. Dreaming of Uruk may signify your spirit of exploration, curiosity, and a thirst for new experiences. It can represent a willingness to step outside your comfort zone, embrace diversity, and discover new opportunities in life.

Search for Roots and Identity: Uruk holds historical and cultural significance in the region. Dreaming of Uruk may indicate a longing to explore your roots, heritage, and ancestral connections. It can symbolize a search for identity, a desire to understand your origins, and a quest for a deeper sense of belonging.

Historical Wisdom and Lessons: Uruk was a center of ancient wisdom and knowledge. Dreaming of Uruk may suggest a need for guidance and wisdom in your life. It can symbolize a quest for deeper understanding, seeking lessons from the past, or a desire to tap into ancient wisdom to navigate present challenges.

Urban Life and Civilization: Uruk was a thriving urban center in its time. Dreaming of Uruk may represent your relationship with city life, civilization, and the complexities that come with it. It can reflect your experiences, challenges, or aspirations related to urban environments, social interactions, and the fast-paced nature of modern life.

Consider the emotions, experiences, and symbols associated with your dream of Uruk to gain deeper insights into its specific meaning for you. Reflect on how these symbolic representations align with your personal experiences, aspirations, and the current circumstances in your life.

V:

Visions: Visions were highly regarded in Babylonian culture and were seen as messages from the divine realm. Dreaming of visions might symbolize revelation, spiritual insights, or the communication of important messages.

Dreaming of visions can carry various symbolic meanings:

Divine Guidance: Visions were considered messages from the divine realm in Babylonian culture. Dreaming of visions may symbolize a strong connection to the spiritual or divine realm. It can indicate that you are open to receiving guidance, wisdom, or insights from a higher source. Pay attention to the symbols, messages, or emotions within the vision as they may hold valuable guidance for your life.

Revelation and Clarity: Visions often bring forth revelations and clarity. Dreaming of visions may suggest a need for clarity or a desire to gain a deeper understanding of a particular situation or aspect of your life. It can symbolize a search for truth, hidden meanings, or a breakthrough in your understanding of yourself and the world around you.

Intuition and Inner Wisdom: Visions are often associated with intuitive knowledge and inner wisdom. Dreaming of visions may indicate that you are tapping into your intuition and trusting your inner guidance. It can symbolize the importance of listening to your inner voice, following your instincts, and relying on your innate wisdom to make decisions and navigate through life.

Spiritual Awakening and Transformation: Visions have the power to awaken and transform our spiritual journey. Dreaming of visions may represent a period of spiritual growth and transformation in your life. It can symbolize a deepening connection to your spiritual path, a desire for personal development, or an invitation to explore higher realms of consciousness.

Messages from the Subconscious Mind: Visions often emerge from the depths of the subconscious mind. Dreaming of visions may suggest that there are hidden aspects of your psyche or unacknowledged emotions that are seeking your attention. It can symbolize the need to delve into your subconscious, explore your dreams, and uncover deeper truths about yourself.

Pay attention to the content, symbols, and emotions within your visions in the dream. Reflect on how they resonate with your waking life and personal experiences. This will help you gain insights into the specific meanings and messages that the visions hold for you.

W:

Wisdom: Wisdom was highly valued in Babylonian culture, and seeking wisdom was an important aspect of life. Dreaming of wisdom might symbolize the pursuit of knowledge, insight, or the need for guidance and understanding.

Dreaming of wisdom can hold various symbolic meanings:

Knowledge and Insight: Wisdom is often associated with deep knowledge and understanding. Dreaming of wisdom may symbolize a thirst for knowledge, a desire to learn and grow intellectually. It can indicate a need for expanding your understanding of certain aspects of life or seeking answers to profound questions.

Guidance and Intuition: Wisdom is also connected to intuition and inner guidance. Dreaming of wisdom may suggest that you need to trust your inner wisdom and rely on your intuition to make decisions and navigate through life's challenges. It can symbolize the importance of listening to your inner voice and following your instincts.

Spiritual Growth and Enlightenment: Wisdom is often associated with spiritual growth and enlightenment. Dreaming of wisdom may indicate a period of spiritual awakening or a desire to deepen your connection to the divine. It can symbolize a call to explore your spiritual path, seek higher truths, and align your actions with your higher self.

Life Lessons and Reflection: Wisdom often comes from life experiences and reflection. Dreaming of wisdom may suggest a need for introspection and self-reflection. It can symbolize a call to examine your past experiences, learn from them, and apply the lessons you have gained to your present and future.

Mentorship and Guidance: Wisdom is often passed down through mentorship and guidance. Dreaming of wisdom may symbolize the importance of seeking guidance from wise and experienced individuals in your life. It can suggest a need for mentorship or the recognition of the valuable insights that can be gained from those who have walked the path before you.

Pay attention to the context and symbols within the dream to gain a deeper understanding of the specific meaning of wisdom in your dream. Reflect on how it relates to your waking life, current circumstances, and personal aspirations. This will help you uncover the significance and messages that the dream holds for you.

Y:

Yoke: A yoke was a common tool used in agriculture to join animals together for pulling a plow. In Babylonian culture, a yoke represented labor, partnership, or being bound to a certain task or responsibility. Dreaming of a yoke might symbolize the need for cooperation, balance, or the acceptance of responsibilities in one's life.

Dreaming of a yoke can hold various symbolic meanings:

Cooperation and Partnership: A yoke is a symbol of joining forces and working together. Dreaming of a yoke may indicate the importance of cooperation and collaboration in your life. It can symbolize the need to form alliances or partnerships to achieve common goals or accomplish tasks more effectively. It suggests that working in harmony with others can lead to greater success and productivity.

Balance and Equilibrium: A yoke is used to distribute the load evenly between two animals. Dreaming of a yoke may symbolize the need for balance and equilibrium in your life. It can suggest the importance of finding a middle ground, avoiding extremes, and seeking harmony in different areas of your life. It reminds you to consider the balance between work and personal life, responsibilities and self-care, or different aspects of your being.

Acceptance of Responsibilities: In Babylonian culture, a yoke represented being bound to a certain task or responsibility. Dreaming of a yoke may indicate the need to accept and embrace your responsibilities. It can symbolize a call to take ownership of your actions and commitments, recognizing that certain obligations come with a sense of duty and dedication. It suggests that by embracing your responsibilities, you can find fulfillment and contribute to the greater good.

Endurance and Hard Work: A yoke is a tool used in labor-intensive tasks. Dreaming of a yoke may symbolize hard work, perseverance, and resilience. It signifies the need to exert effort and stay committed to your endeavors. It reminds you that success often requires dedication, discipline, and a willingness to overcome challenges.

Boundaries and Limitations: A yoke represents a constraint and limitation on freedom of movement. Dreaming of a yoke may symbolize the need to establish boundaries and limitations in your life. It can suggest the importance of defining your priorities, setting clear boundaries with others, and being mindful of your limitations. It reminds you to focus your energy on what truly matters and avoid spreading yourself too thin.

Consider the specific context of the dream and your personal experiences and emotions associated with the symbol of a yoke. This will help you discern the most relevant interpretation and apply it to your waking life.

Z:

Zodiac: The Babylonians developed an early system of astrology, dividing the celestial sphere into twelve sections known as the Zodiac. Dreaming of the Zodiac might symbolize a connection to celestial forces, cosmic influences, or the exploration of one's destiny or personality traits.

Dreaming of the Zodiac can hold various symbolic meanings:

Cosmic Guidance: The Zodiac represents a system of celestial divisions that ancient Babylonians used to navigate the sky and understand cosmic influences. Dreaming of the Zodiac may symbolize a desire for guidance or a connection to higher forces. It suggests that you are seeking wisdom or seeking answers from a higher source. It can be a sign to trust in the guidance of the universe or your intuition when making important decisions in your waking life.

Self-Exploration: Each sign in the Zodiac is associated with specific personality traits and characteristics. Dreaming of the Zodiac may symbolize a desire for self-exploration and self-awareness. It suggests that you are on a journey of discovering and understanding your own strengths, weaknesses, and unique qualities. It can be a reminder to pay attention to the different aspects of your personality and how they influence your actions and relationships.

Destiny and Fate: The Zodiac is often associated with destiny and the belief that celestial bodies can influence our lives. Dreaming of the Zodiac may symbolize a contemplation of your life's purpose, fate, or the idea that there is a greater plan at work. It can be a sign to reflect on the path you are on and consider whether it aligns with your true desires and aspirations.

Harmony and Balance: The Zodiac represents a harmonious arrangement of celestial divisions. Dreaming of the Zodiac may symbolize the desire for balance and harmony in your life. It suggests the importance of finding equilibrium between different aspects of your life, such as work and personal life, or mind, body, and spirit. It can be a reminder to seek balance in your relationships, emotions, and actions.

Awareness of Cycles: The Zodiac is divided into twelve signs, each associated with a particular time of the year. Dreaming of the Zodiac may symbolize an awareness of cycles and the passage of time. It suggests that you are attuned to the natural rhythms and seasons of life. It can be a sign to embrace change, honor the different phases of your life, and be open to the opportunities that each cycle brings.

Consider the specific symbols and elements within the dream related to the Zodiac and how they relate to your waking life. This will help you discern the most relevant interpretation and apply it to your personal circumstances and aspirations.

1. Nisanu was the first month in the ancient Babylonian calendar. Its approximate corresponding time in the modern calendar is **mid-March to mid-April**. However, it's important to note that the ancient Babylonian calendar did not align precisely

with the modern calendar, and the exact dates can vary depending on the specific year and the alignment of lunar and solar cycles.

In the ancient Babylonian zodiac, Nisanu (also known as Nisannu or Nisan) corresponds to the zodiac sign of Aries. Aries is the first sign of the zodiac and is associated with qualities such as leadership, independence, and assertiveness.

Aries: Dreaming of Aries might symbolize assertiveness, leadership, or the need to take charge and initiate new beginnings.

2. Ayaru (also known as Ayaru/Adaru) was the second month in the ancient Babylonian calendar. It roughly corresponds to the period between mid-**April and mid-May** in the Gregorian calendar.

The zodiac sign associated with Ayaru is Taurus. Taurus is known for its qualities such as stability, perseverance, and sensuality.

Taurus: Dreaming of Taurus might symbolize stability, perseverance, or the need to focus on practical matters and material security.

3. Simanu (also known as Sivan) was the third month in the ancient Babylonian calendar. It generally corresponds to the period between **mid-May and mid-June** in the Gregorian calendar.

The zodiac sign associated with Simanu is Gemini. Gemini is characterized by traits such as adaptability, curiosity, and communication skills.

Gemini: Dreaming of Gemini might symbolize communication, adaptability, or the need to explore different perspectives and embrace change.

4. Du'uzu (also known as Tammuz) was the fourth month in the ancient Babylonian calendar. It generally corresponds to the period between **mid-June and mid-July** in the Gregorian calendar.

The zodiac sign associated with Du'uzu is Cancer. Cancer is symbolized by the crab and is associated with qualities such as emotional depth, nurturing, and intuition.

Cancer: Dreaming of Cancer might symbolize emotions, nurturing, or the need to connect with your intuition and create a sense of home and security.

5. Abu (also known as Ab) was the fifth month in the ancient Babylonian calendar. It generally corresponds to the period between **mid-July and mid-August** in the Gregorian calendar.

The zodiac sign associated with Abu is Leo. Leo is symbolized by the lion and is associated with qualities such as leadership, creativity, and self-expression.

Leo: Dreaming of Leo might symbolize confidence, creativity, or the need to express yourself authentically and shine your light.

6. Ululu (also known as Elul) was the sixth month in the ancient Babylonian calendar. It generally corresponds to the period between **mid-August and mid-September** in the Gregorian calendar.

The zodiac sign associated with Ululu is Virgo. Virgo is symbolized by the virgin and is associated with qualities such as practicality, organization, and attention to detail.

Virgo: Dreaming of Virgo might symbolize organization, attention to detail, or the need for self-improvement and service to others.

7. Tashritu (also known as Tishri) was the seventh month in the ancient Babylonian calendar. It generally corresponds to the period between **mid-September and mid-October** in the Gregorian calendar.

The zodiac sign associated with Tashritu is Libra. Libra is symbolized by the scales and is associated with balance, harmony, and justice.

Libra: Dreaming of Libra might symbolize balance, harmony, or the need to seek fairness and make decisions with diplomacy and cooperation.

8. Arakhsamnu (also known as Marcheshvan or Cheshvan) was the eighth month in the ancient Babylonian calendar. It generally corresponds to the period between **mid-October and mid-November** in the Gregorian calendar.

The zodiac sign associated with Arakhsamnu is Scorpio. Scorpio is symbolized by the scorpion and is associated with transformation, intensity, and passion.

Scorpio: Dreaming of Scorpio might symbolize transformation, intensity, or the need to confront deep emotions and embrace personal power.

9. Kislimu (also known as Kislev) was the ninth month in the ancient Babylonian calendar. It generally corresponds to the period between **mid-November and mid-December** in the Gregorian calendar.

The zodiac sign associated with Kislimu is Sagittarius. Sagittarius is symbolized by the archer and is associated with adventure, optimism, and a thirst for knowledge.

Sagittarius: Dreaming of Sagittarius might symbolize adventure, exploration, or the need for expanding your horizons and seeking truth and knowledge.

10. Tebetu (also known as Tevet) was the tenth month in the ancient Babylonian calendar. It generally corresponds to the period between **mid-December and mid-January** in the Gregorian calendar.

The zodiac sign associated with Tebetu is Capricorn. Capricorn is symbolized by the sea-goat and is associated with ambition, discipline, and practicality.

Capricorn: Dreaming of Capricorn might symbolize ambition, discipline, or the need to focus on long-term goals and responsibilities.

11. Shabatu (also known as Shevat) was the eleventh month in the ancient Babylonian calendar. It generally corresponds to the period between **mid-January and mid-February** in the Gregorian calendar.

The zodiac sign associated with Shabatu is Aquarius. Aquarius is symbolized by the water-bearer and is associated with innovation, intellectual pursuits, and humanitarianism.

Aquarius: Dreaming of Aquarius might symbolize innovation, independence, or the need to embrace your unique qualities and contribute to collective progress.

12. Adaru was the twelfth and final month in the ancient Babylonian calendar. It generally corresponds to the period between **mid-February and mid-March** in the Gregorian calendar.

The zodiac sign associated with Adaru is Pisces. Pisces is symbolized by two fish swimming in opposite directions and is associated with intuition, compassion, and spiritual depth.

Pisces: Dreaming of Pisces might symbolize intuition, compassion, or the need to connect with your spiritual side and embrace empathy and creativity.